The Short Stories
of Marcel Aymé

The Short Stories of Marcel Aymé

Graham Lord

University of Western Australia Press

Lord, Graham, 1947-
The short stories of Marcel Aymé.

Index
Bibliography
ISBN 0 85564 180 0

1. Aymé, Marcel André, 1902-1967 — Criticism and interpretation. I. Title.

843'.914

First published in 1980
by the University of Western Australia Press, Nedlands, Western Australia 6009

Agents: eastern states of Australia and New Zealand: Melbourne University Press, Carlton South, Vic. 3053; U.S.A. and Canada: International Scholarly Book Services Inc., Box 555, Forest Grove, Oregon 97116.
Photoset by the University of Western Australia Press, printed by Frank Daniels Pty Ltd, Perth and bound by Printers Trade Services, Belmont, Western Australia.

This book is copyright. Apart from any fair dealing for the purposes of private study, research, criticism or review, as permitted under the Copyright Act, no part may be reproduced by any process without written permission. Enquiries should be made to the publisher.

© Graham Lord 1980

For my wife, Claude, with thanks for the patience she displayed during those hours I spent dissecting the *Contes du chat perché* when I should have been reading them to our children instead

Contents

Acknowledgements	ix
Abbreviations for Aymé's works	x
Introduction	1
1. Faerie and Fantastic: Phenomena and Motifs	20
2. Faerie and Fantastic: Techniques and Themes	57
3. Illusion	95
4. Reality	130
Conclusion	166
Sources of Stories	170
Notes	172
Bibliography	176
Index	179

Acknowledgements

This study was completed with the aid of a research grant from the University of Western Australia.

Some aspects of Aymé's work treated here have been previously touched on in articles in *Essays in French Literature, AUMLA* and the *Australian Journal of French Studies.* My thanks are due to the Editors of these journals for their kind permission to develop the material here.

I would like to express my gratitude to Professor Denis Boak for his comments on the first draft, and especially to Associate Professor Bruce Pratt, who added moral support to constructive criticism. My thanks also to Miss Lisette Nigot and Mrs Unity Beswick, who gave me many hours of proofreading, and to Mrs Naomi Zeffertt at the Press, who made the transition from typescript to printed page surprisingly painless.

Abbreviations for Aymé's Works

AR	*Aller retour* (Paris, Gallimard, 1927)
BI	*La belle image* (Paris, Gallimard, 1941)
BR	*Brûlebois* (Paris, Gallimard, 1948)
CP	*Les Contes du chat perché* (Paris, Gallimard, 1939)
DM	*Derrière chez Martin* (Paris, Gallimard, 1938)
EA	*En arrière* (Paris, Gallimard, 1950)
EJ	*Enjambées* (Paris, Gallimard, 1967)
GU	*Gustalin* (Paris, Gallimard, 1937)
JD	*Les Jumeaux du diable* (Paris, Gallimard, 1928)
JV	*La Jument verte* (Paris, Gallimard, 1933)
NA	*Le Nain* (Paris, Gallimard, 1934)
OL	*Les Oiseaux de lune* (Paris, Gallimard, 1956)
PI	*Le Puits aux images* (Paris, Gallimard, 1932)
PM	*Le Passe-muraille* (Paris, Gallimard, 1943)
RN	*La Rue sans nom* (Paris, Gallimard, 1930)
TC	*La Table aux crevés* (Paris, Gallimard, 1929)
UR	*Uranus* (Paris, Gallimard, 1948)
VG	*Vogue la galère* (Paris, Grasset, 1944)
VO	*La Vouivre* (Paris, Gallimard, 1943)
VP	*Le Vin de Paris* (Paris, Gallimard, 1947)
VR	*Le Vaurien* (Paris, Gallimard, 1931)

Introduction

Marcel Aymé is one of France's underestimated literary figures, a writer who, like Henri Troyat, Hervé Bazin, Jean Giono and perhaps even Jean Dutourd, has never lacked readers, but whom literary critics and above all academics have often greeted with condescension and left largely unexplored. Only in the United States does Aymé seem to have been regarded as a first-rate writer. Aymé certainly deserves better than this and, a decade after his death, intellectual France may be just beginning to realize that solid old-fashioned storytellers like Marcel Aymé, particularly one with his gift of observation and his penchant for laying bare the foibles of his fellow man and the society he has created, may well be read long after the seasonal successes, who eclipsed Aymé in their turns, have faded.

When Marcel Aymé died in 1967 he left behind the image of an extremely shy writer somewhat out of his depth in the publicity-conscious sixties, a rather anti-social personage fleeing not only curious journalists but also the public at large. Aymé guarded his private life quite zealously, considering and hoping that his work needed no artificial support. The ironic Aymé even told his early biographer, Georges Robert, 'Inventez hardiment; cela me distraira.'[1] Journalistic delving behind Aymé's taciturn façade, although it occasionally managed to explain some aspect of his art or subject, has made few discoveries that alter an appreciation of his work.

Marcel André Aymé was born in 1902 in Joigny (Yonne), the youngest of four brothers and two sisters. Both of his parents were from the Jura; his father, a dragoon, was stationed in Joigny at the time of Marcel's birth. Aymé's mother, Emma Monamy, died when he was only two. After her death, Aymé's father put his eldest children into boarding-school and sent Marcel and his sister Suzanne, who was two years older than he, to live with their maternal grandparents in the village of Villers-Robert near Dôle. Their father then went off to live his own life. The six years that Aymé spent with his grandparents are the subject of twenty-two pages of autobiographical material that he wrote for Pol Vandromme's study of his work. In 1910, after the death of his grandparents, Aymé was sent as a boarder to the Collège de l'Arc at Dôle where he quickly earned the reputation of being something of a *cancre*. The following year, while continuing his studies, he and Suzanne were taken in by their Aunt Léa. She was soon to become a mother figure to both of them. Aymé's adolescence was spent in her house, 'Les Tilleuls', in Dôle. The village urchin had become a young lad of the town. His mixed 'origines mi-artisanales, mi-paysannes, mi-citadines, mi-villageoises'[2] were to mark his work quite strongly.

By the age of seventeen, Aymé had become something of a delinquent, frequenting the bars of the lower town and, according to his sister, ruining his health by 'des fréquentations douteuses'. Nevertheless, Marcel finished his *baccalauréat* and in 1919 he won a scholarship to the *lycée* in Besançon for further studies in mathematics. He intended to become an engineer and was even urged to prepare entry to the *polytechnique*, but illness soon interrupted these studies. Despite this period of sickness Aymé completed two years of military service in the occupied Rhineland and then moved to Paris, where he met his future wife. He spent two rather unhappy years in the city struggling to make a living until his ill health forced him back to his aunt's house in Dôle to convalesce in 1925. Aymé's main activity in Dôle was reading. It was during this period that he took to literature quite by chance: 'Je m'étais destiné aux mathématiques. La littérature me laissait indifférent.'[3] The chance was *Brûlebois*. Much to Aymé's surprise the novel was a success and he was soon off to Paris to try to become a writer. He set up house in the rue Paul-Féval with his new bride Marie-Antoinette and soon they had a daughter. By day Aymé was shop-assistant, clerk, film-extra, journalist and even door-to-door insurance salesman, and in the evenings he would write to console himself. His literary efforts were naturally something of a pastime until the success of *La Jument verte* in 1933 assured his literary future.

Aymé quickly took to the image of a rather bohemian and non-conformist writer ('Le Jurassien de Montmartre') living in the village on the Butte with his artist friends: the author and painter Georges Papazoff, the engraver Daragnès, the actor Le Vigan, the cartoonist Ralph Soupault and the proprietor of the Lapin Agile, Max Révol. Except for occasional holidays on the Riviera or in his native Jura, Aymé lived the rest of a very tranquil life in Montmartre. Only when success had brought a slightly bourgeois note into his life did he move up to the rue d'Orchampt, but even then Aymé's life hardly changed. He would walk for hours all over Paris observing his fellow humans, he would play *boule* with Céline on the place des Frères-Casadesus or 421 with the painter Gen Paul in Mme Germaine's café on the rue Paul-Féval. Aymé did not welcome publicity; young reporters who came to pester him as he sat in the Pichet du Tertre listening to the conversation around him usually went back to write that he was extremely reluctant to talk about anything, especially himself, that he wore sunglasses even indoors or else scrutinized the world through drooping eyelids, that he dressed rather eccentrically, had a cat called Alphonse and had spent three weeks in America without being impressed, that he had refused the Légion d'honneur, and that he liked *belote, pétanque*, his granddaughter Françoise and being left alone by journalists.

*   *   *

Aymé's literary career spans the forty-one years from 1926 until 1967. During that period he wrote seventeen novels, twelve plays and three essays as well as eighty-three short stories. Aymé also wrote two little-known musical comedies whose texts have never been published and he occasionally worked for the cinema, writing adaptations, dialogue and sometimes whole scenarios, although almost never for films of his own work. In his less creative moments Aymé adapted translations of the plays of Arthur Kopit, Tennessee Williams and Arthur Miller and was also something of a literary critic. He wrote prefaces to the work of writers as various as Tolstoi, Rabelais, Andersen, Siné, La Bruyère, Brasillach and Madeleine Ozeray as well as a series of articles in *La Parisienne* on the work of his friend Antoine Blondin. As a journalist Aymé wrote for many different periodicals and chose subjects ranging from American puritanism, theatrical subsidies, the discovery of the concentration camps and French foreign policy to capital punishment, the closing of the Paris brothels and the gentle art of fishing in the Seine.

Aymé's novels can be divided conveniently into three main kinds: rural, urban and socio-political novels, although there is such variety in his work that several other divisions might seem just as valid: situational novels, atmosphere studies, psychological studies, social satires and autobiographical novels. The rural novels, *La Table aux crevés*, *La Jument verte*, *Gustalin* and *La Vouivre*, are full of the soul of Aymé's native Jura: small farming villages, Sunday cemetery visits, animals that seem part of the family, stoical peasants with their clogs, their colourful dialects and their Gallic moustaches. They are studies built on a monotonous round of tasks geared to the rhythm of the seasons; they are animated by the prejudices and preoccupations of Aymé's beloved Jurassians and filled with their personal, family and political squabbles. Aymé's view of the Jura is very carefully composed: he balances the small joys and satisfactions of his peasants with the monotony and hardship of their existence; he shows appreciation of the plenitude but also the limitations of their lives. Certainly the ribald *Jument verte* won fame for Aymé by being a rollicking, Rabelaisian tale of bucolic life, full of verve and humour; but like *Gustalin* and *La Table aux crevés* it also underlines a threat to the survival of the peasant culture: the farmers are being inexorably drawn by centralization and mechanization towards the proletarian existence of the suburban factories.

There is constant tension in Aymé's novels between the city and the country. In *Gustalin* he shows the difference in vision between city and country folk and compares the attractions of their two lives. In his gradual move from country novels towards urban studies like *La Rue sans nom*, *Maison basse* and *Le Vaurien* Aymé was exploring his own transition from peasant to Parisian. His novels are an intensification of the duality and the quest for identity that haunted Aymé for many years; novels in both the rural and urban currents betray a man torn between the fascination and corruption of Paris life and his simple Jurassian origins. *La Rue sans nom* and *Maison basse* soon established Aymé's reputation as a serious analyst of the complexes and intrigues, the frustration and corruption of the urban jungle. *La Rue sans nom* is a novel of dimly lit streets, assembly-lines, petrol lamps, resignation, popular slang, dingy tenements and family squabbles. It won Aymé the Prix Populiste. Most of Aymé's urban studies aim a little higher than the working class and the misery they describe is not so much physical as metaphysical. *Maison basse* dissects the desperately impersonal life in a soulless concrete apartment building, with its aggressive concierge, its lift that seldom works, graffiti on the walls, garbage in the foyer and firmly closed doors. Its themes are isolation, anonymity, alienation, despair, escapism and suicide. *Le Vaurien* and

Les Tiroirs de l'inconnu reinforce this atmosphere by relating the aimless wanderings around Paris of characters out of touch with the burlesque, insane world around them and constantly bewildered by the paradoxes they observe in themselves and others.

The socio-political vein in Aymé's novels is best represented by the trilogy of *Travelingue, Le Chemin des écoliers* and *Uranus*, where Aymé covers a ten-year crisis period in French history — from the dashed hopes of the Front Populaire through the dark years of defeat, occupation and collaboration to the vain optimism of the Liberation. It is a trilogy of social and moral dissolution. *Travelingue* describes the crisis of 1936 and condemns the self-centred corruption of the ruling élite and the inherent conservatism of the middle class for combining to stifle the modest social revolution envisaged by Léon Blum. *Le Chemin des écoliers* is Aymé's fresco of the Occupation years, an examination of the physical, moral and psychological pressures experienced by the average Frenchman in this particular crisis situation. The last novel in the trilogy, *Uranus*, is an exploration of the political and moral crisis of the Liberation purges, a national witch-hunt which provides an ironic sequel to *Le Chemin des écoliers* because the F.F.I. and the *comité d'épuration* have simply taken over from the Wehrmacht and the Gestapo.

At the heart of Aymé's novels, whether urban analysis, rural tableau or political statement, there is usually a crisis. Increasing tension and conflict, whether psychological or physical, collective or personal, pervades his work. His most successful novels are often those which concentrate in depth on one particular psychological crisis or situational dilemma and its consequences. *Aller retour* shows nothing else but Galuchey's crisis of self-discovery, the rise and fall of an over-ambitious *pauvre type*; *Le Boeuf clandestin* relates Berthaud's temptation, fall from grace, confusion and atonement; and *Le Moulin de la Sourdine* shows the growing scandal that will destroy an apparently respectable lawyer. These novels, like the fantastic metaphor in *La belle image*, accentuate the kind of psychological crisis which, in less concentrated form, underlines the different themes in most of Aymé's work.

Aymé's modest human comedy is given considerable unity by common themes, motifs, structures and techniques, many of which recur in his plays and short stories. Aymé is concerned with human stupidity, man's twisted visions of reality and the illusions or obsessions that provoke them, and the conflict between reality and appearances. Self-discovery and self-acceptance, moral degeneration and sexual repression are also major themes. Unhappy marriages and disintegrating families are the background for endless personal, spiritual and political quarrelling as harmonious façades crack to reveal sordid human motivations. Other key motifs are: metamorphosis and role change (the second self), the intrusion of someone out of place and the rise and fall of ambitious mediocrity. These motifs are reinforced by recurring structures like the circular return to previous order, and the techniques Aymé exploits to increase the tension in his crises: contrasts between characters and settings, closed atmospheres and external catalysts. Recurring character types give more clues to Aymé's preoccupations. Many of them are an integral part of the themes and motifs already seen: the confused adolescent torn between two worlds, the hypocritical *bourgeois*, the Jurassian lost in the city, the salt-of-the-earth simpleton, the father-figure losing his self-respect or that of his family, the escapist taking refuge in dream or illusion. Aymé's novels are full of people trying to cling on to old values as their world changes, alienated anti-heroes out of touch with their surroundings or quite overcome by their personal crisis or dilemma, lost souls frantically trying to find where they belong, ambitious social climbers making fools of themselves in public.

In 1944 Aymé's career appeared to take a sudden change in direction. He seemed to abandon the novel and turn to the theatre. Like Giraudoux, Camus, Montherlant and Sartre, Aymé allowed himself to be tempted by the theatre as a more direct means of communication than the novel. From the publication of his first play, *Vogue la galère*, in 1944 it appears that Aymé came to the theatre half-way through his career, having already written fourteen novels and five of his seven books of short stories. Yet, although his theatrical début came some twenty years after his beginnings as a novelist, Aymé was clearly thinking of the theatre much earlier. He was writing *Lucienne et le boucher* as early as 1930, only five years after his first novel. By 1932 the play had been refused as 'injouable' by several producers and it was to lie in Aymé's drawer for almost seventeen years before making its very successful stage début. *Vogue la galère*, the first play to be performed, was written in 1936-37, some eight years before its publication and eleven years before its *première*. Aymé's revelation to Parisian theatregoers was clearly not the sudden change of genre that it seemed. Furthermore, it is easy to detect a theatrical orientation in the novelist's predilection for the tense situations of crisis, confrontation and decision that are the stuff of good drama, as well as in the storyteller's taste for dialogue rather than a more narrative means of expression.

There are three general currents in Aymé's theatre: social and political satire, situational melodrama and theatre of fantasy. They do not correspond exactly to the three categories of novel but the two genres are nevertheless integral components of a very unified *oeuvre*. The strongest current in Aymé's theatre is social criticism. *Vogue la galère* is worlds apart from the urban and provincial scenes that had preoccupied him until then, yet it is still just as dependant on personal contrasts and conflicts. The play is a pessimistic look at man's lack of freedom, an almost ideological drama about the physical, social and psychological order of man's life. Its interlude of disorder, like that in *Aller retour*, is a structural and thematic model for much of the rest of Aymé's work. *La Tête des autres* presents the polemic Aymé at his best. Here he develops the personal crisis of a magistrate who must decide between scandal and injustice; in an apparently innocuous intrigue Aymé attacks a corrupt magistrature and an inhuman judicial system whose greatest shame is the guillotine. *La Convention Belzébir* dramatizes a bleak, dehumanized social order that we often glimpse in Aymé's novels. It shows the inhuman excesses of a mechanical, overrationalized totalitarian régime and its final defeat by the force of human instinct and passion. *La Mouche bleue*, a satire in the same vein, highlights the lifeless, frustrated citizens produced by an American society ferociously dedicated to 'le rendement'. We watch an individual's attempt to 'drop out', but his conditioning proves too strong and he is soon recuperated by the offer of a higher salary. The last of Aymé's social satires, *Les Maxibules*, presents a dreaming idealist who upsets all around him until he can be brought back to reality. Against a background of class consciousness and sexual frustration, Aymé propounds a social theory of love that he had already explored in *Images de l'amour* and *Les Tiroirs de l'inconnu*: that woman's interest in man is governed by social considerations while he loves instinctively and indiscriminately.

Aymé's penchant for situational melodrama produced *Lucienne et le boucher, Louisiane* and *Les quatre vérités*. The first of these is based upon a growing personal crisis and on the tension between a social façade and the unpalatable truths it conceals. We finally witness the scandalous explosion of repressed sensuality between Lucienne and her butcher. *Louisiane* depends on a similar threat of scandal; it complements *La Mouche bleue* by attacking the deep-seated racism in the United States and attributes to Americans the same fear of scandal that permeates *La Tête des autres*. *Les quatre vérités* continues this thematic vein by showing the chaos that ensues when 'respectable' *bourgeois* under the influence of a new drug suddenly start to confess the truth about their sentiments and actions.

Aymé's theatre of fantasy reveals the lighter side of his talent. In *Clérambard* he provides a spiritual metamorphosis to match Cérusier's physical face change in *La belle image*. Aymé transforms Count Clérambard's haughty pride and cruelty into humility and love and draws considerable dramatic irony from the consequences. In *Les Oiseaux de lune* he uses the fantasy of a young man who turns people into canaries to explore the flounderings of a reasoning mind confronted by the inexplicable. Both *Clérambard* and *Les Oiseaux de lune* have serious undertones, but this is not the case with the personal metamorphosis in *Le Minotaure*. Like *Consommation*, it is pure entertainment: Gérard Forestier, tired of his life as a trendy socialite, transposes himself back to his beloved Jura and away blow all the city habits he has learned, the artificial crust of hypocritical manners that have choked him and his creator Aymé for so many years.

Aymé's theatre covers everything from pure fantasy to the reality of office routine, with a surprising diversity of setting, tone, character and theatrical style. Yet, despite the mixture of *Clérambard* fantasy with the dry realism of *La Mouche bleue*, the delightful caprice of *Consommation* with the blatant melodrama of *Lucienne et le boucher*, the harsh political satire of *La Tête des autres* with the gentle fable of *Les Oiseaux de lune*, Aymé's theatre is remarkably unified. The unity lies once again in recurring character types, structures, motifs and themes. Common characters are the sexually frustrated woman, the dreaming idealist bringing chaos to those around him, the individual at odds with his environment and variations on the *pauvre type* figure. There is an ever-present antithesis between chaos and disorder, between reason and discipline on the one hand and idealism, illogic, poetry, sex and spontaneity on the other. Aymé often exploits the interlude structure, framing a return to order and compromise after chaotic idealism. This usually involves a variant on the metamorphosis motif with accompanying dramatic irony. Other recurring patterns are the ironic reversal of expected roles or attitudes, the increasing pressure on an individual in a dilemma, the locking together in a closed atmosphere of incompatible or even blatantly hostile elements and the destruction of a hypocritical façade to reveal a scandalous reality beneath. The themes of Aymé's theatre strongly reflect those of his novels: idealism and compromise, the ravages of social, political, sexual or mental disorder, sexual oppression and frustration, the need for natural spontaneity to soften the reasoned, passionless stultification of modern existence, the need for fantasy (whether mental or physical) to balance banal reality, and man's subjective perception of himself and his surroundings.

Despite the initial success of *La Jument verte* in 1933, Aymé has seldom been regarded as a first-rate novelist. Even his own editor Gallimard only once paid him the compliment of featuring his name on the cover of the *Nouvelle Revue Française*, and that was in one of the stigmatized 'collaboration' issues presided over by Drieu La Rochelle. Aymé's career as a dramatist had some high points, *La Tête des autres* causing quite a scandal and *Clérambard* crowning its box-office success with an excellent film version. Aymé's future as a playwright looked quite rosy but somehow he never quite lived up to expectations. Indeed, Aymé himself was disappointed with the theatre. His free spirit felt too restricted by the theatre where an author's direct participation in a text or on the stage was necessarily limited. Towards the end of his career Aymé admitted that his move from the novel to the theatre had been a mistake:

> Le roman est un mode d'expression plus libre. Il permet bien des digressions interdites à la scène. Une pièce enferme son auteur dans un cadre très strict, je m'y trouve prisonnier. On ne peut pas en sortir. Si c'était à refaire, j'hésiterais sans doute à venir au théâtre.[4]

Although performances of Aymé's plays were usually successful and his work attracted serious producers like Douking, Sainval and Barsacq, there were few *reprises*. France has never regarded Aymé as more than a competent dramatist. Most studies of the French theatre simply mention in passing the satire of *La Tête des autres* or the fantasy of *Clérambard* and make comparative references to the work of Salacrou, Achard, Ionesco or Aymé's friend Anouilh.

It is as a short story writer that Aymé has attained lasting fame. The whimsical *Contes du chat perché* have become a milestone in French children's literature, and in the *manuels littéraires*, such an essential part of the French education system, it is excerpts of *Le Passe-muraille* that students will find rather than a scene from

Clérambard or a passage from *La Jument verte*. This is fairly justified. Aymé may not be recognized as a first-rate novelist or playwright but he is certainly a master of the short story. Indeed, as such he has few equals this century. Aymé's short stories naturally reflect many of the key themes of his novels and plays, and to some extent they employ similar techniques to develop his standard crisis situations. But Aymé's short stories are more than just a second fiddle, more than just a frivolous pastime for a self-indulgent novelist and playwright. They are an *oeuvre* in their own right, displaying more variety of subject, tone and mode and much more linguistic skill. It is his short stories that reveal the essential Aymé ever ready to propose an idea and to puncture it with the same stroke of his pen, willing to praise a character's stance and ridicule it with the same breath; it is they that best express the ironic, contradictory dilettante, the taciturn observer hiding behind the clown's mask.

Aymé's short stories belong to a period of eighteen years in the middle of his career. He began as a novelist, publishing six novels before his first collection of short stories. He then spent the years from 1932 to 1950 working on a mixture of novels, essays, plays and short stories before turning mainly to the theatre. His short stories were sometimes published as *contes* and sometimes as *nouvelles* with little distinction between the two. They are grouped into seven main collections: *Le Puits aux images, Les Contes du chat perché, Le Nain, Derrière chez Martin, Le Passe-muraille, Le Vin de Paris* and *En arrière*. There is no evident thematic link within these collections; Aymé seems to have intended a random mixture in each case. He also published a collection called *Enjambées* in 1967 but the story bearing the title 'La Fabrique' is the only previously unpublished one in the collection.

Aymé sometimes published a collection in incomplete form. This means that a complete bibliography of his work is deceptively long and quite repetitive. *Les Contes du chat perché* are the notable offenders here, appearing many times in different combinations until the final collection of seventeen tales was published in 1953. Aymé often republished different groups of these tales with different illustrators. Nathalie Parain was his usual artist but he also used Nathan Altman, Gus Bofa and Touchagues. Many of Aymé's stories were published separately before they were included in a collection. Almost all of the *Contes du chat perché* appeared first in this way but they are certainly not the only ones. 'Rechute' appeared with dry-points by Jean Edelmann a year before it was included in *En arrière*, and 'Traversée de Paris' appeared twice (illustrated by J. Oberlé and then R. Chancel and with different publishers) before it was included in *Le Vin de Paris* the following year. Many stories were first published in less lavish form in the periodicals to which Aymé was a regular contributor. Whenever he was at a loss for a scandal or a *chien écrasé* to fill his column he simply submitted a short story instead. 'Bonne vie et moeurs' and 'Deux victimes' appeared in *Marianne* in 1933 and 'Le Nain', 'L'Elève Martin' and several other stories were published in *Candide* in 1934. Unfortunately, these stories published separately do not always bear their definitive titles. 'Légende poldève' appeared as 'Légende' in *Vingtième siècle* in 1945. 'Porte St Martin', published with 'Avenue Junot' in 1949, is in reality the 'Conte du milieu' that appeared in *En arrière* the next year. 'La Faim du pianiste', which appeared in *Marianne* in 1933 is in fact 'Rue St Sulpice'. Five of these separate stories: 'Un Crime', 'Samson', 'Le Couple', 'Héloïse' and 'Knate' never even appeared in a collection and have usually escaped the attention of commentators.

*   *   *

Aymé's short stories range from the driest realism to the most outrageous fantasy. The material for his stories can be anything from a farmer's reminiscences about his favourite dog or the frustration of a *pauvre type*'s ambitions, to Kafkaesque metamorphoses of the human body and even more frightening obsessions of the mind. Aymé's tone varies from dry mockery to an almost cloying sympathy. His style can be mildly didactic and yet elsewhere annoyingly flippant. The protagonist might be anything from a lazy schoolboy or an axe-murderer to a match-making fairy or a talking cow. Aymé's setting might be a Jurassian farmyard, a slum tenement or anything from a religious statue factory to a futuristic skyscraper village or the court of King Arthur. He may use his short story to sketch the problems of urban adolescence, the tensions of a disintegrating marriage or the hopeless anguish of a man who knows the future. He may exploit his fantastic imagination to underline social criticism or to explore briefly the relativities of time, identity or even existence itself. His extreme variety as *conteur* is such that he has been seen as political commentator, children's author, social historian, psychologist, science-fiction writer and amateur philosopher.

Most of Aymé's short stories are conventional twenty-page sketches of some aspect of life, pithy statements of a human foible or quality, everyday anecdotes with an unexpected twist and perhaps a carefully veiled ironic moral. A typical Aymé story would have a simple plot structure based on one outstanding event or emotional experience. The event could be a simple, unexpected occurrence, it could be a frustration or obsession or it might be a fantastic metamorphosis or the appearance of a dragon in the town square. All of these have the same value for Aymé. He would then follow this initial proposition with an ironic description of its consequences and a reasonably coherent ending.

Whether the subject is physically impossible, mentally disturbing or just improbable and unexpected, Aymé usually creates a situation that will intrigue us and slowly slip out of our grasp. His stories often seem to be a sort of cat and mouse game. Aymé likes to play with the reader and his responses. He exploits his amusing, unusual or disquieting situation as far as the novelty lasts and then quickly withdraws from the web of consequences to escape further responsibility. One of the remarkable aspects of Aymé's stories is their unexpected twists and turns. There is a strong anti-serious vein here:

> Que de fois, au théâtre, au cinéma, ai-je souhaité voir sur la scène ou sur l'écran surgir l'événement insolite qui bouleverserait tout d'un coup les données initiales: l'irruption du fantastique dans le domaine de la réalité étant à cet égard l'inattendu le plus satisfaisant.[5]

Aymé gives the example of a wedding feast where the young bridegroom suddenly plucks off his own head and solemnly places it in the lap of his bride! This is one of Aymé's more flippant manifestations of the unexpected. His symbiosis of unreal and real, his attempt to make the most extreme opposites seem somehow compatible, is usually more subtle than this.

There is a strong element of entertainment in Aymé's stories, entertainment for the author as well as for his readers. Whenever Aymé spoke of his art this is the aspect he tended to stress: 'J'écris pour me faire plaisir',[6] 'Je trouve amusant, quand j'écris une histoire, de me ménager des surprises à moi-même.'[7] Aymé claimed on several occasions that when he picked up his pen he never really knew what was going to happen in his story. He liked to think, rather optimistically, that his tale was evolving spontaneously with a large measure of freedom. Of the novel in particular he says:

> comme toute création libre, il s'achemine vers sa fin sans la connaître, et chaque mouvement nouveau fait surgir une possibilité de choisir imprévue. Matière et personnage échappent en partie à leur créateur, lequel se trouve le premier surpris.[8]

Aymé loves to play with language too. He delights in outrageously detailed descriptions and long accumulations of words; he loves inventing words, punning and arranging incongruous linguistic effects like his Frenchified English words: *chorte, bloudgine, fodeballe, métingue* and *blaquaoute*.

There are many reasons why Aymé was not usually regarded as a first-rate writer, why he has often been dismissed by critics as a 'banal amuseur' and why his work has not appeared prominently on the Sorbonne or *baccalauréat* programmes. The dilettante's variety made Aymé very hard to situate. His work disconcerted critics, who were unable to tuck it safely into a pigeon-hole. Not quite knowing where to start, they often pounced on Aymé's out-of-fashion use of the unreal, his penchant for fairies, ogres and fantastic metamorphoses. Often his taste for the short story itself was mocked. Aymé in turn criticized his intellectual colleagues' sad dependence on dry realism as a mode of expression. He might have felt more at home in the eighties, when the media-magicians are stressing image exploitation to the detriment of reasoned analysis.

Aymé was above all out of place among the anguished 'isms' of the forties and fifties. He detested not only the dull realism but the long, reasoned arguments and the sterile intellectualism of his fellow writers. He complained that they took themselves much too seriously. Aymé preferred the bistros of Montmartre to the cafés of St-Germain-des-Prés. He denied all theories and messages in his work and applied his irony mercilessly to those who allowed their literary creation to be governed by their ideas. Aymé refused to commit himself to any theory because that would necessarily direct the course of his creation and deprive the writer of his only real freedom, that of creator. His stories often plead the cause of poetry, instinct and fantasy in a world of hostile reason. As Aymé has commented (not entirely ironically): 'L'Université pense que Boileau et Gide sont des auteurs infiniment plus importants que Perrault. C'est bien ennuyeux.'[9]

Aymé simply refused to play the intellectual game:

> il commet l'imprudence de composer les refrains d'une opérette au moment où M. Malraux abjure la conscience brésilienne, M. Mauriac la conscience française, M. Duhamel la conscience universelle et M. Sartre la conscience musulmane.[10]

Aymé did not play the success game any better, scoffing at the Légion d'honneur, the Académie Française and invitations to the Elysée. Aymé hardly encouraged the press to like him: he often mocked journalists and snubbed them, insisting that his private life was his own business, and declared that he didn't care whether he was taken seriously or not. He seems to have delighted in welcoming interviewers in stony silence and resisting all attempts to elicit profound, quotable statements from him. '. . . je manque totalement de sérieux',[11] he assured them, and continued: 'Je n'ai de théorie sur rien.'[12] He always denied that he had any message to deliver to humanity, above all in his short stories, and insisted that he was one of those rare writers 'qui noircissent du papier pour leur satisfaction personnelle'. 'Au fond', he continued, 'je n'ai rien à dire.'[13] This reluctance to justify and explain was to find a reflection in Aymé's short story style too.

There were also non-literary reasons for Aymé's lack of success. French literary critics tend to be politically polarized. Just as no one knew where to situate Aymé in the literary spectrum, so he was regarded as politically unstable and no faction wanted to recognize him:

> il ne sert à rien d'être un géant de la littérature si on n'est pas réclamé par la gauche ou si on n'a pas les catholiques dans la manche.[14]

But Aymé did nothing to rectify the situation, openly disavowing both right and left: 'Pour moi la gauche et la droite appartiennent à un complexe d'oppression' and describing himself as someone 'qui n'a pas de religion politique'.[15] He was variously classified with right, left and centre. Once he was even called an 'Anarchiste de droite et réactionnaire de gauche',[16] a paradox which would certainly have pleased him.

Aymé was not kindly treated by the right or the left. After the war he was attacked because of his friendship with the strongly right-wing Céline, whose anti-semitism was construed as being pro-

INTRODUCTION

Nazi and therefore anti-French. Few considered that Aymé might not automatically agree with Céline's views on this subject. In fact Aymé often expressed his sympathy for the plight of the Jews even during the Occupation. Jean-Louis Bory mentions in particular Aymé's courage in publishing 'En attendant' in *La Gerbe* 'en pleine période d'antisémitisme ravageur'.[17] Much political capital was made of the fact that Aymé sold stories to collaborationist journals like *La Gerbe* and *Je suis partout*. As Aymé confessed afterwards:

> A la Libération, j'ai eu la chance qu'on ne me mette pas en prison et qu'on se contente de me maltraiter dans les journaux.[18]

Few people sympathized with the writer who had simply decided to continue living normally, and therefore publishing, despite the Germans. Few critics mentioned that there was absolutely no favourable light cast on the Germans in Aymé's stories and that his fantasies (along with a few thinly veiled patriotic allusions) had surely lifted the Frenchman's morale in a difficult time. Aymé's post-war defence of Robert Brasillach and Maurice Bardèche was also misconstrued. It occurred to very few that this defence might be a question of principle rather than politics. Aymé was in fact obeying his heart and not his head. He always had a soft spot for the underdog, and here were two underdogs who also happened to be fellow writers persecuted for their ideas. Freedom of the pen was a cause dear to Aymé and he stressed that this defence was indeed a matter of principle rather than particular affinity.[19]

The desire to expose the truth was to earn Aymé many enemies. And when he had something to say he did not mince his words. As a journalist he was fond of scandals and was often censored from above:

> je me souviens aussi avoir suivi, pour *Paris-Midi*, l'affaire Stavisky, c'était une franche rigolade. Le procureur, le président, tout le monde était d'accord pour étouffer l'affaire. J'ai voulu l'écrire. On n'a pas marché.[20]

Scandal and the repression of the truth were themes which were to unify much of his work. This was Aymé's strongest affinity with Céline. Aymé saw him as a saviour prepared to shout the truth from the rooftops and described Céline's era (Aymé's own of course) as one that preferred 'l'hypocrisie, le mensonge accepté, la raison d'Etat, la servilité, l'atonie des esprits, l'indifférence au scandale'.[21]

Despite the critical cabal against him, Aymé weakened his position even further by bitter criticism of de Gaulle's post-Liberation régime and its uncontrolled *épuration*. In a vitriolic article entitled 'Le Libérateur', Aymé called de Gaulle 'le geôlier de la nation'. He deplored the personal vengeances and political machinations of the purges and went on to shout the injustice of the persecution of defenceless writers like Brasillach when there were many who deserved more clearly to be shot: the contractors who grew fat by feeding the Wehrmacht or by building the Atlantic Wall. It is hardly surprising that what Aymé called 'la critique officielle', already unkind to his friends Blondin and Céline, was not going to praise Aymé's work along with 'toute cette médiocrité montée en piédestal à la Libération'.[22]

There is clearly a very serious side to the 'banal amuseur'. How could the Aymé of 'Le Libérateur' and *La Tête des autres* remain aloof in his short stories? It is possible to accept outrageous (and possibly a little ironic) statements like 'J'écris pour me faire plaisir' and 'au fond je n'ai rien à dire' in reference to *Les Contes du chat perché* and two or three stories in each of the other collections, but this *conteur* is also the pessimist of *Le Vaurien* and *Maison basse*, the objective political historian of *Travelingue*, *Le Chemin des écoliers* and *Uranus*, the bitter satirist of *La Tête des autres*, the reasoning analyst of *Silhouette du scandale* and the implacably involved polemicist of so many periodical articles.

Aymé's irony prevented many commentators from seeing that his imaginary world is closely linked to its real model and that it is a world as coherent in its own way as literary creations of much greater stature. There is in Aymé a serious counterpart to the storyteller, a moralist who contradicts but also completes the entertainer. Jean Cathelin suggests as an opening to his study that Aymé is 'engageant' rather than 'engagé'. In fact he is both. Behind the smiling mask there is a silent observer pitilessly scrutinizing man's foibles and his society with those penetrating eyes that stare out unnerved from Raymond Moretti's pen sketch on the cover of *Magazine littéraire*.[23]

The short story is an ideal vehicle for the serious Aymé as well as the entertainer; it lets him be serious and pretend not to be. As Jacques Teynier puts it, the short story is an

> Avantage précieux pour un moraliste qui déteste moraliser et

qui tient les moralisateurs pour des 'radoteurs insipides ou des écrivains diminués'.²⁴

Where the more intellectual writer might baulk at the restrictions of character, plot and theme development imposed by the form, Aymé revels in it because he can approach quite serious ideas and shirk the responsibility of sustained comment. Aymé was naturally criticized for this irresponsibility, and such criticism was not totally unfounded; Aymé has demonstrated clearly in some of his longer, more serious works, where he often treats the same themes as his short stories, that he found difficulty in sustaining intellectual development of one idea. These more serious works are far from Aymé's best.

The fact that there is a serious side to Aymé does not make him an intellectual. He is a moralist, but one who tries to balance *joie* and *édification*²⁵ rather than a didactic one. He fits Vandromme's definition perfectly:

> Un vrai moraliste ne fait pas la morale. Il regarde couler la vie. Il explore son flux et son reflux pour en révéler les lois secrètes et immuables.²⁶

Aymé does not often tack a moral on to the end of a story; he prefers to act as a catalyst rather than a teacher, inducing the reader to react rather than presenting a lesson to memorize. Aymé's protestations of innocence must not be taken too seriously. He was simply reacting to those moral-seekers who tend to find messages where there are none. What Aymé was really trying to say was that the reader will ruin the balance of the story if he looks too insistently for a deep moral lesson.

*   *   *

This study is an attempt to describe, analyse and evaluate Aymé's short stories. It will judge to what extent the short story was a toy for the entertainer or a tool for the more serious writer, how the short story was used in each way and what advantages or disadvantages it brought the *amuseur* and *moraliste*. It will also isolate thematic and artistic patterns that might bridge the gap between fantasy and reality in Aymé's stories and give unity to his work. It will determine whether Aymé constructs a coherent *comédie humaine* (Aymé confessed that Balzac's was 'le roman de ma vie')[27] or whether his extraordinary variety defies analysis.

Many pages could be written on some of Aymé's individual stories. Space and ambition here are more modest. In order to make sense of variety it will be necessary to deal with as many stories as possible, often sacrificing some comment on the individual story in order to situate it in a wider context. This analysis is not intended as a reference source on individual stories. The total comment on any one story may sometimes seem fragmented because of that story's use as an illustration of several different trends. It will be necessary to generalize, despite several contradictions and countercurrents. A limited amount of comment on Aymé's plays and novels will also be inevitable because they often illustrate the same trends. They are part of the context of Aymé's short stories, often being more detailed, more theoretical expositions of the same themes.

The main problem arising from a project such as this is just how to approach the extraordinary variety of Aymé's stories. There is a disadvantage in proceeding chronologically, collection by collection, because of their lack of internal thematic unity. Each one is a mixture not named for a unifying theme but for one of the stories included. The most convenient division to impose on Aymé seems to be to move from his more striking fantasy, through the more subtle inventions, towards his more ordinary realism. This is a purely artificial division by subject matter, created in order better to express the underlying unity; it does not correspond in any way to a chronological evolution in Aymé's short stories.

The few commentators who have written about Aymé's short stories have been dazzled by the striking fantasy images that characterize approximately half of his stories. The psychological complexities and the subtle realism that express an equally important side of Aymé have often been glossed over. There has also been a sad preoccupation with thematic questions. It would be wrong to place too great an emphasis on analysing Aymé's stories according to the themes and phenomena involved without also taking into account the storyteller's approach to his material and the structures and techniques involved. There has been a frustrating lack of interest in this aspect of Aymé's work. Just what sort of situation does he find most appealing? How is the material made into a story? How is the reader led to accept it and how is he intrigued? How far can such a situation be pursued without becoming tedious? How does Aymé arrange a satisfying ending without becoming too predictable? The storyteller's art is the more interesting side of Aymé's creation but is much harder to analyse than his themes. The charm of his stories is easy to feel but hard to isolate and define, especially as it so often lies in the humour of irony.

* * *

To avoid any confusion between a short story and a collection which may bear the same name, individual stories will be referred to thus: 'En arrière', and collections of stories (as well as novels and plays) thus: *En arrière.*

A list of all Aymé's short stories giving their source will be found on page 170.

1
Faerie and Fantastic Phenomena and Motifs

Les fées sont agréables à fréquenter. Les hommes aussi.
Marcel Aymé

It is the physical fantasies that are most commonly accepted as Aymé's trade-mark. All three pastiches of his work stress this kind of story.[1] Commentators trying to analyse Aymé's extremely varied use of the physically unreal have had recourse to a multitude of terms to qualify it: *fantaisie, merveilleux, surréel, fantastique, fabuleux, absurde, non-sens, miraculeux, féerique, science-fiction*. This list makes the analysis of Aymé's unreal stories seem a particularly daunting project, but in fact many of these terms are wrongly or too vaguely applied. Aymé's unreal has little connection with the vogue of Surrealism, the 'literature of the Absurd' or the rather anglophone trend towards verbal nonsense, and the theoreticians of the unreal tend to condemn the terms *merveilleux* and *fantaisie* as being too general, along with the once precise but now vague use of *miraculeux* and *fabuleux*.

Part of Aymé's originality is that he dabbles in several different currents of fantasy. Apart from a thin vein of science fiction, Aymé's imagination can be divided between the two widely accepted currents of *féerique* and *fantastique*. It is important to make a clear distinction between these two because Aymé tends to disregard literary convention by mingling them and adapting them to his own purposes. The *féerique* implies a world apart, like C. S. Lewis's Narnia or J. R. R. Tolkien's Middle Earth, a world inhabited by fairies, unicorns and sorcerers. Its normal phenomena are spells, magic lamps and moonlight. Describing the faerie world of Perrault, Marcel Schneider writes of 'un monde où tout vit, où tout parle, où tout agit. Ce monde a un sens.'[2] It is also a moral world where man's causality is absent even though his attributes may be reflected in humanized animals; Isabelle Jan underlines the tradition of 'L'Ours-valeureux', 'le Cochon-tyran', 'le Renard-fripon' and 'le Chat-brigand'.[3] Man's presence is not obligatory but Aymé obviously finds that faerie is much more relevant and interesting if man participates. Yet this participation will usually be temporary; man will return to the security of his own world at the end.

The literature of the fantastic tends to be taken more seriously than faerie because it talks of our world, our own time and space coordinates. Humans provide most of its protagonists even if they have some frightening new power, and where there are monsters — vampires and werewolves — they often reflect man in their creation. Several common themes recur: metamorphoses, time manipulation, invisibility, voyages to a 'beyond', statues that come to life, pacts with occult powers, monstrous psychological reflections of human feelings or experiences. The essence of the fantastic is the intrusion of something strange and frightening into our secure world. The fear is stressed because our security is threatened; man himself is closely involved and usually helpless before the fantastic. He could kill a fire-breathing dragon but the spectres that he encounters now are often part of himself, the *fantastique intérieur* that is so important in the work of Hoffmann and Poe.

There are elements of both faerie and the fantastic in the stories of Marcel Aymé. He admits appreciation of the work of Andersen and Perrault and has written prefaces to the stories of both. In his comments on his own childhood Aymé refers to the influence of fairy stories as well as to his penchant for Jules Verne and the comtesse de Ségur. All of these influences are to be seen in borrowings of material, but what is more interesting is the way Aymé adapts, distorts and often parodies that material.

*   *   *

Aymé's most recognizable borrowings are from faerie literature. He does not exploit faerie very often, perhaps because the inventive and nonconformist *conteur* felt constrained by the particularly strong rules of a tradition which 'n'admet pas d'acte vraiment créateur ou vraiment libre'.[4] What is more, Aymé is essentially a humanist and faerie is too far removed from man. He has exploited only a few truly faerie characters: a water-sprite, a wicked ogre and a centaur; but several stories are infected in a more general way by the faerie spirit.

Aymé's break with tradition starts very early. The water-fairy Udine in 'Au clair de la lune', after nine hundred years at the bottom of her river, enters man's time and space scale. She is quite a conventional fairy: long blonde hair 'comme elles ont toutes', magic wand, crystal and jade chariot drawn by white rabbits. One of Aymé's recurrent themes is the clash between reality and fantasy. This is accentuated here by bringing Udine out of her traditionally closed context into our world. Udine is quickly threatened with a fine for driving on the highway without lights. An evil fairy, smiles Aymé, would have turned the gendarme into a merino ram or a coffee-grinder, but Udine is a kind fairy: she adapts to his world by telling him she is 'la femme du préfet'. The clash of real and fantasy continues as Udine tries to help young Jacot win the hand of his Valentine. Reality threatens to turn her *conte rose* into a *conte gris*: she sees her rabbits beaten by Jacot's sports car and then she is so disturbed that she muddles up her magic spells. Aymé's sad smile persists at the end: Udine does manage to bring the lovers together but must go on her way discouraged by a world where man's law requires head-lights even though 'la lune éclate au firmament étoilé comme la rose livide dans un parterre de jasmins' (PI 171) and where Jacot cannot go and 'chanter la romance éternelle sous les fenêtres de Valentine (. . .) dans ces jardins tout parfumés de blanche aubépine et de tendre péché' (PI 179) because Valentine's father has set traps in the flower-beds!

Aymé's ogre in 'Conte du milieu' suffers even more than Udine in his confrontation with man's world. This ogre no longer inhabits a cave in Fairyland but runs a café near the Porte St Martin. His particular vice is to touch young ladies on the cheek with his magic ring and mutter the incantation 'Calvados, Cognac, Fine Champagne' to shrink them and store them in his salad bowl until he wants to take his pleasure or eat them. After bringing this faerie out of its context into the reality of Paris Aymé almost parodies a conventional fairy-story plot. The young hero's mistress is spirited away and Janot sets out to rescue her, turns the ogre's own weapon against him, rescues Riri la Blonde and they live happily ever after as proprietors of a brothel. We do not need Pierre Berger's ribald etchings in the separate edition of this tale to realize that it is pure entertainment.

Aymé enlivens several of his more serious short stories by borrowing faerie accessories and effects from their traditional context and applying them in a very real frame. At the end of a rather lengthy account of an unmarried mother's sacrifices to give her young son enough to eat, Aymé introduces magic into 'Les Bottes de sept lieues' to provide a happily-ever-after ending that he shows to be sadly impossible if we remain tied to reality. The boots enable young Antoine to escape his life of poverty and bring back poignantly simple treasures to his mother in their cold attic:

> En dix minutes, il fut à l'autre bout de la terre et s'arrêta dans un grand pré pour y cueillir une brassée des premiers rayons du soleil qu'il noua d'un fil de la Vierge.
> Antoine retrouva facilement la mansarde où il se glissa sans bruit. Sur le petit lit de sa mère, il posa sa brassée brillante dont la lueur éclaira le visage endormi et il trouva qu'elle était moins fatiguée. (PM 230)

Magic tears, gestures and incantations are used in *Les Contes du chat perché* as well as the eerie sound-effects that accompany the metamorphosis in 'L'Ane et le cheval': rattling chains, a music box and the howling of a non-existent storm. Aymé further mixes his genres by applying moonlight effects to the fantastic time jump in 'La Fabrique' and the strange storm motif accompanies the time movement and metamorphosis in 'Le Décret', which by its structure and theme belongs well and truly in the fantastic vein.

The novels *La Table aux crevés*, *Gustalin* and *La Vouivre* are coloured by elements of Aymé's native Jurassian mythology that should clearly be classed as faerie. Yet, despite its influence on his childhood, this pagan faerie with its mysterious trees and rocks, its enchanted ponds and snake-charming nymphs, touches only one short story, 'Les mauvaises fièvres', and there as hardly more than an accessory. Aymé more often exploits the faerie of classical mythology. 'Fiançailles' is the story of a young centaur called Aristide who has the torso and face of a charming adolescent but the body of a stallion. Here, too, the intrusion of fantasy into reality and man's own reaction are underlined. Aristide has been born to the marquise de Valoraine and then hidden away to avoid social scandal. The story describes his discovery of the outside world, his sexual coming of age and his choice between the two sides of his nature. He becomes excited by the budding young god-daughter of the local bishop and thinks that it must be his 'âme' that he feels stirring at the sight of her rounded 'croupe'. His spontaneity, candour and evident lack of social conditioning provide some rather amusing situations, the best of which is the proposed marriage of real and fantasy. The bishop is at first shocked by the proposition, seeing nothing but 'péché' and 'animalité' in the uneducated Aristide, but soon jumps at the opportunity to marry off his ward.

Aymé turns this story into a light-hearted dig at the religious and social constraints that the untutored centaur cannot comprehend. Aristide relives Udine's experience with the representative of society's law and order: the gendarme in this case regards Aristide's very existence as an affront to authority and threatens to arrest him for 'attentat à la pudeur publique'. Aristide is confused and instinctively decides that his animal half must be the better one. He rather symbolically breaks out of the park and runs off into the forest with the first real mare he meets, leaving poor Ernestine to have her stirrings repressed by the nuns of the école Sainte-Thérèse de l'Enfant-Jésus.

Just as recognizable as Aristide or the seven-league boots are several images which are biblical or at least religio-moral in origin while being *féerique* in spirit. Aymé's preface to the stories of Andersen shows that he regarded this as a legitimate extension of faerie material. Whether his irreverent story is to be based on Samson's magic hair, a comic-strip God astride a cloud, the Devil riding up to the pearly gates on a broomstick to parley with St Peter, or St Francis of Assisi appearing to a sadist to ask him to read his *Vita* (Editions du Ciel, of course), Aymé's parodic exploitation of the image is similar to his use of more conventional material.

'La Fosse aux péchés' exploits the biblical parable tradition with a story of allegorical monsters acting out the battle between good and evil. Aymé uses a dream to frame a ribald pastiche of the whole tradition. This is one of several stories where the ironic Aymé subjects a pure character to temptation. The hero this time is Martin, a 'professeur de pureté' who gives in to temptation in a very familiar pattern: he sells his soul to the Devil for a golden calf but the Devil snaps him up on his way to spend it. The following scene in hell, where an English pastor does battle with the Devil's seven deadly henchmen, allows Aymé to indulge his Rabelaisian streak of verbal amusement. The pastor vanquishes one by one the grotesque sins which take the form that the sinner imagines them to have. Here is Aymé's vision of pride:

> Son corps avait la forme d'une commode Louis XV. (. . .) Il avait le derrière empanaché d'un flot de tentacules multi-

colores où dominaient l'or et la pourpre. Ses jambes de pierre étaient d'un blanc laiteux, ses pieds et ses cuisses couleur merde d'oie. Il portait en sautoir, imprimé sur la peau, un grand cordon violet fileté de blanc et, sur son torse Louis XV, deux rangées de décorations qui étaient ses excroissances naturelles aux coloris des plus chatoyants. Ses cornes étaient dorées, ses oreilles de veau d'un rouge éclatant. (VP 138-9)

At the end of the epic struggle hell vomits its prey, but this ending is deceptive. Aymé's target is once again the constraints placed on man by a religio-social educative process, so he arranges a reversal of the standard moral ending: the Devil's pleasure-creed 'Le péché est la substance essentielle de la vie' wins the day. Once back among his disciples, Professor Martin tells them:

— Déchirez mon traité de prophylaxie de l'âme. (. . .) Si vous voulez vous garder des mauvaises tentations, ne haïssez pas le péché, mais familiarisez-vous avec le péril. Ne soyez pas bêtement modestes, ne méprisez pas les bonnes nourritures, ne fuyez pas les femmes, etc. (VP 150)

Hypocritical conceptions of virtue are ridiculed more bitterly when Aymé uses the décor of heaven and an imaginary country for his 'Légende poldève'.[5] The exaggerated virtue of the old maid Mlle Borboïé is Aymé's target. Her virtue is constrained, ritual and above all egoistic. All her actions are directed towards her own entry into paradise. Aymé's satire of her self-righteousness continues right up to the gates of a heaven that is disturbingly like an administrative office. She pleads her 'dossier' with St Peter as with any other public servant and tries to get him to take a personal interest in her case:

— . . . Prière du matin, action de grâces, puis messe de six heures par tous les temps. Après la messe, invocation spéciale à saint Joseph et remerciement à la Vierge. Chapelet à dix heures, suivi de la lecture d'un chapitre des Evangiles. *Benedicite* à midi . . . (. . .)
— Ecoutez, dit ce bon archange, votre cas me paraît intéressant. Je veux tenter quelque chose pour vous. (PM 156-7)

Aymé subjects the hypocritical old maid to a final test: to attain paradise she must pretend to be whore to a regiment of hussars! In

'Légende poldève' Aymé is very close to Voltaire in his blend of ironic humorist and bitter moralist. This is visible not only in his imitation of the style of *Candide* and his satire of the spinster and her heaven, but also when he describes the comic-strip war fought for national honour:

> Un petit garçon de Molletonie pissa délibérément par-dessus la frontière et arrosa le territoire poldève avec un sourire sardonique. C'en était trop pour l'honneur du peuple poldève dont la conscience se révolta, et la mobilisation fut aussitôt décrétée. (PM 151-2)

Wartime God-on-our-side sentiments and the idea that wholesale slaughter becomes moral when backed by a 'noble' cause are mocked as Aymé reveals the ignoble side of militarism: the swaggering local soldiery assault, rape and plunder the very civilians they are supposed to be protecting. And of course all combatants (and only combatants), automatically 'morts pour la patrie' and also 'pour le bon droit' even if they are the enemy, are admitted to heaven with no questions asked.

True to Voltairian tradition, Aymé works through irony rather than direct statement. Certainly he is exploiting the faerie mode to satirize reality, but faerie is only a ruse. Aymé's main weapon is his language itself. His attitude is conveyed by tone rather than by the actual events that are narrated. A good example of this is his treatment of the contrast between Marichella Borboïé and her nephew Bobislas. The nephew is a thorough scoundrel: we follow his career through lechery and drunkenness to theft, rape and pillage. Aymé appears to have created an obvious candidate for the fires of hell and yet the joyous, flowing narrative contradicts these appearances: it provokes a smile which lures the reader into feeling a certain sympathy for the ribald Bobislas:

> Un chapelet d'abominables jurements l'annonçait du bout de la rue où demeurait la vieille demoiselle. Titubant, son grand sabre cognant et s'embarrassant à tous les meubles, sans autre bonjour qu'un blasphème, il lui signifiait, éructant et braillant, qu'elle eût à sortir son argent et à se hâter. Plusieurs fois même, comme elle tardait à s'exécuter, il avait à moitié dégainé son bancal et menacé la sainte fille de la partager en deux dans le sens de la longueur (PM 153)

while the dry irony of the sentences devoted to the 'virtuous' but stupid old spinster and her misguided faith leaves no doubt as to Aymé's opinion of her:

> Pendant cinq ans, Mlle Borboïé voulut croire qu'il s'amenderait un jour et lui prodigua inlassablement les bons conseils et les pieuses exhortations avec tout l'argent qu'il fallait pour les faire fructifier. (PM 151)

The theme, the reversal structure and above all the rather *féerique* accessories of 'Légende poldève' recur in the very similar 'L'Huissier'. The comic potential of the heavenly décor is more fully realized here; it is brought into more profitable contrast with reality. Aymé opens the story with another light-hearted parody of a Last Judgement trial scene. The magistrate is St Peter with his book of records, the defendant is an over-zealous, cynical and self-righteous bailiff called Malicorne, the evidence is a large vat full of the tears of the widows and children he has evicted, and the appeals judge is God, who enters on his cloud to the accompaniment of a roll of thunder. Malicorne's refusal to be cowed by the situation provides some rather splendid dialogue. Undeterred by St Peter's opening remark that there are hardly any bailiffs in paradise, he suavely assures the guardian of the gates that he does not really insist on being with his colleagues . . . . Asked about his 'bonnes oeuvres', he searches back fifteen years in his memory and cites the occasion when he gave ten *centimes* to a beggar. The objection that the coin was counterfeit leaves him unperturbed too; the beggar would have passed it on quite easily. Naturally there is also a dark side to this humour. Malicorne's cynical defence is that he was only doing his job to the best of his ability ('Dieu merci, mes affaires marchaient bien et je n'ai pas chômé', PM 232), but he was obviously rather too zealous a bailiff. St Peter is all for stoking up the fires of hell and washing down Malicorne's burns with the salt water from the vat, but Malicorne appeals against this judgement. The appeal is heard, because 'La procédure est la procédure', even in heaven. God deems that St Peter was rather too hasty in his condemnation: it is not the bailiff (over-zealous or not) who is at fault, but the human laws whose agent he is. Yet they can hardly allow a bailiff into heaven because 'Ce serait un scandale'.

Malicorne is sent back to earth to redeem himself. He tries to buy his way back into heaven by performing good deeds and he records these for St Peter in a little notebook drawn up with debit and credit columns:

> 'J'ai, spontanément, augmenté de cinquante francs par mois mon clerc Bourrichon qui ne le méritait pourtant pas.' (PM 236)

At the end of his first day of reprieve Malicorne has performed twelve of these empty 'bonnes oeuvres' at a noted cost of 600 francs. It seems that the only good deeds he can think of involve money. Aymé is not only using his faerie borrowings, complete with suggestive dream frame, to scourge those hypocrites who would purchase salvation with their 'charité intéressée'; he has also treated us to a neat ironic reversal. We have before us a miser who is now determined to part with his fortune. It is almost as if Aymé had started a new story by suggesting that 'Il y avait, à Paris, un méchant huissier qui, un jour, décida de devenir bon.' This is a particularly fruitful premise because Aymé has chosen a rather excessive bailiff to start with:

> Il y avait, dans une petite ville de France, un huissier qui s'appelait Malicorne et il était si scrupuleux dans l'accomplissement de son triste ministère qu'il n'eût pas hésité à saisir ses propres meubles. (PM 231)

Obviously there is great potential for humour in this reversal. Imagine the bewilderment of the bailiff's staff when their tyrannical master suddenly doubles their salary! Malicorne sets his target of good deeds at twelve a day, but increases this whenever an ache or pain makes him afraid his end might be near. At the end of a year he has filled six exercise-books, and Aymé indulges in a superb parody of the classic Scrooge image: Malicorne gloating as he weighs his tally-books and leafs delightedly through their pages (PM 241).

Here, too, there is a dark side to the humour, a sombre dramatic irony in the bailiff's first post-metamorphosis encounter with his client, the landlord Gorgerin, who does not know that Malicorne is now working against his interests. There is even more bitter irony in the comparison between the two men's ambitions: Malicorne is trying to be known as 'bon' while Gorgerin is desperately trying to avoid it. Money is the only tool Malicorne knows. As the bailiff does his rounds dispensing alms to the poor, Aymé builds a case against

Malicorne's former clients, the heartless slum landlords like Gorgerin who exploit the poor in their defenceless misery. Malicorne is received in heaven at the end but it has nothing to do with his false generosity. He is finally moved by the poverty of a tawdry seventh-floor garret and, in his first truly spontaneous gesture, turns on Gorgerin shouting 'A bas les propriétaires'. He is shot dead for his treason and of course goes straight to Aymé's anti-serious heaven that is reserved, like his sympathies, for the meek and the downtrodden:

> Dieu, émerveillé, commanda aux anges de jouer, en l'honneur de Malicorne, du luth, de la viole, du hautbois et du flageolet. Ensuite, il fit ouvrir les portes du ciel à deux battants, comme cela se fait pour les déshérités, les clochards, les claque-dents et les condamnés à mort. Et l'huissier, porté par un air de musique, entra au Paradis avec un rond de lumière sur la tête. (PM 245-6)

This unexpected reversal motif, already visible in 'La Fosse aux péchés' and 'Légende poldève', is a favourite one with Aymé. He uses another faerie image to pursue it in 'Conte de Noël', where 'l'enfant Noël' distributes joy to the ladies of a brothel instead of to spoilt little rich children, and again in 'Dermuche' where 'le petit Jésus' comes down to die instead of a morally innocent criminal. 'La Grâce' explores the same thematic area with a hero who is so virtuous that he is awarded a halo. He has to wear it around the streets of Montmartre. Here Aymé is again combining two genres; the halo is essentially a faerie accessory but the situation—a mortal has a strange gift conferred upon him within his own context—is clearly fantastic. Duperrier is quite embarrassed by his distinction. At first he replaces his bowler hat with a wide-brimmed one to hide the halo, but finally tries to get rid of it. This is where the common notion of virtue comes under fire. It seems reasonable to the victim that he should simply sin to get rid of it. This neat paradox—a saint trying desperately to sin—provides Aymé with some very comic situations. Duperrier is innocent of lust, for example, and has to consult 'un livre révoltant où se trouvait exposé, sous forme d'un enseignement clair et direct, l'essentiel de la luxure' (VP 95). He tries pride, anger, greed, envy, laziness and avarice as well as lust but all to no avail. He finally becomes a pimp on the boulevard de Clichy, counting the night's takings by the light of his halo. Aymé's notion of sin and virtue is no ordinary one. His spokesman is perhaps the Devil in *Les Jumeaux du diable* when he says to St Peter:

> — Vraiment le monde est trop vertueux. C'est un scandale. Tu ne recevrais pas dix âmes par an, si le monde allait raisonnablement. (JD 10)

In 'Samson', Aymé pastiches the biblical story line while adapting it to his own ends. His hero has magic hair and a lucid knowledge of his destiny, but Aymé adds to the psychological interest of the theme by describing a superman who is 'désespérément seul', who aspires to mediocrity and anonymity and whose submission to Dalila is quite conscious. 'Samson' is a rather heavy tale and not as typical of Aymé's style as the lighter hearted and much freer adaptation of the same motif in 'Le faux policier', where Martin's mistress Dalila insists he shave off his moustache, thus changing his appearance and bringing catastrophe.

The entertainer in Aymé is very fond of parody. This comes out again in 'Le Mendiant', which adapts the biblical Nativity theme to a modern American setting. Aymé's intermediary is the *pauvre type* (American style) Theo Bradley who is pitied by all his friends because he has to drive a car that is several years old. One night Bradley is visited by an angel who takes him to a ramshackle Detroit garage where a young couple are just putting the finishing touches to a car that has taken them nine months' effort. We witness the ecstatic moment of completion ('il est né!') and the arrival of three worshippers from afar bearing petrol, oil and water. From what seems to be a dream, Bradley wakes with a sense of purpose: he will be the prophet of 'Le Grand Moteur' and will found 'La Grande Eglise Motorisée'. The tale grows bitter now as Aymé satirizes the commercialization of the new religion and acidly underlines the American worship of the motor car. He sketches the repressed, hypocritically puritan, racist matriarchy that preoccupied him in the plays *Louisiane* and *La Mouche bleue*. Aymé was criticizing the United States from first-hand experience. In 1949 he had been invited to the United States by *Collier's* magazine, which planned to publish his impressions in article form. 'Le Mendiant' was part of his offering. It was politely declined.

Aymé's rather liberal attitude towards literary convention is visible again in the special case of *Les Contes du chat perché*. This collection is one of Aymé's best-known works. It won him the Prix

Chanteclair and has been consistently re-edited ever since its first publication. In 1979 several of the tales were even adapted for the theatre by a young Parisian troupe, the Compagnie de la Licorne. Outwardly, these stories seem to have been written for children. Aymé intimated quite early that they were part of 'l'art d'être grand-père' and that they were written for his granddaughter Françoise, but he later confessed: 'Mes contes pour enfants, je les ai écrits pour moi-même. Je ne crois pas à la littérature enfantine.'[6] His second *prière d'insérer* to these tales was probably more honest: like so many so-called children's books, *Les Contes du chat perché* were 'écrits pour les enfants âgés de quatre à soixante-quinze ans'. For Marcel Aymé there was certainly an element of personal nostalgia in them too: they harked back to his games of 'chat' in the Cours St Maurice at Dôle and to the happy days of his early childhood in Villers-Robert and his adventures with his cousins in his uncle's mill.

These tales are special in two ways: firstly, because Aymé makes a faerie world apart out of a very real setting, and, secondly, because some of the unreal within that world is distinctly fantastic in character. The seventeen stories are set in a special farmyard and centred on the farmer's two young daughters, Delphine ('l'aînée') and Marinette ('la plus blonde') and their animal friends. This is an ideal frame for faerie. Aymé encourages the feeling of this being a world apart not only by setting the action in the farmyard and its surrounds but also because the stories feature an esoteric child's point of view. The farm is a children's world like so many that have been exploited in literature, an

> univers enfantin séparé, replié sur lui-même et où peuvent faire irruption l'improbable, l'étrange et même l'impossible.[7]

We are much closer here to the Wonderland of Peter Pan or Alice than to a Fairyland of giants and magic spells. Alice and Wendy are surely related to Delphine and Marinette and a long line of young girls whose imagination and sensitivity have been exploited to link fantasy and reality.

The magic of the farm mainly surrounds the animals. It is not the simple magic proposition of Aymé's earlier novel *La Jument verte*, where he proposed a storytelling horse with a highly refined sensuality; here it is much more episodic. The animals can talk and play humanized roles and to a certain extent they can use their reason.

Aymé is clearly conscious of the tradition which produced the 'Cochon-tyran' and the 'Renard-fripon' but he varies his characterization. His fox is the traditional wily creature but his pig is usually stupid, vain and rather nasty, his duck very clever and helpful, his cat rather passive and his rooster proud, arrogant and even treacherous. Yet any stability from story to story depends on Aymé's whim and on the girls' imagination. The pig turns out smart enough to play the detective in 'Les Vaches' and the ass, normally stupid and obstinate of course, appears as sensitive and intelligent in 'Le mauvais jars'.

Most of the action depends on contact between the girls and their animal friends. There is complicity and understanding only between them. The girls try to educate an ox; the animals help the girls with their homework and troop into the classroom to see the results. As well as occasionally adopting human roles, the beasts change roles among themselves: a deer swaps with an ox, a panther comes to live on the farm, a wolf wants to play 'chat perché' with the girls and a duck turns world-traveller. Animals talking and thinking is not an end to the magic. Aymé waves his wand once more and we see blindness transferred by telepathy, a hen that changes into an elephant, two white cows that disappear and a horse that shrinks to the size of a rooster. The fantastic even touches Delphine and Marinette to change them into an ass and a horse. This potentially frightening situation is eased somewhat by the fact that it occurs within a frame where such events seem almost acceptable.

The magic often starts with mischief; one of the girls' pranks backfires on them or one of the animals does something unnatural. A frequent story pattern starts with the parents going to town for the day and warning their daughters against doing one particular thing in their absence. Of course Delphine and Marinette disobey and promptly get into a fix. Their situation worsens as they try to repair the damage and the ominous moment when their parents will return approaches. This tension is usually eased by a convenient last-minute solution. It is the girls' curious predicaments and the inventive solutions that provide much of the charm of these tales.

Delphine and Marinette's pranks are caused by their very innocence. Aymé is presenting the world through unconditioned eyes. He has created a frame where the girls can question the constraints, the conventions and the routines of the adult world and find them lacking. There is fantasy not only in the metamorphoses but also in the girls' minds: perhaps the wolf would make a nice playmate after all; perhaps the donkey is really quite clever despite what people say; and why should a panther not live on the farm? It is their fecund and strangely logical imagination that often provokes the magic. In 'Les Boîtes de peinture' Delphine and Marinette try to draw the two white cows, but it is not possible to draw them on white paper, say the girls, or at least they would not be visible: 'C'est comme si vous n'existiez pas.' So the offended animals promptly disappear. The animals apply the same innocent process to the girls' homework. The problem is to calculate how many trees there are in a hypothetical forest, so the animals simply set out to count the trees in their own real forest. And when the girls want it to rain so they will not have to go and visit their nasty old aunt, what more natural solution than to ask Alphonse the cat, transposed from the Aymé apartment on the rue Paul-Féval, to wash his whiskers?

Naturally the parents cannot participate in this innocence. They are depersonalized, being referred to and even addressed as 'les parents'. In fact the other adults suffer the same fate, becoming 'la maîtresse', 'l'inspecteur' and 'l'aveugle'. Even aunt Mélina and uncle Alfred tend to be stereotyped figures. When they are active, the parents are always enemy figures. They seem hard-hearted, suspicious and miserly. What little dialogue they are accorded is unsympathetic: they spend their time scolding the girls or else rather optimistically warning them to 'soyez sages . . .', and they whisper ominously to each other as they watch the pig or the chicken growing plumper each day. There is a communication barrier represented by different attitudes to the animals. For the practical parents they are beasts of burden and work and candidates for the cooking pot, while for the girls they are playmates. The parents' main function in this faerie is obviously to represent the parallel, real world, the world of farm chores, homework and the threatened 'pain sec', a world to which the girls usually return after each episodic tale.

Strange things may occur and the girls will get into all sorts of scrapes, but in the end all will be put right. The animals will be restored to their proper forms and proportions, Delphine and Marinette will cease to be a horse and an ass and the blind man will retrieve his blindness. The kidnapped hens are brought back, the lost cows are found and the little black rooster can employ all the guile he can muster but will end up *au vin* in the pot all the same.

Often a return to reality includes a moral ending. Good deeds are rewarded and pride, hard-heartedness, arrogance and treachery are suitably punished whether in the pig, the rooster, the drunken soldier or the parents. Yet these moral punishments almost never involve Delphine and Marinette. Grandfather Aymé is clearly trying to teach the girls a lesson without actually punishing them. The threatened punishments for disobedience are miraculously waived (an exception: their 'affreux péchés' of falsehood and disobedience in 'Le petit coq noir'). Sometimes this is simply because Aymé finds the parents too malicious: the girls fool their parents and allow Alphonse the cat to escape his drowning in 'La Patte du chat' because the parents were being quite unjust. Sometimes it is because the girls have had a fright and already learned their lesson: they are temporarily eaten by the wolf in 'Le Loup', harshly whipped as animals in 'L'Ane et le cheval' and made to feel thoroughly ashamed in 'Les Boîtes de peinture'. But more often it is simply that the girls have got into a fix through their own innocence or generosity: they are led into mischief in 'Le Loup' and 'Le petit coq noir'. Good intentions and the saviour figure of uncle Alfred retrieve the situation in 'Le Mouton'. The girls seem to deserve punishment in 'Les Cygnes' because they have again disobeyed their parents, but their pure hearts and good intentions save them once more.

Delphine and Marinette are not wilfully disobedient; it is just that girls will be girls . . . . This same reasoning is even applied to the animals. The pig's raving vanity should perhaps be punished in 'La Buse et le cochon' but he is let off because Nature made him the ugliest of all; and when the wolf eats the girls he is only being his natural self. So when he is painfully cut open to free them he is sewn up again instead of being left to die. And in any case, he seems to have learned a lesson so why punish him? It is he, rather than the scolding parents or a moralizing Aymé who rounds off the tale: 'Je vous jure qu'à l'avenir on ne me prendra plus à être aussi gourmand. Et d'abord, quand je verrai des enfants je commencerai par me sauver' (CP 182).

The reprieve in 'Les Cygnes' gives the entertainer in Aymé a chance to show off his talents in a superb ending. The girls have crossed the road in spite of their parents' admonitions and are being held prisoner by some swans who turn out to be harsh disciplinarians. They are finally liberated by a wise old swan and returned to the farmhouse just in time to welcome their parents. But the effort costs their liberator his life: it is his swansong that will enchant the parents just long enough to let the girls scurry home. The final irony lies in the parents' comment: 'Quel dommage que vous n'ayez pas traversé la route tout à l'heure. Un cygne a chanté sur les prés' (CP 325).

Les Contes du chat perché are the work of a storyteller much more than of a moralist. This is clear above all in his endings. When the animals cause an uproar in the classroom trying to help the girls with their arithmetic homework, the teacher gives them 'zéro de conduite'. But the inspector, fortuitously present that day, saves the story by giving them the 'croix d'honneur' for their originality! This is the Aymé who, having allowed an ass a certain measure of cunning to teach the nasty gander a lesson, rounds off his tale with:

> Aussi n'est-il plus question, depuis ce jour-là, de la bêtise de l'âne; et l'on dit, au contraire, d'un homme à qui l'on veut faire compliment de son intelligence qu'il est fin comme un âne. (CP 264)

Aymé has often been called a fabulist more than a moralist. Indeed there is something of the simple world of La Fontaine or the medieval *fabliaux* in stories like 'Le petit coq noir', 'Le Paon' or 'Le mauvais jars', where the animals interact among themselves. The moral character of this world cannot be denied. It has been stressed by almost all those who have written on Aymé. Yet for him the purity lies not so much in the moral character as in the lack of artificial adult preoccupations. In his first *prière d'insérer* Aymé wrote:

> Je les écrivais pour reposer mes lecteurs éventuels de leurs tristes aventures où l'amour et l'argent sont si bien entremêlés qu'on les prend à chaque instant l'un pour l'autre, ce qui est forcément fatigant. Mes histoires sont donc des histoires simples, sans amour et sans argent.

The fact that we are adventuring in a moral world should not necessarily provoke a search for an individual lesson at the end of each story. This has been a common failing among commentators, who have felt obliged to label as many stories as possible. The formulae 'A chacun sa fonction dans la vie', 'la sottise des gens qui vont à l'encontre de leurs talents naturels' or the more complicated 'la dangereuse séduction dont jouissent les révolutionnaires dans les milieux intellectuels'[8] may not be actually wrong, but to sum up

Aymé's tales like this is absolutely to miss the essence of his talent. This kind of formulation (and thus limitation) quite destroys the *conteur*'s nostalgic, whimsical, grandfatherly charm. Such activity is as futile as the criticism of André Rousseaux, who missed the point entirely when he accused Aymé of 'lèse-réalisme', asserting that 'Si les bêtes parlaient, elles tiendraient un tout autre langage.'[9] Aymé's ironic reply is contained in his second *prière d'insérer*:

> Il avait bien raison. Rien n'interdit de croire en effet que si les bêtes parlaient, elles parleraient de politique ou de l'avenir de la science dans les îles Aléoutiennes. Peut-être même qu'elles feraient de la critique littéraire avec distinction.

* * *

Jules Verne and the comtesse de Ségur are two of Aymé's most often avowed sources of inspiration. Ségur's influence is easily seen in the *Contes du chat perché*, but it is only when we move towards Aymé's fantastic vein that we encounter a thin vein of science fiction which might be a product of Aymé's penchant for Verne. For Aymé, science fiction seems to be an extension of the fantastic. He avoids the traditional thematic material—interstellar invasions, space stations and one-eyed Martians:

> Habituellement, je n'éprouve pas de sentiment bien vif pour le genre science-fiction. Dans la réalité, les exploits des spoutniks ne m'ont jamais fait battre le coeur.[10]

Aymé's science fiction is more humanized, like his faerie and like the more traditional fantastic. He often uses future man to focus attention on present man.

Aymé's most significant contribution to the science fiction genre is a long and serious *nouvelle* called 'Pastorale'. He launches into the futurism of a seventeenth Republic where a series of skyscraper villages shelter the whole of France. On the surface this is pure fantasy but on closer examination it is an Orwellian world closely based on reality, reflecting present problems like over-population, centralization and government control of all aspects of life. Aymé describes a society where the social authorities exercise total control over the individual, the kind of society that Aymé foresees and criticizes not only in stories like 'La Carte' and the play *La Convention Belzébir* but also in several polemic articles devoted to civil liberties.

It is a society where nothing is left to chance. The number and sex of all children are regulated, dreams are monitored, excess population is exterminated, all desires find immediate satisfaction and poets are re-educated in mathematics and the physical sciences in case they upset society's logic. The ugly buildings and lifeless inhabitants of 'Pastorale' allow Aymé to exercise his acid wit against many of our social and political customs and institutions.

Futuristic imagination sparkles even more darkly in a story called 'La Fille du shérif' and subtitled 'Le roman que je n'écrirai jamais'. This is an undeveloped sketch for a longer story, rather clumsily blending Aymé's black humour and his post-Liberation political views. Several of his magazine and newspaper articles of the period strongly criticize the government's attempts to tie France's defence to America and N.A.T.O. Written in 1951 and supposedly set in 1953, 'La Fille du shérif' tells of an atomic war between Russia and America using France as the battleground. France is obliterated and then abolished by the U.N. Most of the French have been killed and the rest are enslaved by the United States. Aymé once again takes the opportunity to scourge de Gaulle: during the atomic war a government of 'la France libre' is set up in Missouri and their radio broadcasts tell the French to give their lives willingly for France. Their post-war *épuration* executes 100 000 and imprisons twice that number.

The fantastic genre seems to be less governed by literary convention than Fairyland or Flash Gordon and more widely accepted as a tool of 'legitimate' literature. Aymé takes full advantage of this freedom. In Fairyland, Aymé's man has worn seven-league boots, made love to a dryad and defeated a magic ogre, but here his Everyman, so often called Martin, will be more personally and more disturbingly involved. Yet Aymé still anchors his fantastic creations in reality. Reality is his source material even more visibly than it was with his faerie. One of the rules accepted by most writers of the unreal is that one must not get too far from the recognizably real:

> Pour arriver à créer une oeuvre viable, en quelque domaine que ce soit, il est nécessaire de s'éloigner assez du réel pour le dominer, tout en restant assez près de lui pour ne pas le perdre de vue.[11]

Like most creative minds, Aymé starts with known elements and rearranges them rather than indulging in total creation. He can suggest that two minds may inhabit the same body or that one being can have multiple bodies, but they will be real bodies. They will never have three arms or two heads. Aymé never goes as far as the grotesque. Man may be given a halo or a changed face, but not green horns or a tail. Aymé's fantastic images are usually either extensions or reversals of reality. An extension is proposed in 'Le Décret', where instead of the government advancing the clock one hour in summer, the move proposed is seventeen years in order to reach the end of an interminable war. 'La Liste' is an extension of a different kind: a poor farmer has so many daughters that he has to have a list to remember their names. When one name is accidentally torn off the list, he forgets the particular daughter and the poor girl disappears. A reversal of reality is the basis of 'La Grâce', where Duperrier wears his halo despite what is normally regarded as a life of sin. Mostly Aymé tries to reverse or extend the more certain elements of man's existence—death, space, time, identity—so that our shock is all the greater.

Spectres, vampires and werewolves, the traditional fantastic creatures, do not interest Aymé much more than 'les exploits des spoutniks'. The closest he comes to this tradition is in *Les Jumeaux du diable* with its supernatural twins. It is man and his society that concern Aymé. Much of his fantastic is concerned with giving new capacities to man and then exploring the consequences. Just as the faerie of 'L'Huissier', 'La Fosse aux péchés' or 'Légende poldève' and the science fiction of 'Pastorale' were used to mask social criticism, so Aymé's fantastic is put to this use. In 'Dermuche' capital punishment and the cruelty of prison authorities chained by impersonal regulations come under strong attack. The simpleton Dermuche is condemned for a triple murder but he has no comprehension of a crime he committed simply because he liked the tinkling of a music box. He is morally innocent, having 'une petite âme claire comme une eau de source' (VP 122). Dermuche has long talks with the prison chaplain about 'le petit Jésus' and on the eve of his execution he writes to heaven to be allowed to have his little music box when he reaches paradise. That night Dermuche's soul dominates his body to the extent of transforming him into a new-born baby complete with the same tattoos. It seems that the soft-hearted Aymé has granted Dermuche a reprieve, and this would be a typical Aymé ending, but this time he is not in the mood for reprieves. The chief warder is stubbornly unmoved: 'je ne veux pas d'histoires'. The rules are the rules even in the face of a miracle. We are treated to several pages of Aymé's blackest irony as the guards coldly verify Dermuche's birthmark and fingerprints and carry the child up to the guillotine regardless. As with 'Pastorale' and 'La Fille du shérif', Aymé is using the unreal mode to complement the real mode; he criticized the judicial system and capital punishment in several polemic articles[12] and in his notorious play *La Tête des autres*.

Aymé's satire is not quite as bitter when he underlines the commercial exploitation of creative artistry in 'La bonne peinture'. The fantastic premise of this *nouvelle* is a concretization of the intellectual satisfaction derived from the contemplation of a work of art. Lafleur's canvases have very special qualities:

> sa peinture était devenue si riche, si sensible, si fraîche, si solide, qu'elle constituait une véritable nourriture et non pas seulement pour l'esprit, mais bien aussi pour le corps. (. . .) Le menu variait selon le sujet du tableau, sa composition et son coloris, mais il était toujours très soigné, très abondant et il n'y manquait même pas la boisson. (VP 171)

Like 'Avenue Junot', 'La bonne peinture' is a rambling frolic through Aymé's familiar Montmartre with his artist friends, but here there is more direction to the tale. The basic situation is familiar: the poor but happy artist whose lifestyle is threatened by fame and fortune and the grasping parasites—critics, gallery-owners and journalists—who are attracted by his success. Aymé exploits his premise for its comic potential by satirizing the American scientists who try to analyse Lafleur's gift and the art critics who are nonplussed by the tangible qualities of his work. In another comic scene the dealer Hermèce gets indigestion from feasting his eyes.

Of course there is a darker side to this humour. Hermèce and his fellow parasites think of nothing but profit. The dealer doesn't even want to tell Lafleur about his talent, and buys up the paintings as fast as he can. The state soon puts a stop to this by nationalizing Lafleur, and Aymé's cynical wit now describes the artist as one of France's 'instruments de production' with a factory and the associated bureaucracy. Art has become 'efficace', a political tool and a means to material rather than intellectual comfort.

Aymé obviously found the *conte fantastique* well suited to social criticism. More than with his faerie, the entertainer now often takes second place to a more serious side of Aymé. Many of his ridiculous situations are used to present parallel realities through which Aymé can snipe at the corresponding real situations. This process is used particularly well in 'La Carte'. Yet in general, Aymé's fantastic is still much more personal than his faerie; it is above all the more individual human failings that he underlines. The social or political criticism is often accessory to his story's primary effect.

The little ironic twists introduced into reality often provide Aymé or his protagonist with a rather special position, a privileged point of view from which to reassess reality. The short story seldom allows room to discuss this advantage and it is the novel *La Jument verte* that provides Aymé's most explicit comments. When the painter Murdoire endows a canvas of a green mare with the gift of observation so that she can spy on the Haudouin family from her wall, the mare offers her remarks directly to the reader:

> Je m'appliquai à observer mes hôtes, à réfléchir sur le spectacle qu'ils me livraient de leur vie intime. (. . .) Tandis que l'observateur ambulant ne peut s'attacher à découvrir dans le monde que les harmonies des grands nombres et le secret des séries, l'observateur immobile a cet avantage de surprendre les habitudes de la vie. (JV 21)

A much more personal advantage is gained for Cérusier by his change of face in *La belle image*. Since his friends no longer recognize him, he can overhear what they say about him behind his back. But what he hears is not always to his liking:

> Tiens, dit Joubert le sculpteur, voilà la bonne de Cérusier. A propos, qu'est-ce qu'il devient, ce pauvre Cérusier?
> — Pauvre, protesta Garnier. Il n'est pas à plaindre.
> — Je ne dis pas qu'il soit à plaindre, mais c'est quand même un pauvre type.
> Quoiqu'il en eût dit, le ton de ses paroles exprimait une commisération à mon égard. (BI 43)

Cérusier, too, has time to reflect on this new ability to see beneath his own façade, 'examiner sa vie avec un lucide regard d'outre-tombe et pénétrer en étranger dans ses propres secrets' (BI 85).

The novel *La belle image* deserves in many ways to be treated as a short story. It starts with the same absurd premise and proceeds to explore the consequences and the protagonist's reactions. It is almost as if an ideal short story situation has been stretched and padded artificially to fill a novel. In fact this kind of situation is much better suited to the pace and concision of a short story. Much the same could be said of the play *Les Oiseaux de lune* except that there Aymé stretches his situation with much more subtlety and variety.

An almost identical advantage is engineered in 'Le Nain', where the dwarf Valentin suddenly grows up and is not recognized any more. The truths he overhears are more flattering than Cérusier's but equally revealing. Delphine and Marinette are given an unpleasant insight into what it is like to be an animal on their parents' farm in 'L'Ane et le cheval', and a spoilt young *bourgeoise* in 'La Fabrique' is given a much more instructive appreciation of her own existence by means of a jump in time. Valérie is told that if she does not stop biting her fingernails by Christmas there will be no presents this year. We see her wake on Christmas Eve to discover that she has indeed bitten them again:

> Elle eut un mouvement de retraite comme pour échapper à la triste réalité, et croyant s'enfoncer sous les couvertures, elle s'enfonça dans la nuit des temps et de cent vingt ans en arrière, en sorte qu'elle se retrouva en 1845. (EJ 121-2)

This trip is a lesson in humility. Valérie is put in the position of invisible observer of a day in the life of an underprivileged family. This new reality chills her to the bone. The youngest son is dying of consumption but he is still sent to work in the freezing factory because the family needs the pittance he will earn and above all because if he is left at home his retarded brother will probably assault him. Hippolyte knows he is going to die, just as many of his young colleagues have that winter, but he has heard of the visits that 'l'enfant Noël' pays to little rich children and wants to see a Christmas tree before he dies. At the end of his terrible day's work, the speechless Valérie follows him home. On the way, he hears hammering: 'C'est Papa qui cloue mon arbre de Noël', but in fact his father is making a little coffin. Valérie can bear it no more: taking him by the hand she succeeds in translating them both back to her century. On Christmas morning she gives him her tree and her presents and is just about to tell her parents she has a little brother for Christmas when his exhaustion and happiness finally kill him and he disappears. 'La Fabrique' is a rarity in Aymé's work, a story completely devoid of humour. It was the last short story Aymé ever wrote and was published after his death. One of the most moving of Aymé's tales, 'La Fabrique' was very successfully adapted for television by Pascal Thomas and shown on Christmas Eve 1979.

Cérusier's 'coup d'oeil oblique' is also reflected throughout the *Contes du chat perché* in the innocent, unconditioned eyes through which Delphine and Marinette interpret the world, but a richer exploitation of it is found in 'Le Décret', with its voyage seventeen years into the future and abrupt return. The anti-serious Aymé uses this premise to provoke several comic situations. The narrator tries to return a cycle he hired during his stay in the future and discovers that the shop still sells umbrellas! The owner, who has the same name as the cycle seller, finds rather ridiculous the idea that one day he might sell 'bécanes'. Seriousness returns as the narrator continues:

> Tandis qu'il parlait ainsi, je comparais à ce jeune visage frais et rieur, un autre visage de dix-sept ans plus âgé, dont un lupus déformait tout un côté. (PM 116)

It is this ability to see through present appearances to a future reality that is the most disquieting aspect of the narrator's position and the most fruitful for Aymé's social commentary too. Here he meets a friend in the *métro*:

> Il est très déprimé et me confie qu'il est dans une situation extrêmement difficile. Je regarde avec curiosité cet être minable qui, dans une dizaine d'années, se trouvera à la tête d'une fortune colossale, malhonnêtement gagnée à de scandaleux trafics. Tandis qu'il me parle de sa misère présente, je le revois dans sa future opulence. (. . .) je suis partagé entre la compassion et le dégoût que m'inspire sa brillante carrière. (PM 123-4)

The splitting effect of this privileged position is the main theme of this long humanist *nouvelle*. The victim can see things that are invisible to others. He does not always like what he sees; he quickly rejects his privilege, effectively 'forgetting' the future. Like Samson, he wants to be nothing more than an ordinary man.

Aymé's physical unrealities also serve him particularly well by providing a tangible image for an abstract process, sentiment or quality. This often borders on the traditional role of the *fantastique intérieur* with its physical representations of psychological activity.

Aymé is not so much a moralist here as a very serious humanist. 'Le Décret' gives a physical dimension to the feeling of *déjà vu* and, as young Valentin changes more and more of his friends into birds in *Les Oiseaux de lune*, we are afforded a bleak look at the effects of absolute power on man's soul. Both of these show a particularly serious Aymé. His lighter tone returns in the use of Duperrier's halo to represent his inner virtue in 'La Grâce', or in the concretization of inner satisfactions in 'La bonne peinture'. 'Le Romancier Martin' is perhaps the most fruitful example of the mental becoming physical. Here Aymé uses the fantastic to give a concrete dimension to the experience of artistic creation. He adopts the Pygmalion gift of life motif (akin to what the French theoreticians call the *statue vivante*) in portraying a novelist who creates his characters so thoroughly that they come to life and manage to exist on the same plane as their author. They have a will of their own and try to change the course of their novel. Finally some of them even escape from Martin's control. The powerless novelist confesses: 'J'abandonne mes personnages, mais leur vie continue.'

The special experience of childhood is to some extent made concrete in *Les Contes du chat perché* and Aymé proposes a tangible image for the next stage of the human cycle in 'Le Nain'. Valentin's body becomes adult but he still has the innocence of a child. Like the narrator in 'Le Décret' and the centaur in 'Fiançailles', he is torn between what he was and what he is becoming. His metamorphosis also reflects Aristide's potentially traumatic discovery of sex through the eyes of someone who knows nothing of social convention and constraint. His clumsy but spontaneous advances to Germina are rejected. The ex-dwarf tries frantically to learn another circus trick so that he can stay in the circus and win back the love that Germina bore him. But that love was innocent and can never be the same. He reluctantly leaves the artificial, protected, childhood life of the circus where he no longer belongs and goes to face the adult responsibilities of earning a living and forming mature relationships. M. Barnaboum finally announces: 'Le nain est mort.'

The physical image in 'Le Couple' intensifies the next stages in the human cycle: marriage and divorce. Antoine and Valérie love each other so much that their bodies fuse together into one. Society's sexism is reflected in the choice of Antoine's body to express the union. Valérie lacks physical presence and effectively loses her identity in this marriage. She finds no fulfilment wearing her husband's body so the union disintegrates after a few weeks. The experience of death is explored somewhat less seriously in 'La Carte' and 'Le Temps mort', which propose a sort of relative death through the total disappearance of a victim for a short period. But Aymé is more interested in the manipulation of time in these stories and, apart from touching on man's egoistic resentment that the world will keep on turning when he is gone, hardly explores the notion of death any further.

Man's solitude, a strong element in the modern literary conception of man, is often Aymé's primary target in these fantastic intensifications. Newly unrecognizable characters are placed in a situation where their isolation from others is increased by their fantastic affliction. After his face change, Cérusier feels that 'Cette solitude soudaine dans un monde qui ne vous connaît plus, c'est une chose épouvantable' (BI 90) and the dwarf Valentin feels cut off in the same way when his metamorphosis removes him from his friends:

> Valentin regardait Mlle Germina galoper sur la piste. Debout sur son cheval, et le bras tendu vers la foule, l'écuyère répondait par des sourires aux applaudissements, et Valentin songeait qu'aucun de ces sourires n'était pour lui. Il se sentait las et honteux de sa solitude. (NA 27)

Valentin is not spared Aymé's irony: his happiness lay in his deformity itself.

The most striking intensification of man's solitude is probably the image of the superman Samson who feels cut off from other men because of his magic hair and wants to return to the ranks of ordinary mortals to discover 'la sensation d'équilibre que procure une force musculaire à la mesure de l'homme'.[13] Despite its rather faerie character, Samson's magic hair serves as a fantastic intensification of the absurdity of his condition and provides a physical metaphor for his frustration when faced with the forces of a destiny he cannot control. This is another reason why he tries to have his magic hair cut off: his superhuman strength is too strong for his merely human will. He is not in control of himself:

> Ma force m'apparaissait comme une personne surajoutée à la mienne, un maître qui se servait de mes membres, de mes mains, de mon corps et disposait sans discussion de ma volonté. Ecrasé sous la pression de ce géant et emporté par son élan imbécile, je n'étais qu'une créature dérisoire, reléguée dans un

coin de mon être et moins libre que ne peut l'être un paralytique.[14]

Samson has a split image of himself as man and superman, 'assis entre deux sièges'. He is very conscious of his destiny as national liberator but he wants to be just human. The impossibility of this is brought out by his symbolic attempt at suicide: he goes to Gaza looking for a girl who will sell him to the Philistines. Shaved, blinded and chained to a mill-stone, he seems to have escaped the 'présence étrangère' and found his human self. But his hair is beginning to grow again . . .

Aymé had already tried to give a physical dimension to grace and free will by describing man's life as predestined and controlled by a guiding master in *Les Jumeaux du diable*, but the novel's length and heavy style negate the potential advantage of Aymé's graphic image. *Les Jumeaux du diable*, like *La belle image*, is easier to appreciate if it is considered more as a short story mistakenly stretched to novel length. The opening of the novel reflects the tongue-in-cheek tone and the easy style that were to become the trade-marks of the *conteur*:

> A travers les infinis où les dimensions se reposent, Satan chevauchait un manche à balai qui est le véhicule ordinaire aux créatures infernales d'occident. Il avait hâte, murmurant à chaque instant: Keibal, Ikal, formule incomparable pour presser l'allure des manches à balai (JD 9)

and Aymé follows up the image with the sort of proposition that was to become the backbone of his short stories:

> — Céphas, j'ai rêvé un jeu amusant. J'imaginais deux hommes de la Terre, deux hommes tout pareils, d'âme et d'apparence, (. . .) Je n'ai pas imaginé plus avant, Céphas. Seulement, je m'interrogeais s'ils étaient promis au Ciel ou à l'Enfer.
> Le Diable sourit.
> — Même, je me suis demandé s'il se pouvait que l'un fût damné et l'autre élu de Dieu. (JD 10-11)

But what follows is an over-long and rather unimaginative exploitation of the early momentum of the story and is totally lacking in the charm of Aymé's later developments of this kind of proposition. The novel is a clumsy mixture of the mysterious and the banal.

Aymé clearly sensed the failure of this, his first venture into the unreal: he always refused to have the novel reprinted, calling it 'un très mauvais roman'.[15]

'Le Romancier Martin' shows what *Les Jumeaux du diable* might have become had it been written ten years later. Aymé explores a similar thematic area through the image of a god-author who cannot refrain from ending his novels with a massacre:

> Il y avait un romancier, son nom était Martin, qui ne pouvait pas s'empêcher de faire mourir les principaux personnages de ses livres, et même les personnages de moindre importance. Tous ces pauvres gens, pleins de vigueur et d'espoir au premier chapitre, mouraient comme d'épidémie dans les vingt ou trente dernières pages, et bien souvent dans la force de l'âge. (DM 9)

Siné's humorous sketch on the cover of the Livre de Poche edition shows bodies sandwiched between pages of manuscript while Martin eyes off the fleeing remnants of his characters, wondering whom to impale next with his giant pen. The main action of this story is a revolt by Armandine Soubiron, who comes to plead with her creator and 'maître' in a prayer situation. She is upset by her 'fatalité' and Martin's excessive use of arbitrary power over his characters' destinies. Martin protests that he is not really in control and Armandine comes to realize that she is free as long as she doesn't regard herself as a prisoner of destiny. She finally escapes completely from Martin's novel.

The frantic running out of time as man rushes towards his absurd death is given a physical dimension in 'Le Temps mort', where another Martin simply ceases to exist every second day. Aymé has also given a solid dimension to the relativity of time. For Martin, time actually does pass twice as fast as for everyone else. His solitude is intensified by the difficulty of communication with those around him. His mistress is used to bring out the way two people develop at different rates:

> Son amour, qui durait depuis deux années pleines, n'avait ni la fraîcheur, ni l'élan que gardait celui de Martin, âgé d'une année seulement. (DM 107)

Aymé exploits Martin's predicament, drawing brief glimmers of comedy from his pathetic ruses to make time go more slowly and from the situations he finds himself in when he suddenly comes back to life.

The fantastic time rationing of 'La Carte' is probably Aymé's most striking attempt to give a concrete dimension to the abstract. Here, too, the relativity of time is intensified. He describes the inhuman logic of a governmental decree that institutes time rationing, a situation reminiscent of the authoritarian excesses of 'Pastorale'. Those citizens whose work is regarded as socially productive will live full time while all unproductive consumers will be rationed by time cards and 'tickets de vie'. The relativity of time is well underlined by Aymé's marvellous stretching month. A humble painter may experience a month of only fifteen days while the necessary butcher lives the full thirty-one and a corrupt official or a wily black-marketeer may stretch the month even further! This relativity leads to interesting problems of communication. How can the painter and the butcher share their experiences, since for one of them time goes twice as fast as for the other and a month only contains half as much experience? How can Flegmon arrange a rendezvous with his mistress when the day in question will have a different date for each of them?

This kind of intriguing invention allows Aymé to touch on potentially complicated concepts of time and then move on quickly before the story is slowed down by intellectualism. Aymé's story of fluid time is also a pretext for him to explore the humorous consequences of his premise: Monsieur Dumont arranges to have his fifteen days of existence in the second half of the month so as to avoid his shrewish wife, while the Roquenton couple come back to life in their bed separated by Lucette's lover. The guilty pair pretend not to know each other but the outraged husband finds their story 'bien invraisemblable'. But Aymé is a realist as well as a humorist; there will always be serious consequences too. The government's draconian decree only remains valid for as long as it takes the resourceful few to profit by it or find a way around it. One of Flegmon's rivals takes advantage of his temporary annihilation to manoeuvre against his candidature for the Académie Française. All efforts to change to a useful job are soon declared illegal, and very few citizens succeed in their attempts to obtain additional time tickets. So we soon see more sinister solutions. Flegmon and many others take to living at twice the pace, eating twice as much to make up for the days when they will not exist. To his credit, Flegmon also tries to work at twice the pace. Trading in time tickets begins, soon to blossom into a flourishing and well-organized black-market. The rich and the wily exploit their weaker fellows and amass large numbers of tickets, and they find themselves able to lengthen a month beyond its normal thirty-one days. Finally the decree has to be repealed because the expected economy of food has not been realized, but not before Aymé has used the consequences of his premise to highlight man's inhumanity, his lack of courage and moral fibre and his blatant egoism, all illustrated by the intellectual Flegmon.

Of course Marcel Aymé is using his fantastic time rationing to comment on reality. 'La Carte' is not one of Aymé's frivolous fairy tales; it is a very dense story and contains some of his most serious socio-political commentary. And far more than just being a pseudo-philosophical glance at the relativity of time, Aymé's tale is an indictment of events in the France of 1943. The time being taken away by decree in 'La Carte' is a metaphor for the human life that was being so callously disposed of during the Deportation. Of course the time rationing in 'La Carte' is a reflection of food rationing, but is not food a source of life? Aymé's pattern of trading, hoarding and black-marketeering closely follows the real patterns induced by wartime food rationing. But Aymé's story of relative death (so it is christened by the trendy set at their death soirées) is really an indictment of French acquiescence in deportation and extermination. The arbitrary but rationalized nature of the time decree:

> Afin de parer à la disette et d'assurer un meilleur rendement de l'élément laborieux de la population, il serait procédé à la mise à mort des consommateurs improductifs (PM 71)

could not fail to suggest Hitlerian policies to the Frenchman of 1943. The economic reasons given reflect some of the lame justifications advanced by the Nazis for their persecution of the Jews in the 1930s. Aymé's choice of victims for the fantastic rationing reflects the Nazis' deportation priorities too: among them are artists, prostitutes, intellectuals and of course Jews. The latter are allowed only half a day's existence per month.

It is above all people's reactions to this crisis that interest Marcel Aymé. Frenchmen who peeped from behind curtains (or worse, who stood and stared in the market-places) as their Jewish countrymen were trucked to the Vélodrome d'Hiver must have felt a little guilty on reading Aymé's fantasy: in 'La Carte' no one who is untouched by the decree pleads for the victims, no one protests, all are silently thankful that they are not on the list. Not even the Church, in the person of its bishop (a stand-in for Pope Pius XII, who was criticized for not denouncing Hitler's policies forcefully enough) is prepared to condemn the measures. Indeed, many people stand to gain from their colleagues' temporary deaths, just as neighbours and competitors must have often benefited from the Jewish deportations. To the sinister reactionary Maleffroi, society as a whole has benefited from the decree:

> On se rend compte alors à quel point les riches, les chômeurs, les intellectuels et les catins peuvent être dangereux dans une société où ils n'introduisent que le trouble, l'agitation vaine, le dérèglement et la nostalgie de l'impossible. (PM 83-4)

Nor are the victims of the decree totally blameless. None of them seem revolted by the ghastly inhumanity, the absurdity, the arrogance of the decree; they are all too busy trying to gain some personal advantage. Collective resistance is undermined by individual egoism. In Flegmon's diary entry for 18 February Aymé reiterates the often-voiced suggestion that Europe's Jews went into the Vélodrome d'Hiver, the cattle trucks and even the gas chambers without putting up much resistance. That day's entry describes a queue of victims waiting to register for their card. It is very like a *rafle*, complete with French police doing the dirty work and the victims' faces seeming to say, 'Je ne veux pas mourir encore.' But no one really resists. Flegmon tells us of his own 'cri de révolte', but adds that it was bellowed 'mentalement'. This suggestion of the victims' resignation to their fate blends into a brief, pessimistic comment on the speed with which man can adapt to and passively accept this kind of measure, his perception of injustice dulled by the fact that the decree is official and perhaps by the knowledge that many of his fellows are similarly afflicted. Flegmon gets used to his fate with rather unhealthy rapidity: just before his first disappearance he is 'angoissé' but the very next time he expresses 'Aucune appréhension'. Roquenton's second experience of death is even greeted with 'bonne humeur'.

Aymé's experiments with time also lead him to indulge in conventional time travel. He matches Valérie's trip backwards in time in 'La Fabrique' with a double time movement in 'Le Décret'. Cathelin stresses the *conte philosophique* aspect of both 'La Carte' and 'Le Décret' and Dumont devotes a whole chapter to Aymé's time manipulation, referring to the theories of Lavelle, Bergson and Bridoux, but in fact Aymé's stories are much more human, more personal than these critics suggest. Just as Aymé avoids Jules Verne or H. G. Wells time machines, so he avoids getting out of his depth with philosophical complications. The first half of 'Le Décret' is Aymé's only failing in this respect. The story starts very slowly because Aymé spends several pages telling of man's growing awareness of compressible, relative, physiological and subjective time and his efforts to control it (including a reference to the previous tale, 'La Carte'). It is only after eight pages that Aymé's victim starts to tell of the trip to the Jura and the inexplicable (and for him gratuitously mysterious) reversion to 1942, and it takes him several more pages to ascertain that he is in fact the only person who has retained a memory of the future.

At this point the orientation and quality of Aymé's story changes. It is almost as if the learned arguments about time, the narrator's difficulties in adapting to 1959, his trip to Dôle with its mysterious forest and strange fall back through time were nothing more than a pretext. Aymé's *conte philosophique* is really about man's loss of control in his attempts to master time, and his subsequent confusion. Psychological chaos results for a narrator split between time zones and not really knowing where he belongs. As he says, belonging is not just a matter of changing the clock:

> 'Etre d'une époque, pensai-je, c'est sentir l'univers et soi-même d'une certaine manière qui appartient à cette époque.' (PM 112)

The discussion of time in the first half of this long *nouvelle* leads to a much more human discussion in the second half. More explicitly than in 'L'Huissier', Aymé seems to start a new story: 'Il y avait, à Montmartre, en 1942, un homme qui connaissait l'avenir.' Once again, Aymé sets out to discover the human consequences of the special gift. The same loss of control is visible in 'Rechute' when time is reversed by a similar governmental decree. The Assemblée Nationale institutes a 'projet de loi visant à instituer l'année de 24 mois'. This seems reasonable enough except that in Aymé's world it means that everyone's age in years is thereby halved! The result is the kind of split already seen in stories like 'Fiançailles', 'Samson',

'Le Nain' and 'Le Décret': Josette now has the body of a child but the experience of an eighteen year old. For her it is not only disconcerting but humiliating:

> 'Si mon bébé pleure, j'appelle le grand loup méchant', disait maman. Et papa: 'Comme tu dois être contente! C'est si charmant d'être une vraie petite fille!' Leur enjouement m'était odieux, j'enrageais d'entendre leurs sottises. J'aurais voulu les écarter, les chasser d'auprès de mon lit, mais, en face de ces grandes personnes, je n'étais qu'une fillette de neuf ans que ses larmes ne protégeaient pas. (EA 51)

Youth stages armed revolt against the egoism of their elders' abuse of power and the law is abrogated.

'Rechute' is a longer, more complicated *nouvelle* than many. The rather high-handed and egoistic actions of the adults, and above all their official hypocrisy and lies, are certainly criticized here. Yet a more pertinent theme in 1950, when the story was published, was young Bernard's collaboration. Aymé describes Bernard's situation and justification very fairly. The young man's metamorphosis leaves him with naturally divided loyalties: while Josette and Pierre revert fully to physical childhood despite their emotional advance, Bernard was just old enough to keep his 'réalités physiologiques' as well as the memory of what they were for. So, although partly a child, he is tempted to side with the adults. When he is accused of collaboration and threatened with the *comité d'épuration* (a practice that Aymé's polemic articles describe as being hardly better than the excesses of the Occupation forces),[16] his defence is that of so many Frenchmen who simply tried to pick the winning side and lost:

> — Je n'ai pas collaboré! proteste-t-il. Comme tant d'autres, j'ai eu tout d'un coup treize ans, j'ai dû m'accommoder d'une situation moralement très pénible et, matériellement, des plus menaçantes. Bien sûr, l'idée ne m'est pas venue qu'un coup de force pouvait rétablir l'ordre légitime, mais je ne suis pas le seul à n'y avoir pas pensé. (EA 90)

Josette forgives him but only because he is part of the sexuality that she is just rediscovering.

The confusion provoked by these manipulations of time is also a feature of several stories where Aymé explores the multiplicity of man's personality. The duality of someone who is placed in the position of having to choose between two sides of himself recurs in 'Le Passe-muraille'. Dutilleul is an unassuming *pauvre type* whose monotonous existence is divided between his job as civil servant (third class) and his leisure hours reading the paper and sorting his stamp collection. Aymé has created a particularly ordinary character in order to use him as a vehicle for the clash between reality and fantasy. One day, Dutilleul discovers that he has the ability to walk through walls without encountering the slightest resistance. At first he has no idea what to do with this 'étrange faculté qui semblait ne répondre à aucune de ses aspirations' (PM 8). His early, hesitant steps in the world of fantasy provide Aymé with some rather hilarious moments. First of all Dutilleul scares his tyrannical superior Lécuyer by appearing head and shoulders on the wall of his office like a hunting trophy. Having whetted his appetite, Dutilleul takes his crusade to extremes: he terrorizes Lécuyer to such an extent that within a day the poor fellow has lost a pound in weight. Within a week he is fading away, having taken to eating his soup with a fork, and he is spirited off by men in white coats. This light-hearted vein in 'Le Passe-muraille' is the one chosen by Jean Boyer to exploit in his film version of Aymé's story, made in 1950. Unfortunately, the adaptation made by Boyer and Michel Audiard takes some quite unjustified liberties with Aymé's plot and characters. It fails completely to reproduce Aymé's symbiosis of solid reality and outrageous fantasy, leaning towards the tradition of boulevard comedy instead. It is worth seeing only for Bourvil's performance as Dutilleul.

Aymé's 'Le Passe-muraille' does not rely much on comedy. Dutilleul's next step is to become a burglar — an ideal profession for someone with his particular talents. By day he continues as the modest Dutilleul but by night he becomes the romantic Garou-Garou who grandly autographs each crime in red chalk. This second self is of course the antithesis of the meek civil servant from which it sprang. Dutilleul soon has the police baffled, and provokes the resignation of the Minister for the Interior, since he can escape at will through the challenging walls of the Santé prison. Dutilleul's adventure is of course a revolt against mediocrity and anonymity. He longs to be someone. When the mysterious Garou-Garou starts to become famous, Dutilleul cannot resist confessing to his colleagues at the ministry, 'Vous savez, Garou-Garou, c'est moi.' Mortified by their scornful laughter, he allows himself to be arrested and is vindicated by the appearance of his photograph on the front page of the paper. His colleagues start growing little goatees like Dutilleul's in homage and admiration; Dutilleul has acceded to full existence. Soon he abandons his dual life, preferring that of Garou-Garou. He buys different clothes, shaves off his beard and takes a new apartment. His metamorphosis seems complete. In reality, of course, Dutilleul is still there beneath the mask.

The duality light-heartedly sketched in 'Le Passe-muraille' is made tangible in a different way in 'Le Cocu nombreux'. A vagabond traveller arrives in a village where the relationships between the people he meets begin to seem rather complicated. Slowly he realizes that each person has two complementary bodies. Here is Aymé's description of one of the women he meets:

> C'était pour un quart, une petite femme sèche, à la voix pointue, et pour les trois autres quarts, une gaillarde ventrue et fessue, aux bras énormes, à la voix de tonnerre. (DM 131)

Always on the lookout for the most outrageous side effects of his inventions, Aymé describes a husband who has been cuckolded by another of his own bodies! The traveller tries to question them about their multiplicity but they cannot communicate because they have not the same 'notion de personne'. But there is a still more troubling aspect of the side effects. Aymé underlines society's conditioning towards 'normality' and the repression of the individual: the only person to live by the one body-one mind ratio has a black cross painted on his house and is known as 'le fou'.

'Héloïse' provides an excellent image of fluidity with its Martin who changes into a woman (Héloïse) every night and then back again every morning. 'Les Sabines' intensifies the same fluidity of identity and gives Aymé the opportunity to pursue the consequences of his initial situation much further through the metamorphosis motif. Variety of experience is given a physical dimension by Sabine's ability to multiply her body at will. She starts by creating a twin 'pour la commodité d'examiner son visage, son corps et ses attitudes' (PM 23) but soon tastes the joys of a varied existence, wanting ever more variety. Here, again, the humorist gives free rein to his penchant for Rabelaisian enumeration: Sabine is

> dans le même instant, lady Burbury, assise à une table de bridge en face du comte de Leicester; la bégum de Gorisapour, étendue dans son palanquin porté à dos d'éléphant; Mrs Smithson, occupée dans l'Etat de Pennsylvanie à faire les

honneurs de son château Renaissance synthétique; Barbe Cazzarini dans une loge de l'Opéra de Vienne où ténorisait son illustrissime; Rosalie Valdez y Samaniego, couchée sous la moustiquaire, dans une hutte d'un village de Papouasie, . . . (PM 41-2)

'Les Sabines' is perhaps rather long, given the premise Aymé is working from, but he succeeds in rescuing his tale to some extent by bringing it back towards a more easily manageable duality. He does this by describing a moral struggle taking place within Sabine: she is tempted by her infinite, luxurious variety but deep down she feels she should belong to one man. Aymé develops the struggle between 'la Providence' and 'le Péché'. Some Sabines turn to charity and repentance to make up for their sinful sisters. Dark realism contrasts with fantasy when Louise Megnin, one of the repentant ones, goes on a mission of charity and self-sacrifice to the *zone* St Ouen, 'ce dernier cercle de l'enfer terrestre' (PM 59) where she is abused, raped and finally murdered to atone for the excesses of her other embodiments.

In these exploitations of the fantastic to underline certain aspects of reality there are clearly some very serious themes involved, yet the anti-serious ironist is always hovering nearby and the result is often an irritating refusal to pursue them. The essence of Aymé's *conte* is still the invention of a disturbing situation and a brief exploration of its most interesting consequences. Social commentary and pseudo-philosophical discussion take second place to this. The confusion in stories like 'Le Décret', 'Le Cocu nombreux' or 'Les Sabines' is the final stage; Aymé proposes no solutions, offers no intellectual discussion. His primary goal is to find an image that will intrigue us, disturb us, increase our awareness and amuse us.

It seems inevitable that with this questioning of what is often regarded as stable and absolute — one of Aymé's greatest short story successes — he should venture further than confusion of time and identity. Indeed, the stability of reality and existence themselves suffers half mocking, half serious distortion too. In 'La Clé sous le paillasson' Aymé exploits a less exaggerated image of fluidity than in 'Les Sabines' but moves the reader further towards a fluid reality. The basic movement of the story is a gentleman burglar's search for his lost family and his true identity among all the aliases that he has been using:

'J'ai eu tant d'états-civils, depuis que je cours l'aventure, et tant

de faux parents respectables que je ne suis pas fichu de m'y retrouver. Aussi bien, je me demande quel est mon nom véritable?'
Il porta la main à son front et cita rapidement une cinquantaine de noms. (NA 251)

To add to the confusion, Rodolphe is initially proposed as a character who has escaped from between the pages of a detective novel to arrive in a real country town! His search involves a constant mingling of two levels of reality.

Aymé pursues this transfer between two levels of reality much further in 'Le Romancier Martin'. Not only do the novelist's creations now leave their fictional frame to attain the same level of reality as their author, but Martin has the power to remove people from real life and imprison them in a purely literary reality. A thorough mingling results: Martin's editor falls in love with one of his characters and another friend wants the novelist to translate his mistress Jiji into a 'personnage de troisième plan' so that he can be rid of her. It is rather surprising that an author so interested in images of mingled identity and fluid reality should have missed the ideal figure of a spy; maintaining two or three identities at once and living in an unstable world of changing loyalties and disintegrating façades, the spy could have combined Cérusier, Rodolphe and the bewildered time traveller in 'Le Décret' to become Aymé's greatest creation.

Most of Aymé's short stories question reality to some extent. He often seems to create absurdities in order to have them accepted as realities, whether by the victim, who hardly has any choice, or by the reader, who is equally bound if he wants to read on. Cérusier is at first bewildered by his face change and goes through a period of confusion when he concludes that 'le monde feint d'exister' (BI 85). Finally he accepts Roland Colbert, his new self, as a 'nouvelle réalité'. In 'Le Décret' Aymé does not just aim at confusion of time for his victim but goes as far as the brief suggestion of a parallel existence:

J'arrivais à cette conclusion baroque qu'il existait simultanément deux villes de Dôle, l'une vivant en 1942, l'autre en 1959. (PM 114)

Aymé suggests very strongly that this other reality is perhaps only ever mental; the deeper reality is in the eye of the beholder. 'Oscar et Erick' deals directly with this important theme. Oscar has for a long time been painting only imaginary things, but the people of the northern kingdom of Ooklan where he lives hardly appreciate his inventiveness and (shades of the villagers of 'Le Cocu nombreux') call him 'Oscar le fou'. One day his Viking brother comes home from the sea bearing real objects that appear to be the exact models for Oscar's fantasy canvases. The unreal has become real, or what is unreal in Ooklan exists as reality elsewhere.

It is this fantastic vein that is most often regarded as typical of Aymé's short stories. The three successful pastiches of his stories all stress this vein of the unreal. Yet anthologists of the fantastic have tended to ignore Aymé, probably because his fantastic is so often anti-serious and contains so little of the deep-rooted fear that is so essential in Poe, Hoffmann and even marginal writers like Lovecraft. There are occasional thematic similarities but Aymé's attitude to his material and his adaptation of it to accentuate reality is different. Because of Aymé's disarming, anti-serious, anti-intellectual stand it would also be wrong to align him too closely with the Surrealists who were often among his friends and who used similar processes in arriving at their strange images, or with the dramatists of the Absurd whose phenomena and situations so often resemble his own. Aymé has created his own distinctive blend of faerie, fantastic and reality. The accumulation of unreal imagery in his fictional world gives the impression that it is a special world apart where any absurdity is allowed. Exploring story after story, the reader feels that the fantastic is really quite banal and, what is worse, even expected. Masson's pastiche best captures this atmosphere when it describes a world where

> Le merveilleux est partout. Seulement il se cache. Et le plus souvent, vous mourrez avant de vous être aperçu du don que les fées vous ont donné au berceau.[17]

So we see his hero Mouton (read Martin) wondering what his next gift will be — transmutation of cobblestones into gold or the power to stop a bus with nothing more than telepathic commands. Sadly enough, Masson was right: after reading a lot of Aymé we are tempted to expect phenomena whose charm should really be in their unexpectedness.

2
Faerie and Fantastic Techniques and Themes

> *je pars sur des données imaginaires avec une conscience paisible et une foi robuste dans la vérité du dénouement.*
> Marcel Aymé

The usual critical approach to stories like these has simply been to analyse according to the beings created (werewolf, invisible man, automaton) or according to the motifs or phenomena represented (spatial displacement, time manipulation, modification of solids). As Tzvetan Todorov has pointed out in his *Introduction à la littérature fantastique*, such functional analysis is only half way to an appreciation of a short story. Not only is there a great variety of possible phenomena[1] but this approach tends to neglect the way the material is made into a story: the author's intentions and his attitude to his material, the type of narration used, the level of credibility or reader acceptance required and the techniques involved in obtaining it. All of these are crucial aspects of Aymé's art. Jean Bellemin-Noël's definition of the fantastic: 'L'intrusion de l'inadmissible dans le monde communément admis',[2] supports Todorov's contention that with the unreal especially, material and approach are indivisible. The intrusion (a structural element) is just as important as the fact of being inadmissible (an attribute of the material).

Aymé's fantasies are liable to make the reader baulk, so the presentation of this intrusion is just as important as its invention. Aymé has to smuggle the reader past the moment of revelation and hold his interest once the surprise or novelty wears off. The techniques used obviously depend on the level of unreality, as the more shocking the proposition, the more expensive our collaboration will be. The art of constructing these short stories depends also on the author's intentions (we have seen Aymé mocking or parodying his material) and also on the familiarity of the unreal (fairies and dragons being more acceptable than some of Aymé's more original experiments with human powers).

Aymé has an apparently dual approach to the presentation of the unreal: the anti-serious, almost mocking approach of the entertainer and the false-serious approach of the moralist. The two may seem incompatible but are not. Aymé only wants us to accept his absurdities as realities for the duration of the tale and thus participate in his creation. One of his favourite devices is a sort of challenge to the reader, to warn him of the absurdity and at the same time dare him to accept it. This ruse can be applied to a novel like *La Vouivre* where there is a rather clumsy, drawn-out discussion of the mythical origins of the Jurassian dryad, but it is more subtle in its two- or three-line form at the beginning of a short story:

> Il n'est pas bien rare qu'un romancier soit visité de ses personnages, quoiqu'ils ne se manifestent pas couramment avec une présence aussi certaine. (DM 17)

> N'exister qu'un jour sur deux est une chose qui révolte le bon sens. Martin lui-même en était choqué et croyait dangereux de mettre le monde en demeure d'accepter une réalité aussi absurde. (DM 95)

The same kind of light-hearted challenge is involved when Aymé increases our consciousness of our imminent removal from reality. This is often implicit in his use of the 'Il y avait . . .' formula. He is very conscious of its frequency in his work and occasionally parodies it by using it in situations that would not normally demand it:

> Il y avait dans la ville de Blémont, rue de la Ferronerie, une petite fille de six ans prénommée Valérie qui se rongeait les ongles. (EJ 121)

Our consciousness may be provoked by the use of a title like 'Légende poldève' or even of a subtitle: 'La Liste — histoire d'une jeune fille qui ne pouvait pas tenir dans un conte fantastique'. The setting too may warn us that we are about to leave reality — the town called Cstwertskst in 'Légende poldève' or the strange northern kingdom called Ooklan in 'Oscar et Erick'. Elsewhere, Aymé may use the opening of a dream frame ('Le Mendiant'), a self-conscious allegorical parody ('La Fosse aux péchés') or the story-within-a-story ploy ('Conte du milieu') to achieve the same end and remove the absurdity from his immediate responsibility.

The other approach to our acceptance of the story, the mock-serious opening, is more interesting and requires more art and guile from the storyteller. Here we see the straight-faced joker, the *pince-sans-rire* façade where Aymé seemingly agrees with Tolkien that the creator of fantasy should not mock his own magic.[3] Aymé likes the challenge of treating the unreal as an everyday occurrence, proposing his outrageous premise 'avec un sérieux et une crédibilité qui font vaciller notre raison'.[4] This is one of the most commented upon aspects of Aymé's art. He gives no smile, no wink, no warning:

> Un cambrioleur mondain échappa une fois d'entre les pages d'un roman policier, et, après d'admirables aventures, arriva dans une toute petite ville de province. (NA 249)

> Le meilleur chrétien de la rue Gabrielle comme de tout Montmartre était, en 1939, un certain M. Duperrier, homme si pieux, si juste et si charitable que Dieu, sans attendre qu'il mourût et alors qu'il était dans la force de l'âge, lui ceignit la tête d'une auréole qui ne le quittait ni jour ni nuit. (VP 83)

Aymé even borrows the fairy-tale formula for the same treatment in 'Le Passe-muraille'.

The surprise is not necessarily at the beginning of a story. The same kind of presentation works in 'Le Romancier Martin' when Aymé calmly announces that Martin's characters have attained physical existence. The initial presentation of Martin only mentions his habit of killing off his characters at the end of his novels, but this is a ruse to push the story along; the real absurdity is to be revealed towards the middle. In 'Avenue Junot' the flying horse is proposed with similar, carefree understatement right at the end:

> En effet, le percheron Pégase attendait à la porte de l'atelier. Les amants, avec légèreté, sautèrent sur l'abside. (EA 123)

Most often Aymé offers no comment, no tongue-in-cheek discussion of the proposal. His comments on the work of writers as different as Andersen and Simenon suggest that he is very conscious of his own economical presentation. Of his fellow *conteur* Andersen he writes:

> le conteur ne s'y embarrasse pas d'explications, et le merveilleux surgit, pour ainsi dire, naturellement[5]

and of Simenon's detective stories, a genre which usually depends on reasoned explanations, he says:

> L'auteur se garde, d'ailleurs, d'expliquer ses personnages et de démonter devant son lecteur les rouages d'un mécanisme psychologique. Il se contente de donner des renseignements, des indications, des repères, et non sans économie.[6]

Aymé's own style is even and unconcerned. It is perhaps a legacy of his short career as a young journalist. He just gives us the facts, as his editor had taught him, but now they can be the 'facts' as he creates them. Whatever the level of reality, the tone and the 'présentation naturelle' that Jacques Teynier has compared to Voltaire's[7] remain the same:

> Il y avait à Montmartre, dans la rue de l'Abreuvoir, une jeune femme prénommée Sabine, qui possédait le don d'ubiquité. Elle pouvait à son gré se multiplier et se trouver en même temps, de corps et d'esprit, en autant de lieux qu'il lui plaisait de souhaiter. (PM 23)

> Pendant la guerre de 1939-72 il y avait à Montmartre, à la porte d'une épicerie de la rue Caulaincourt, une queue de quatorze personnes. (PM 247)

> Il y avait, dans un village du pays d'Arbois, un vigneron nommé Félicien Guérillot qui n'aimait pas le vin. (VP 101)

Naturally the introduction of magic into one of the *Contes du chat perché* poses less of a problem because magic is more or less expected once we realize what sort of world we are to move in. Yet we find the same natural smoothness in the way Aymé introduces magic into the first of the stories, 'La Patte du chat'. We are treated to a page of the parents' scolding monologue directed at the lazy cat, and when the cat finally moves himself to reply and convert the monologue into a dialogue Aymé passes it off as naturally as can be. From that moment onwards in the seventeen tales, anything can happen. One of Aymé's best linguistic trumps here is his natural participation in the girls' logic, a sympathy which soon engenders reader-participation too. Here is the girls' conception of the duck's globe-trotting:

> Le canard partit d'un bon pas sans se retourner et, comme la

terre est ronde, il se retrouva au bout de trois mois à son point de départ. (CP 233)

Naturally, if a pig were to put on a false beard he would not be recognized, and when the vet is summoned to examine the transformed animals it seems quite a matter of course that he will see through the girls' prank:

> Ce vétérinaire était un homme extraordinairement habile. On pouvait être sûr qu'après avoir regardé les bêtes dans le blanc des yeux et palpé leurs membres et leurs panses, il n'allait pas manquer de découvrir la vérité. Il semblait aux petites l'entendre déjà: 'Tiens, tiens, dirait-il, j'aperçois en tout ceci comme une maladie de peinture; quelqu'un aurait-il, par hasard, fait de la peinture ce matin?' (CP 90)

Except where the unreality is introduced as an ironical joke or tender gleam of hope at the end of a serious story, Aymé builds quite an elaborate structure on the original premise. The intrusion is to become the story itself. This means that the moment following the introduction of the absurdity is crucial. He protects our passage with a guile that anaesthetizes our reason. Jean Cathelin has dubbed Aymé's usual ruse 'la technique de l'évidence',[8] because of the façade of recounted facts and also because Aymé likes to call a witness. Sometimes a friend of the victim corroborates the story. Elsewhere, rather than have the author-observer recount the tale, Aymé appoints the victim-protagonist himself. This detaches Aymé and lessens his responsibility, while also increasing our participation. We share the victim's confusion, joy or despair. There is little author-comment, just the victim's impressions, and for him the events are terrifyingly real. In 'Le Décret', the victim of the disquieting leap forwards and backwards in time recounts Aymé's cruel farce in the most convincing manner possible, and 'Rechute' benefits from the same first-person involvement. The ruse of the private diary is appropriate too; we find Aymé using it to lend credibility to Jules Flegmon's experience of life rationing in 'La Carte'. Flegmon and the narrator in 'Le Décret', both writers, are in fact partial reflections of Aymé: his friends appear in 'La Carte', and in 'Le Décret' we wander with the narrator in the forest of Chaux and the village of La Vieille-Loye that Aymé knew so well.

Acceptance of the absurd by the victim himself is often exploited by Aymé as he tries to persuade the reader to continue on past the barrage of magic spells and metamorphoses. His protagonists, who are much more closely concerned than we are, do not baulk more than a moment at Aymé's new realities, so why should we? The parents of Delphine and Marinette are clearly quite level-headed and reasonable, yet they only find it 'curieux' that their daughters should turn into animals, so who are we to object? 'La Carte' illustrates a skilful double manipulation of the victim's reaction. Aymé's first sentence announces a 'nouvelle restriction', as if what we are about to read is only the latest of several, and ostensibly more acceptable because of this. Already the reader is drawn into participation. Then comes the outrageous proposition: in a dire economic crisis all unproductive consumers are to be put to death. This premise is quickly and cleverly modified to understate a much more absurd proposition:

> Naturellement, il n'est pas question de mettre à mort les inutiles. On rognera simplement sur leur temps de vie. Maleffroi m'a expliqué qu'ils auraient droit à tant de jours d'existence par mois, selon leur degré d'inutilité. (PM 72)

It is of course this seemingly second-rank shock ('simplement') that Aymé intends to exploit, but his narrative trickery goes even further. The victim, an unproductive consumer with inflated ideas of his own usefulness, is still unaware of his degree of implication. He happily accepts the absurd decree because he regards the non-producers as 'them'; it is 'their' lives that are to be rationed. His outrage ('C'est une infamie! un déni de justice! un monstrueux assassinat!' PM 72) on discovering that he, too, is regarded as useless, distracts our attention even further from the implications of Aymé's premise. Flegmon's hypocrisy, comic at this early stage although it is later to become sinister, serves the same purpose: he discovers that writers and artists are on the list:

> A la rigueur, j'aurais compris que la mesure s'appliquât aux peintres, aux sculpteurs, aux musiciens. Mais aux écrivains! (PM 72)

and above all to him!

Aymé uses his protagonists' reactions to strengthen his treatment of the absurd as real. They seldom question the possibility of their situation, but react as if it were (as it is) a *fait accompli*. When Martin suddenly discovers that he changes into a woman at night in

'Héloïse', his wife only worries about what her mother will think. 'Ce qui m'embête', says the victim himself, 'ce sont mes affaires.'⁹ Duperrier the saintly Parisian is quite untroubled by the how and the why of his halo; it is his wife who reacts:

> — A quoi ça ressemble? disait-elle. De quoi va-t-on avoir l'air, je te demande un petit peu, aussi bien pour les voisins et les commerçants du quartier que pour mon cousin Léopold? (VP 83)

When the criminal Dermuche is changed into a baby just before his execution, the guards and the politicians are quite untroubled as to how or why. His miracle simply ranks with all other 'histoires' that are to be avoided or suppressed. In fact everybody involved reacts with soul-destroying realism: there is nothing in the prison regulations about babies or metamorphoses, so off with his head! The use of a character who mistakenly or intentionally avoids the real issue is a standard trick of Aymé's. Like the victim of Kafka's *Metamorphosis* and the untroubled townspeople in Ionesco's *Rhinocéros*, Aymé's Martins cleverly side-track the reader with irrelevant accessory problems. This not only eliminates troublesome questions of how and why but brings further benefits:

> C'est du même geste qu'on intensifie le retentissement des événements et qu'on esquive l'accusation d'invraisemblance en posant en écran un faux problème (ou du moins un problème accessoire).¹⁰

Aymé is careful to exploit the comic side of his characters' reactions too. When Sabine reveals her multiplicity to her lover she is apprehensive lest he be angry. On the contrary, he sees how lucky he is to be about to enjoy so many different Sabines. She will be all things to one man! But then comes the comic reversal: he sees that she can cuckold him in many different ways too:

> — Est-ce que je sais, moi, où tu peux être en ce moment? Est-ce que je sais si tu n'es pas à Javel ou à Montparnasse, dans les bras d'un truand? ou à Lyon dans les bras d'un soyeux? ou à Narbonne dans la couche d'un vinassier? ou en Perse dans celle du schah? (PM 29)

'Fiançailles' provides another example of the accessory problem that leads to humour. When Aymé proposes the marriage between Ernestine and her centaur, the bride's godfather swallows his pious shock at the chance to marry off his ward. Then comes the false objection: Aristide's grandfather says it is a 'mésalliance', but his reasons are not those we might expect. He finds nothing wrong with a centaur marrying a human, but claims that Aristide's noble blood is much too good for the likes of a plain Mademoiselle Gorin!

This is all part of the process of playing down the absurd premise, the techniques of understatement that Robert Brasillach admired so much in Aymé's work and that contribute to the highly original symbiosis of real and unreal.[11] We are in a world where astounding propositions are treated as banal. At the beginning of 'Le Passe-muraille' Dutilleul's wall-penetration is introduced as 'singulier', but by the next story Sabine's much more striking attribute hardly rates a comment. Understatement is a source of considerable humour in Aymé's stories.

Aymé's 'présentation naturelle' involves not only the understatement of the absurd and its treatment as reality but also the technique of surrounding it with banal accessory facts and events to camouflage it. He tells how, during the making of a film of the face change in *La belle image*, he insisted that the metamorphosis be filmed to put it on the same level of reality as all the other events in the film. Aymé claims that he could not understand the director's objection that the spectator would baulk at this.[12] Perhaps Aymé's colleague Marcel Schneider was right when he confessed that most writers of fantasy end up confusing real and unreal.

Happily, this camouflage or equalization of the absurd works much better in a short story. Aymé skips over and plays down the main absurdity so that we do not register it until too late. Even before the surprise in 'Le Passe-muraille' Aymé is busy side-tracking us with little details:

> Il y avait à Montmartre, au troisième étage du 75 *bis* de la rue d'Orchampt . . .

and immediately after the shock he pursues the same vein:

> Il portait un binocle, une petite barbiche noire et il était employé de troisième classe au Ministère de l'Enregistrement. En hiver il se rendait à son bureau par l'autobus et, à la belle saison, il faisait le trajet à pied, sous son chapeau melon.
> (PM 7)

Similarly, in 'Héloïse' Aymé side-tracks us with Martin's address and by telling us that he votes M.R.P. and owns an umbrella! All of this is quite plausible but hardly relevant.

Sometimes the accessory facts are not merely plausible but actual. Aymé's penchant for setting his fantastic propositions in recognizable décor is another way of dulling our objections. Many of his absurdities evolve in or around the apartments, bistros and shops of the rue de l'Abreuvoir, the rue Caulaincourt, the avenue Junot and the rue Paul-Féval where Aymé lived. This process of 'actualization' is taken further when the anti-serious Aymé, like his counterpart in 'Le Romancier Martin', transposes his own friends into his stories. In 'Le Passe-muraille', 'La Carte', 'Avenue Junot' and 'La bonne peinture' we find many of Aymé's friends and colleagues: the writer Céline, the painter Gen Paul, the editor Daragnès, Max Révol, René Fauchois, André Villeboeuf. He even actualizes 'Le Passe-muraille' to the extent of saying that Dutilleul is still there, stuck in the wall lamenting, and that Gen Paul goes to console him from time to time with his guitar. Duperrier and his lady still ply the boulevard de Clichy and Sabine is buried in the tiny cimetière St Vincent where her creator lies. Having anchored his creation in reality, Aymé calmly moves on. He continues his outrageous tale as straight-faced as ever. The reader is lulled by a style often compared to the fast-moving fluid language of Céline, and by his playful and reassuring tone.

Aymé can sometimes maintain our interest by stretching out the revelation of the full extent of his proposition. This long drawn out discovery is used well in 'Le Cocu nombreux' and 'La Carte'. In the first, we slowly realize the full extent of the situation with the vagabond himself. From clues like strange quantities of washing hung out to dry and ambiguous remarks made by his hosts, the stranger finally deduces that the two 'cocus' are manifestations of the same personality and that one is cuckolding the other. But how can a man be cuckolded by himself? and should he be jealous or proud? Aymé also exploits the verbal humour of his invention:

> Le vagabond sentit que le cocu le considérait, de ses deux paires d'yeux, avec stupéfaction (DM 124)

and then proceeds slowly through the stranger's discovery that not only is the unfaithful wife 'nombreuse' too, but so is everyone in the village! In 'La Carte' we gradually move closer to the absurdity with the diarist Flegmon. His first experience is third-hand: Lucette Roquenton tells him how her husband vanished at midnight leaving only his rumpled pyjamas and a denture on the pillow. Next he experiences second-hand contact as he watches Lucette die her relative death; and finally he himself vanishes while writing in his diary:

> Ce pourrait être l'occasion d'un joli poisson. Je me sens pris d'un horrible panique et je . . .
>
> 1er avril. — Me voilà bien vivant. (PM 79-80)

Aymé introduces Flegmon and his reader to the stretching month with similar care. Firstly the actress Mélina tells him she has lived thirty-six days in May. He can dismiss the notion because he has always found her rather frivolous, but the 'fable' takes on added strength when it is confirmed by Laverdon 'qui est pourtant un homme digne de foi' (PM 91). Flegmon's next diary entry, headed '32 juin' shows that his first-hand experience has begun.

Aymé also draws us along by using a recognizably real structure or pattern to develop his story. His fantastic stories, like his fairy tales, reflect that deep reality that Bruno Bettelheim has underlined in *The Uses of Enchantment.* Once the reader realizes that it is reality that is under examination he is less likely to baulk. The age law in 'Rechute' is followed by recognizably real consequences: firstly private discontent, then clandestine resistance, armed insurrection, civil war and finally abrogation of the law. The terribly real deportation of Jews and other 'undesirables', as well as the real pattern of food rationing are used as models in 'La Carte', commercial exploitation is the basis for the development of 'La bonne peinture' and we easily recognize the model when Sabine's experiment leads to addiction and finally to an overdose.

One of the more skilful ways of developing a premise is to heighten the initial confrontation between real and unreal once it is accepted. This can be done by developing the absurd proposition against a very real background like Montmartre or more often a particularly sordid reality like the prison in 'Dermuche', the factory in 'La Fabrique', the bleak garret in 'L'Huissier' or the *zone* in 'Les Sabines'. The contrast is heightened even further in this last story as Aymé continually brings us back to the original Sabine in Paris after watching her sisters in Rio, Gorisapur or Sydney. The alternation between office routine and the farfetched burglaries in 'Le Passe-muraille' produces the same effect.

A conflict or contrast of two characters is one of Aymé's standard development techniques. His usual pattern is to remove his victim, alter him in some way and replace him in the niche he occupied before. Not only is there a conflict between what he is and what he was, but the surrounding reality (and above all the surrounding people) clash with him too. Martin with his temporary death, Duperrier with his halo, Aymé's *alter ego* with his knowledge of the future, all face a potentially hostile society, especially in the persons of their wives and close friends who are not affected and who cannot understand. Germaine Buge ('Les Bottes de sept lieues'), Pataclac ('Le Nain'), Dermuche's almoner ('Dermuche'), Bradley's wife ('Le Mendiant') and Udine's gendarme ('Au clair de la lune') are all used to underscore the fantasy of the main character. The mathematician Aymé pursues his technique as far as a controlled experiment with his two animals in 'Les Boeufs': one ox takes a fantasy trip (he is educated by the girls) while the other is left unchanged for comparison, to measure the distance travelled from reality by the other. The same technique is even more rigorous in the play *Les quatre vérités* where one character remains unaffected by the truth drug.

Aymé sustains interest in his story by increasing the confrontation with our static reality. This is done by adding to the initial situation, whether by developing the absurdity itself or by pursuing its consequences. 'J'écris pour me faire plaisir', says Aymé, and much of his pleasure is taken at the reader's expense. His stories are often constructed as reader traps: we are lured into accepting the proposition $2 + 2 = 5$ 'for the sake of the story . . .' and then we have no defence when subsequently asked to accept $2 + 2 = 55$ or even 555. Since Delphine and Marinette's oxen can talk, why shouldn't they be taught to read and write? This ironic reasoning is quite explicit at the beginning of 'Le Décret':

> Ce qui, au premier examen, parut le plus remarquable, ce fut l'extraordinaire facilité avec laquelle on avançait l'heure d'été d'une ou de deux unités. A la réflexion, rien n'empêchait de l'avancer de douze unités ou de vingt-quatre, voire d'un multiple de vingt-quatre. (PM 96)

And here there is an additional trap: Aymé asks us to accept that with a jump of seventeen years there will be physical changes involved, conveniently forgetting that there were none engendered by the one-hour summer-time change. Aymé exploits this sleight of pen as much as possible.

Aymé favours the geometric progression or chain reaction for his unreal stories. This is not entirely original but is still very effective. Once the reader is hooked, Aymé gives him plenty of line, developing his premise as far as possible. And once we accept that Sabine can have two bodies 'pour la commodité d'examiner son visage' why not twenty or 200 in order to live life to the full? Once it has forced its way into our real world, the absurd runs riot. We are trapped by Aymé's joyous multiplications:

> des cowboys, un champion d'échecs, des athlètes scandinaves, des pêcheurs de perles, un commissaire du peuple, des lycéens, des toucheurs de boeufs, un matador, un garçon boucher, quatorze cinéastes, un raccommodeur de porcelaine, soixante-sept médecins, des marquis, quatre princes russes . . . (PM 52)

Sabine only stops when she gets to an incredible 67 000 separate existences. This typical multiplication is the main element satirized in Masson's pastiche of Aymé. He describes a man who, like Valentin in *Les Oiseaux de lune*, changes his fellow humans into animals at an ever-increasing rate. Indeed, Aymé satirizes his own trend in 'Les Sabines':

> Bientôt, la malheureuse ubiquiste fut saisie d'une frénésie de luxure et eut des amants sur tous les points du globe. Le nombre en augmentait au rythme d'une progression géométrique dont la raison était 2,7. (PM 52)

Aymé knows that stories like these, drawing so much of their appeal from surprise and novelty, must move forwards or founder. Man's reaction to his gift provides much of the movement, as Aymé suggests in 'Le Passe-muraille':

> l'homme qui possède des dons brillants ne peut se satisfaire longtemps de les exercer sur un objet médiocre. (PM 12)

But the inexorable movement also comes from the nature of the gift itself:

> C'est le départ d'une aventure, qui appelle une suite, un développement et, en somme, une rétribution. (PM 12)

So, after suggesting that Dutilleul had himself arrested in order for his identity to become known, Aymé suggests that there was in fact more to it than this: 'en réalité il glissait simplement sur la pente de sa destinée' (PM 15). Starting by insulting and then terrorizing Lécuyer, Dutilleul moves from office partitions to bank vaults and prison walls and even greater things: 'il rêvait de s'enfoncer au coeur de quelque massive pyramide' (PM 18).

The multiplication of the real consequences of an absurd premise is an alternative to the extension of the absurdity itself. Aymé's victim in *La belle image*, Raoul Cérusier, talks about this role of the absurd as nothing more than a starting-point: 'Après avoir fourni à la réalité un départ sur des données nouvelles, il s'effaçait discrètement' (BI 42). Aymé proposes a strange situation and draws out all its potential consequences, both as comic situations and as the more serious confusion where he hides the barbs of his satire. Then he quickly abandons it for another novelty. When Martin changes sex in 'Héloïse' Aymé exploits the situation for both verbal and situational comedy. His victim is often obliged to refer to himself with feminine adjectives despite Aymé's continuing 'il', and his wife ends up calling her husband 'une pauvre fille'. This strange *ménage à trois* (or is it one and two halves?) produces some hilarious situations: Martin ends up in drag when his evening change occurs before he reaches home; the postman who inadvertently witnesses a change goes mad; Martin wakes one morning in bed with a bearded photographer who seduced Héloïse the night before; and he later has to spend several months visibly pregnant with Héloïse's child!

Behind this comedy there are of course more serious implications. Conflict between Martin and his jealous wife is the starting point, then Martin's split personality begins to weigh on his mind. His male and female halves have a different outlook on life, different experiences and soon even different memories. Communication between them becomes very difficult. Since they never meet, they have to write letters to each other. The gap widens when Héloïse discovers that she is autonomous; Martin is no longer in control of his other half.

This multiplication of real consequences in a combination of comedy and sinister implications is also a standard development pattern for the faerie of *Les Contes du chat perché*. Once the girls disobey their parents they set in motion a kind of *machine infernale* and their attempts to repair the damage tend to involve even more situational complications. We are treated to several hilarious little images: two pairs of horns wander the fields stuck onto invisible bodies, a hussar gallops off to war on a sheep and the little white hen wins a croix d'honneur at school. We watch as blindness moves from man to dog to cat to mouse and back to man, we see the white cow stop the plough in mid-furrow to work out a complicated physics problem, and we remain helplessly laughing as 650 chickens troop off to live in the wild forest 'protected' by the fox and the weasel.

Aymé's better comic contrasts lead directly to the more disquieting aspects of the absurd. In 'Le Loup', for example, a superb parody of the Seven Little Billy-Goats theme, there is a scene where the wolf pleads with Delphine and Marinette to be let into the warm kitchen to play with them now that he has become 'bon'. It is one of Aymé's linguistic gems, but the humour takes on a sombre note towards the end. After much comic fluctuation (will they open the door or won't they? Will the wolf resist his natural impulses or not?), the wolf's sighs, tears, smiles and wily, indignant arguments to support his project finally win the girls' trust. Thus we see the wolf singing *comptines* and playing 'la main chaude', 'la ronde' and 'le chat perché' with the girls. But when they decide to play 'Loup y es-tu?' the situation gets out of hand, 'ce qui ne manque jamais d'arriver quand on reçoit le loup en cachette de ses parents' (CP 176), smiles Aymé. The wolf takes his role too seriously and another *conte rose* becomes a *conte gris*. He confuses the game with reality:

> Devant ses yeux luisants, passaient et repassaient les jambes des deux petites. Un frémissement lui courut sur l'échine, ses babines se froncèrent. (. . .) déjà les idées se brouillaient dans sa tête. Il ne voyait plus les jambes des fillettes, il les humait.
> — . . . Loup y es-tu? m'entends-tu? quoi fais-tu?
> — Je monte à cheval et je sors du bois!
> Alors le loup, poussant un grand hurlement, fit un bond hors de sa cachette, la gueule béante et les griffes dehors. Les petites n'avaient pas encore eu le temps de prendre peur, qu'elles étaient déjà dévorées. (CP 182)

This development pattern of acceleration away from the girls' initial disobedience becomes sadly familiar in the *Contes du chat perché*. By half-way through the collection the situations begin to have an air of *déjà vu*, a predictability which tends to diminish their charm, but they are saved by Aymé's style. Their charm depends not only on the novelty of the situation but above all on the way they are recounted. Aymé is a master of language, although the level of excellence here varies from episode to episode.

The essence of the *Contes du chat perché* lies in the way Aymé participates in Delphine and Marinette's reasoning, in the way he induces even the adult reader to participate in the plot against the parents and in the way he leads us smoothly from one complication to the next by manipulating tension and relief. Aymé is completely in control of his irony in these tales. The cynical irony of many fantastic stories is eliminated to be replaced by little asides or else brief images of dramatic irony, both of which are essentially humorous attacks on the parents; we know the truth but the parents are never to find out.

The dialogue with which Aymé endows his animals is particularly worthy of comment, all the more so after the remarks of M. André Rousseaux. Some of the more strikingly realistic dialogue is given to the wolf as he tries to convince Delphine and Marinette to let him inside:

— Vous savez, dit-il, on raconte beaucoup d'histoires sur le loup, il ne faut pas croire tout ce qu'on dit. (CP 169)

And the lamb he ate in La Fontaine's fable?

— L'agneau que j'ai mangé? Lequel? (. . .) naturellement que j'en ai mangé plusieurs. Je ne vois pas où est le mal. . . Vous en mangez bien, vous! (CP 170)

And Little Red Riding-Hood?

— (. . .) un péché de jeunesse. Il y a si longtemps, n'est-ce pas? A tout péché miséricorde. . . (CP 171)

And the way he licks his chops?

— (. . .) c'est une mauvaise habitude que je tiens de famille, mais ça ne veut rien dire . . . (CP 172)

The wolf passes from defence to attack as soon as the girls give him the chance:

— Moi je prétends qu'on n'a pas le droit de décourager les bonnes volontés comme vous le faites. Et vous pouvez dire que

> si jamais je remange de l'enfant, ce sera par votre faute. (CP 172)

The linguistic heritage of La Fontaine and the *fabliaux* is equally visible in 'Le petit coq noir' when the fox convinces the rooster to bring his chickens into the forest. Starting with little snippets of verbal humour like the fox's evocation of the rooster's *coq au vin* destiny ('j'en ai la chair de poule'), Aymé develops a superb dialogue between fox and rooster. The fox talks the rooster down from his refuge branch and then sacrifices the immediate but small meal for something better:

> — Te manger? mais tu n'y penses pas! Je n'en ai pas la moindre envie. (. . .) Certes, il m'est arrivé trop souvent de croquer quelqu'un d'entre vous, mais c'était par amitié, pour le préserver d'une mort indigne dans la casserole. (CP 338)

He is banking on the feast that will await him when he convinces the rooster (and the girls) that the chickens should be liberated from what they stupidly see as their 'mort naturelle' in the cooking pot, and brought to the forest. There they will have free food, no more masters and will even grow teeth to defend themselves! Cleverly working on the rooster's vanity, the fox manoeuvres him into working for the fox's own designs. And when the chickens start disappearing into Mr Fox's belly the rooster cannot complain because he might be next, and anyway, it was he who brought them! The girls have been put into the same position: one thing has led to another, and then another, and now they are trapped as accomplices.

Aymé's development of these consequences has been called 'un développement logique sans défaillances'.[13] 'Logique' may be too strong a word, but the development of his stories is often disturbingly realistic. Many of his consequences start as the realistic reactions of his characters. Brasillach appreciated this technique when he wrote of 'Le Cocu nombreux':

> Supposons que cet événement puisse se produire. Croyez-vous que cela empêcherait le pauvre mari trompé d'être bafoué? Pas du tout, et plutôt deux fois qu'une, diront les mauvais plaisants. En deux corps, comme en un, les lois éternelles des farces de Molière peuvent se vérifier chez Marcel Aymé.[14]

In 'L'Ane et le cheval' it is the darker side of the realistic farce that is stressed. Since the girls are now animals, their parents must adapt to the new reality. They start by housing their daughters in the stable instead of the bedroom. And why should they get more to eat than the productive animals? And in fact why should they not be put to work like the others? ('On a un cheval ou on n'en a pas.') Naturally, they are soon whipped when they don't go fast enough and finally the parents even try to sell them.

The consequences of Aymé's time rationing in 'La Carte' are sadly realistic too. Draft dodgers immediately try to change to more productive jobs to be granted exemption from the decree that will shorten their life. Others try to profit from their fellows' absence. And of course there is soon the inevitable black-market in 'tickets de vie'. But Aymé's realism of development is seen above all in the movement of time itself: if the month can be halved then it can be doubled. So the generous month of June stretches to the thirty-fifth, the forty-fifth and the sixty-sixth and soon we are faced with the extreme of the rich profiteer Wadé:

> qui aurait vécu entre le 30 juin et le 1er juillet, mille neuf cent soixante-sept jours, soit la bagatelle de cinq ans et quatre mois. (PM 94)

In her study of Aymé's satire. Hélène Scriabine underlines the sad realism of this time gathering by the rich and the resourceful: 'de même que dans la réalité certains favorisés n'ont jamais autant mangé et fumé qu'à l'époque du rationnement'.[15]

Perhaps the clearest example of Aymé's pursuit of the realistic consequences of his imagination is the exploitation of Lafleur's talent in 'La bonne peinture'. The painter sees what is in store for him but cannot stop his gift running its full course. After a painting banquet and a painting restaurant, the commercialization continues with the move to nationalize Lafleur, and soon there is the factory with its production and distribution bureaucracies. Forgeries and scandals follow until Lafleur is finally returned to the private sector. Having exhausted his satiric pursuit of the consequences, Aymé now turns to the expansion of the original premise: Lafleur attracts disciples who learn his gift and soon apply it to sculpture, music and even literature.

Aymé's stories are not logical. One only has to examine the time manipulations in 'Le Décret' or 'Rechute' to see that it is only an ironic façade of logic. His stories are simply 'réalistes'. In his *prière d'insérer* to *Derrière chez Martin* (containing, among others, the fantasies of 'Le Romancier Martin', 'Le Temps mort' and 'Le Cocu nombreux') Aymé explains this private realism:

> J'ai réuni sous ce titre neuf nouvelles très résolument réalistes. La première, par exemple, est l'histoire d'un romancier réaliste qui prend ses personnages dans une réalité si dure qu'ils s'animent d'une vie réelle, matérielle, et, retirant à l'auteur son libre arbitre de romancier, imposent à son oeuvre les exigences de la réalité vécue. Je ne crois pas qu'on ait encore écrit sur un thème aussi réaliste.

There is a hint of seriousness behind the irony here, above all when the ex-mathematician continues:

> C'est justement dans les apparentes défaillances de la vraisemblance que mon réalisme se montre le plus vigilant, car il ne fait (en réalité) qu'emprunter une forme rigoureusement et sévèrement mathématique. En effet, selon la méthode analytique consistant à traiter un nombre absurde, imaginaire, pour en faire jaillir des équations comestibles ...

Aymé has made the unreal part of the real. He is realistic because he is only moving just far enough away from reality to get a more objective view of it. He maintains constant reference to reality and returns to it at the end of most stories:

> je pars sur des données imaginaires avec une conscience paisible et une foi robuste dans la vérité du dénouement, de sorte qu'en achevant la nouvelle, j'ai le droit (parce que j'ai été réaliste tout le temps) d'ignorer les absurdités auxquelles j'ai feint de me laisser aller.[16]

The endings of these stories are usually simple and natural. When Lafleur's talent affects all branches of art or when Wadé's month stretches to several years Aymé has reached the end of his consequences. He loses interest and quickly puts down his pen: '6 *juillet* — un décret supprime la carte de temps. Ça m'est indifférent.' These endings are often engineered rather suddenly but they are seldom entirely unexpected. The multiplication or acceleration has usually been built to such a pitch that we feel that a dénouement is both morally and aesthetically inevitable. When Sabine attains 67 000 selves, a whole town is progressively transformed into birds and snails or Delphine and Marinette are about to be sold as animals we feel that the situation must be rectified before the end of the story. The interlude seems to be the only reasonable structure.

The application of this structure to the fantastic is a fairly traditional ploy. Our well-being insists that the unreal be terminated. Fantasy can be a fearful weapon, not to be left within reach of children. So when a mother of two finds she is suddenly fifteen years old again she must revert to her correct age. Valérie must return to her own century after her lesson in humility, Delphine and Marinette must be changed back to their human forms and the bailiff Malicorne must finally go back to heaven for judgement after his rather unconvincing interlude of reprieve. A majority of Aymé's fantasies are simply and abruptly terminated: Martin in 'Le Temps mort' is conveniently run over at the stroke of midnight, Barbe reappears, the skyscraper comes back to life in 'Pastorale' and Dutilleul ends up stuck in his wall. Order is restored quickly and simply:

> Heureusement, le loup ne savait pas ouvrir les portes, il demeura prisonnier dans la cuisine. En rentrant, les parents n'eurent qu'à lui ouvrir le ventre pour délivrer les deux petites. Mais, au fond, ce n'était pas de jeu. (CP 182)

Marcel Aymé is far too varied a *conteur* to be tied down to the reassuring return to reality as a short story ending. Part of his charm lies in his unpredictability. So, instead of ending up in the butcher's window, the two oxen find employment for their new talents in a circus, and instead of Delphine and Marinette having to face the reality of a visit to aunt Mélina once Alphonse stops the rain, they are reprieved:

> Ayant eu l'idée de raser sa barbe, la tante Mélina avait trouvé sans peine à se marier et s'en allait habiter avec son nouvel époux à mille kilomètres de chez les petites. (CP 28)

An abrupt ending can be used to provide humour instead of reassurance, especially if it comes from one of Aymé's frequent reversals: having a bailiff shout 'A bas les propriétaires', insisting that the over-pious Mlle Borboïé enter heaven as the regimental whore or awarding a halo to a pimp. Here again it is Aymé's calm, unflinching statement of the situation that provides much of the humour.

Occasionally the whimsical Aymé will allow his absurd propositions to run through the story and even beyond the word 'Fin'. So the novelist Martin's characters finally leave their fictional frame to live on in the real world. In a way Aymé is speaking for himself when he has Martin confess that even though he abandons his characters their life continues. Lafleur's talent spreads to make all art 'efficace' and Aristide goes off to the forest to give free rein to his equine half. There is a strong element of reader teasing in the way Aymé leaves stories up in the air like this. Admittedly Dutilleul ends up stuck in his wall, and for him the interlude of fantasy is over, but for us the unreality lingers on in the clever irony of Aymé's ending. Quite early in the tale Dutilleul consults his doctor, who diagnoses 'un durcissement héliocoïdal de la paroi strangulaire du corps thyroïde', a parody if ever there was one. For an absurd illness, an absurd remedy: he prescribes lots of strenuous exercise and two pills a year of 'poudre de pirette tétravalente, mélange de farine de riz et d'hormone de centaure' (PM 8). Dutilleul takes one of the pills and then forgets the rest in a drawer; and of course collecting stamps and reading the newspaper is hardly strenuous exercise. So when Dutilleul suddenly gets stuck in a wall it calls for an explanation. In fact Dutilleul had just swallowed more of the pills by mistake, needing aspirin for a headache. And then he spent a night with a young lady indulging in unaccustomed and indeed strenuous exercise. The absurd remedy worked after all! The fantastic is also allowed to survive in 'Le Cocu nombreux': at the end of his story Aymé opens up limitless horizons and then frustrates our curiosity by firmly putting down his pen. He has the 'fou' warn the vagabond to go back the way he came before it is too late:

> La route opposée vous mènerait à d'autres villages pareils à celui-ci, et pires encore. Il en est où une personne habite quatre, dix, vingt corps et davantage ... (DM 134)

Aymé even finds the introduction of a physical absurdity at the end of a story a satisfying way of putting down his pen with humour. Thus the rather strange 'Avenue Junot', with its many courtships of Adélaïde, only ends when she flies off on Pegasus' back after his sudden appearance at the studio door. The poignant ending of 'Les Bottes de sept lieues' is rather less of a surprise: Antoine dons his magic boots and strides off to gather his sunbeams, but since moral justice has been done Aymé can let the unreal continue while we slip away. Not only these whimsical escapes and the last-minute reprieves and 'It's lucky you didn't disobey us or you would have got into trouble' endings of so many of the *Contes du chat perché*, but also the suspended dénouements of 'Le Cocu nombreux' and 'Le Passe-muraille' must have been at the back of Aymé's mind when he commented that 'Les plus beaux contes' are rounded off by 'une brume de mélancolie'.[17] One such ending crowns 'Légende poldève'. Indeed, the whole story, like 'L'Huissier', must have been conceived with a view to its ironic dénouement. Military satire aside, the story relates a major test of Marichella Borboïé's convictions. At the gates of heaven Marichella's faith is severely shaken. Firstly she is shocked at not being acclaimed by the angels upon her arrival: 'Bel ange, vous ne savez pas qui je suis, sans doute. Je suis Mlle Borboïé, de Cstwertskst' (PM 156). Secondly she discovers that Bobislas and his fellow hussars are streaming through the gates bellowing obscene songs while she and her virtue are firmly turned away. The final, superbly ironic humiliation is that to gain entry to paradise she will have to accept the help of the ignoble Bobislas and she will have to employ 'ruse' and 'artifice' on St Peter. 'Les desseins de la Providence sont impénétrables' (PM 162), muses Marichella, with more than a suspicion of hypocrisy, and finally agrees to masquerade as the regimental whore. 'Ah, bon, passez', says St Peter.

*   *   *

It is clear from Aymé's repetition of patterns and techniques that he is not just using his vivid imagination to amuse himself and his readers, nor only to underline man's individual or collective foibles. Despite socio-political satire or moral lessons sketched in individual stories, the thematic key to Aymé's absurdities is not to be found in this direct expression but rather in the impressions communicated by an accumulation of stories. It is already possible to isolate several thematic currents which bind this limited group of stories together and lend coherence.

J. R. R. Tolkien underlines one of the overall unities of Aymé's imagination when he remarks that one function of fairy stories is to enable us to look at sheep and horses refreshed from having seen dragons.[18] This is one advantage of the creative imagination that Aymé appreciated in the work of his friend Pierre Véry:

> Sur les ailes de son imagination, il se plaît à franchir les hauts murs entre lesquels l'homme reçoit une lumière avare sur les mystères de l'univers.[19]

Aymé often betrays his humanist orientation in individual stories, and it seems true to say that collectively they lead us to take another look at man. Aymé gives new capacities to man to explore his limitations; he constructs social absurdities which parallel man's collective reality; he provides concrete images for what is abstract and difficult to grasp; he places his observers in privileged positions from where they and we can penetrate façades and reassess reality. Aymé's absurdities, taken as a whole, amount to a unique, oblique perspective on man himself and man in his social context.

It is not hard to see a more precise thematic unity behind the many changes that Aymé brings to the supposed certainties and absolutes of man's existence. They are often used to reflect man's hidden desires and aspirations. Sometimes this is only an implication, but elsewhere the tongue-in-cheek Aymé speculates quite openly. Of Martin's sex-change he says: 'Probablement que son subconscient l'avait travaillé',[20] and then intrudes as a first-person 'je' into the tale to discuss the subconscious causes of metamorphoses before proceeding with his story. His use of these changes as a cumulative exploration of man's desires is a fairly traditional ploy. Pierre Mabille has described this expression of man's quest for freedom:

> Le merveilleux exprime le besoin de dépasser les limites imposées par notre structure, d'atteindre une plus grande puissance, une plus grande jouissance, une plus grande durée. (. . .) Il est la lutte de la liberté contre tout ce qui la réduit, la détruit ou la mutile.[21]

It would be a mistake to complicate this psychological aspect of Aymé's absurdities with talk of psychoses and complexes. As always, the storyteller in Aymé holds him back. Excessive psychoanalytical interpretations of Aymé's unrealities involve two major pitfalls. Firstly, they tend to stress the significant to the detriment of the equally important expressive side of the story. Secondly, such interpretations tend to postulate Aymé's characters almost as case histories, or at least as people much more real than their obvious artistic intensification suggests. In *L'Imaginaire et le merveilleux*, Pierre-Maxime Schuhl describes the attempts of literary analysts to trace the unreal in contemporary literature (above all magic causality and metamorphoses) back through Freudian psychoses to primitive mythology, research which continually confuses the expressive and the significant.

The simple human desires described by Marcel Aymé should not be interpreted as complexes. His fantastic metaphors of desire are much simpler. They spring straight from the omnipresent, frustrating clash between fantasy and reality. They spring from the real world around them, from the 'infirmités de la condition humaine'[22] rather than from the depths of man's psyche. Pierre Mabille puts it as simply as Aymé could have wished:

> Le merveilleux trouve son origine dans le conflit permanent qui oppose les désirs du coeur aux moyens dont on dispose pour les satisfaire.[23]

Aymé's short stories harbour some of the more traditional aspirations expressed in fantastic literature. The desire to manipulate time is the most recognizable. The time traveller in 'La Fabrique' does not express this aspiration nearly as well as the decree in 'La Carte' and above all 'Le Décret', where the time movement also satisfies a desire to know the future. Man's desire to transcend his physical limitations is explicit in Dutilleul's 'besoin nouveau, impérieux, qui n'était rien de moins que le besoin de passer à travers les murs' (PM 12), which later becomes 'un besoin d'expansion, un désir croissant de s'accomplir et de se surpasser' (PM 12). Dutilleul's actions once he starts exploiting his gift betray other simple aspirations: the desire to be taken seriously by his colleagues (the desire to 'be someone'), the desire to be famous, seen in his burglaries and his intentional capture, and the desire to be sexually successful:

> A Paris, comme en province, il n'y avait point de femme un peu rêveuse qui n'eût le fervent désir d'appartenir corps et âme au terrible Garou-Garou. (PM 13)

This sexual aspiration is more strongly suggested when Dutilleul decides to take a mistress. He falls passionately in love with a ravishing blonde and is even more determined to win her when his friend Gen Paul warns him that she is married to a jealous brute who follows her whenever she goes out and double-locks her bedroom when he himself goes out on the town. She represents a sexual challenge: 'Hélas! Monsieur, c'est impossible' (PM 20). So Dutilleul moves from anonymity to existence on a sexual plane too, and his fall is directly linked to his desire for this 'beauté blonde' who seems to be forbidden fruit for several of Aymé's ambitious bumblers. It is their first night of strenuous activity together ('jusqu'à une heure avancée') that causes the headache that Dutilleul mistakenly calms with the 'poudre de pirette tétravalente', and it is their second night of love that finishes him off.

This sexual ambition is equally visible when Raoul Cérusier changes faces in *La belle image* and suddenly has much more success with women, and is even more explicit in 'Rechute', when the ageing senators decree the year of twenty-four months to regain their lost youth (another standard fantasy theme also seen in 'Le Décret') and revolt against the asexuality of old age. The insurgents who take to the streets are the children who were just discovering their sexuality and who now face the prospect of years of waiting. As Sabine develops her gift of self-multiplication we soon realize that each new Sabine represents a new love affair. She achieves in fantastic terms a varied sex-life that would make Casanova quite jealous.

A particularly interesting aspiration that links several stories of unreality is the desire to be someone else, to create life anew. This is an extension of the accessory theme of the split personality that has been seen running through 'Le Décret', 'Le Nain', 'Samson', 'Fiançailles', 'Héloïse', 'Rechute' and 'Les Sabines'. The extremes reached in this last story are of course quite outrageous, Sabine reaching 67 000 selves in her attempt to live more fully. The humble clerk Dutilleul pales in comparison, limiting himself to a modest Jekyll and Hyde split. In 'La Clé sous le paillasson' Aymé ironically reverses both these patterns: Rodolphe is an adventure novel hero who has tasted the power, the diversity and the riches of Sabine's multiplied self and tries to reject it all for reality. He sets out to find his one true indentity. The fictional 'cambrioleur mondain' not only steps out of his novel, thus relinquishing special powers, but also decides to become honest. The ironic opposite of Dutilleul, Rodolphe the fantasy burglar dreams of mediocrity:

> il rêvait qu'il était sous-chef de bureau dans une administration importante, et décoré des palmes académiques. (NA 254)

Finally, Rodolphe feels the helplessness of mere mortality; confronted by a family injustice he feels the lack of his former fictional prerogatives:

Il lui souvenait d'avoir été un fameux redresseur de torts, au temps où il disposait de la lettre anonyme et de toutes les combinaisons de coffre-fort; il lui suffisait d'écrire: 'Monsieur le Comte. J'interdis toute promesse de mariage entre votre fille Solange et le jeune Alexis. Signé: LA MAIN DE FER.' (NA 267-8)

Behind the camouflage of these very graphic images, a hesitant mosaic of human ambitions, capacities and limitations can be seen taking shape among Aymé's stories. Yet, despite the serious implications of some of the pranks that Aymé plays on his hapless creations, it would still be wrong to interpret individual short stories too zealously. Some of Aymé's longer, more wearying texts might permit this; Jacques Teynier judges that the novel *La belle image*

> illustre intégralement et sans didactisme les vues existentialistes sur la nécessité — et la difficulté — d'inventer, dans la lucidité et le courage, une vie qui n'est jamais au pouvoir que de soi.[24]

Certainly, Aymé places some of his protagonists in a position where their fantastic gifts oblige them to recreate their lives, to make a conscious and responsible choice, but he would surely baulk at the idea that Sabine, Rodolphe or Dutilleul might be seen as existentialist heroes.

In many of Aymé's fantasy stories there is a marked current of escapism. This is not only the escape from man's physical condition, the one body and the four walls that combine with the march of time to contain him. There is also escapism on a more personal level and with quite varied motivation. Dutilleul does not just walk through walls. That is a means to let him escape his routine, his mediocrity and anonymity, and accede to a more poetic existence. A rather anti-serious vein of escapism can be traced through many of the whimsical *Contes du chat perché*. Through the magic of the cat Alphonse the girls are spared their visit to the nasty aunt Mélina, and only slightly more serious is the grace accorded to the pig who escapes the butcher's knife with buzzard wings glued to his back with the aid of magic words.

A more serious side of Aymé's escapism is reflected in 'Les Bottes de sept lieues', where the comfort that the boots bring into the life of the Buges is an escape from the poverty, hunger and cold of their bleak existence. Aymé almost inflicts an overdose of pathos on his reader in several pages of darkly realistic details of Germaine's physical and social condition. The worn-out clothes, the sparsely furnished garret, the concierge's scorn, the job as cleaning-woman where she is allowed to eat the leftovers that the dog used to get; all are described with an ironic understatement which only serves to accentuate the misery even more. When Germaine learns of Antoine's accident all she can say is 'Ça devait arriver. J'étais si heureuse' (PM 201). Naturally, the fantasy of 'Les Bottes de sept lieues' also provided Aymé's original readers with an escape from the rigours of the Occupation. Indeed, when the director Marcel Carné formed the project of making an escapist fantasy film in 1942, he wanted to adapt this story of Aymé's. He worked on the project for some time but was unable to find sufficient financial backing. He made his masterpiece *Les Visiteurs du soir* instead. This aspect of escapism is much more explicit in 'Le Décret', where the time change enables the protagonist to escape the harsh reality of a war that is beginning to seem interminable. Given that the story appeared in 1943 this escapism, like the Buges', is not his alone. His readers must have participated very closely as he tried to escape the 'cercle enchanté' of the German presence and reach a dreamed-of time when the grey-green uniforms would have disappeared from France. Aymé's fantastic premise gives his narrator the rather intriguing ability to talk about the present Occupation in the past-tense:

> — Tu n'étais pas encore née, toi. C'était la guerre. La France était vaincue. Les Allemands occupaient Paris (. . .) Et sur la place et aux Champs-Elysées, partout, il y avait des uniformes verts. Et les Français qui étaient déjà vieux pensaient qu'ils ne les verraient jamais partir. (PM 102)

And just to drive the comment home, after the return from 1959 to 1942 a Jurassian farmer can seem to address the Germans with much more conviction: 'Vous êtes foutus. Y a les Américains qui vont arriver. Feriez mieux de rentrer chez vous tout de suite' (PM 107). The physical fantasy of *La belle image, La Vouivre* as well as much of *Le Passe-muraille* (it contains in particular 'Le Passe-muraille', 'Les Sabines', 'Le Décret', 'La Carte', 'Les Bottes de sept lieues' and 'Légende poldève') must have been typical escapist reading in the bleak war years when they were published. Indeed, given the anti-German fantasy of 'Le Décret' (which first appeared in *Candide* in October 1941) and the fairly explicit commentary on the deportations in 'La Carte', it is a wonder that *Le Passe-muraille* ever received the German imprimatur.

The escape from reality is a strong thematic link in Aymé's fantasies. It is not often as explicit as when Valérie skips back in time: 'elle eut un mouvement de retraite comme pour échapper à la triste réalité' (EJ 121-2) but it is a common enough element for Michel Perrin to have distilled it into the rather symbolic beginning of his pastiche:

> Il y avait une fois un héros de roman qui, fatigué de la Série noire et désireux de mener une vie plus pure, profita d'une nuit sans lune pour s'évader de chez Gallimard et s'introduire chez Hachette, où il s'installa dans la Bibliothèque rose.[25]

This movement away from black reality towards the rosy unreal is indeed one of the most characteristic elements in these stories. Through this recurring motif Aymé has woven a fairly extensive study of man's relationship with the physically unreal. His inventions are not merely a mode of expression, a means of exploring various facets of man's existence, or even just a way to amuse. The unreal is clearly the subject too. Dutilleul moves away from reality; his fantasy self preoccupies him more and more until it dominates his routine, mediocre real self. The same movement is seen in the increasing unreality of the stretching month in 'La Carte' and in the mounting confusion in 'Le Décret' as reality recedes further and further from the narrator's grasp. A personality split is a common element of this confusion, as is the acceleration which is the first sign of an impending disaster.

Man's loss of control during this movement is very characteristic. Even in the harmless faerie of *Les Contes du chat perché*, Delphine and Marinette consistently get out of their depth and are overtaken by events of their own making; but it is above all Aymé's fantastic guinea-pigs who are ill equipped to handle his special gifts. Once the novelist Martin has created a character he can no longer really direct the course of events. He watches, helpless, as Armandine Soubiron slowly discovers the true extent of her freedom from him. Each character is a potential monster: Dutilleul loses control of himself, Sabine indulges in compulsive multiplication and Lafleur cannot direct the exploitation of his talent. Aymé's condemnation of this loss of control is implicit in the structure that he so often applies to the stories. His dénouement ensures that the escapist's respite from reality will be temporary. Admittedly, the protagonists may occasionally deserve their respite, but they are only sorcerers' apprentices and do not comprehend the power they wield: they abuse their privileges and are quickly brought back to reality.

Aymé has a predilection for underlining man's stupidity. He has weakly protested his optimism[26] but the sum of his work contradicts him. He sets up his victims like Aunt Sallies just to knock them down again. The Devil in 'La Fosse aux péchés' seems to speak for Aymé when he says at the beginning of the story:

> — La vie n'est qu'un test, (. . .) l'occasion offerte à tout être de donner la mesure de ses aptitudes à l'éternité. Qu'avons-nous à faire, dans l'au-delà, des incapables, des ratés et des impuissants? Qu'ils retournent au néant. (VP 131-2)

Indeed the test or temptation theme (with the Devil as the usual tempter) recurs quite often. It seems to be the Devil disguised as 'l'homme qui guérissait le mal de pendaison' who teases the three 'coquins' in 'Enfants perdus'. This tale, like 'L'Huissier', is based on a reprieve from death: the Devil brings the three criminals back from the grave for another chance at life, only to see them waste their gift in pointless squabbling among themselves. They save him the trouble of intervening, as they conveniently kill each other.

Aymé may often seem to be giving his protagonists a brief respite so that they may better face reality once more, as both Brodin and Cathelin have stressed, but in fact the respite usually backfires and the return to reality is constantly cruel. After all, who can be content to live on earth after a fleeting glimpse of heaven? Cérusier's privileged position turns against him:

> ce coup d'oeil oblique qu'à la faveur de ma métamorphose je viens de jeter sur le centre de ma vie me fait froid au coeur. (BI 85)

When his face reverts to its original ordinary exterior and his new mistress no longer even deigns to look at him, he feels 'la sensation d'être enterré vivant, d'agoniser sous un poids sans pouvoir manifester ma présence' (BI 172). Pol Vandromme has very succinctly described the final stage of the typical adventure:

> Entre le souvenir de ce qu'ils furent et l'espérance de ce qu'ils

voudraient bien être, il n'existe pas de point de ralliement. Ils errent, plus solitaires, plus démunis que jamais — isolés à la fois des autres et d'eux-mêmes.[27]

The victim of Aymé's generosity in 'Le Décret' is a very explicit illustration of this point. Far from being an advantage, his knowledge of the future turns out to be an affliction. After living for a while in the future he is arbitrarily sent back to the middle of the Occupation to what was his present, and still is the present for his friends, but has become the past for him. After several near misses talking about friends and events that the others do not 'know' about yet, he realizes that he cannot reveal his situation or he will be treated as mad. He is obliged to play a role that splits his personality and leads to increasing confusion in his mind. He ponders the idea of tampering with reality too: since he knows about the future perhaps he can change its course. Yet this advantage too proves to be illusory. He meets a future friend in the street, smiles, but of course is not recognized. So why not introduce himself and start the friendship earlier than 'before'? He does not do so, feeling restrained by 'je ne sais quel respect humain ou quelle soumission à la fatalité'. He reluctantly leaves things to 'l'ordre fixé par le destin' (PM 123). Like Arsène and his friends trying to envisage immortality in *La Vouivre*, he finally sees that knowledge of the future has no real attraction. Life will be *déjà vu* and *déjà vécu* for seventeen years. His regained youth is illusory:

> 'Illusion, pensais-je. La jeunesse qui n'a rien à découvrir n'est pas la jeunesse. Avec ce champ de dix-sept années qui s'ouvre devant moi, mais dix-sept années déjà explorées, connues, j'ai plus d'expérience que tous les vieillards de France et de Navarre. Je suis un pauvre vieil homme. Il n'est pour moi lendemains ni hasards. Mon coeur ne battra plus de l'attente des jours à venir. Je suis un vieux. Me voilà réduit à la triste condition d'un dieu.' (PM 115)

Too few of Aymé's Martins are allowed to profit from his generosity. Either they go too far, the gift turns out to be an affliction, or they themselves lack the necessary imagination. Aymé has a sad tendency to single out undeserving subjects for his attention. It is usually only in longer stories like 'Le Décret' or parallel novels like *La belle image* that Aymé's victims can afford to muse openly on their plight. Cérusier can be seen as typical of his more briefly sketched cousins when he reflects on how limited his horizons were considering the potential of his situation.

In these frequent returns to reality there is more than just the description of individual or even collective stupidity, more than a condemnation of the escape or of the fantasy chosen in preference to reality. There is a feeling of overall order, almost a feeling of ordered reality that reasserts itself with a vengeance at the end of a story, reinforcing Aymé's decision to bring the dreamer back to earth. It is most clearly a feeling of natural order that dominates these physical fantasies. We often see a demonstration of the strength of the order that is temporarily upset. But again Aymé seldom becomes didactic; the notion of a necessary order is not a theory but an impression conveyed by an accumulation of cases. Physical chaos tends to provoke a return to order. The failure of the unreal tends to become an apology for the real. Description of chaos tends towards an apology for order. This position is certainly not unique to Marcel Aymé. In his comments on the fantastic in general, Roger Caillois evokes the movement of an ordered reality that tries to stifle a scandal:

> Le fantastique (...) manifeste un scandale, une déchirure, une irruption insolite presque insupportable dans le monde réel.[28]

The impression of a necessary order is very strong in Aymé's world. Nature will not tolerate body multiplication or metamorphoses any more than she will permit a man to walk through walls or disappear every second day. At the end of most stories there is a strong feeling that the situation must be rectified. As Aymé comments at the beginning of 'Le Passe-muraille', the situation cries out for 'une rétribution'. The natural order to be respected is more subtle than the simple reversal of a metamorphosis. Certain natural cycles must be respected too. 'Le Nain' uses the transitions of puberty and adolescence to insist that however much Valentin wants to remain in the sheltered circus world of childhood he must eventually go out and face the real adult world. This is essentially the same age cycle that is upset in 'Rechute' by the senators' attempts to regain youth, thus unjustly benefiting from both hope and experience. Real youth revolts and sets the cycle moving in its right direction. As Aymé says in *La Vouivre*: 'La Nature ne se perd pas. Ce qui se défait d'un côté, se refait d'un autre' (VO 117).

The disorder that lies at the heart of many of Aymé's absurdities is more complex than its more obvious manifestations. There is often an upset harmony that is less visible than the multiplicity of Sabine or the marriage of Aristide and which cries out less stridently for revenge. Valentin's metamorphosis is again an illustration. The most immediate problem for the ex-dwarf is that he is now useless within the circus. All his friends are special—snake-man and bearded lady—while he has become ordinary and no longer feels he belongs. He tries desperately to learn a new role for the circus but the only one he can fill now is that of spectator. He belongs in the grandstand. He finally accepts this and harmony returns.

The upsetting of a subtle harmony or belonging is also seen in many of the outrageous situations into which Delphine and Marinette get themselves. In 'Les Boeufs' it is not so much the absurdity of teaching an ox to read and write that makes the story, but what happens to the ox afterwards. Not only does the educated one want time off from the plough to study, but even when he is harnessed he pulls unevenly, composing poetry while the plough wanders instead of going in a straight line. This is one of Aymé's little symbols of imbalance and it recurs in 'Le Cerf et le chien'. This story tells of the deer and the ox who decide to reverse their roles. They exchange the work, discipline and security of the farm for the freedom and dangers of the wild forest. But the ox gets stuck in the undergrowth of the forest and the deer makes an uneven plough pair with the remaining ox. Not only that but the spirited deer takes unkindly to the parents' harsh use of the whip. Finally he deserts.

The strength of the same kind of roles is visible again when the wolf tries to take part in the girls' games. Of course the wolf's instincts are too strong; to eat tender young girls is his natural role. This same feeling of not belonging is underlined when the chickens go to live with the fox and the little travelling duck brings back a panther to live on the farm. The panther's stay is fatal to her because she is not equipped for a winter, but a more interesting aspect of her presence is the upsetting of the ordered hierarchy whereby the parents control the caprices of Delphine and Marinette: at one stage the panther obliges the parents to reverse normal discipline and say to their daughters: 'Venez jouer, (. . .) vous ferez vos devoirs une autre fois' (CP 238). This situation cannot be allowed to last.

There is a clear social element in some of these upsets of physical harmony. This does not simply mean that the neighbours will gossip if Duperrier cannot get rid of his halo or that Martin will be locked up if he claims to live only one day in two. It is more a feeling of allotted, almost predestined social (as well as natural) roles. The disappearances in 'La Liste' are not only a matter of physics but a social phenomenon. It is at the morning roll-call that the farmer's omission of one name takes effect. It is then that the daily chores are allocated and the girl whose name is forgotten realizes that she no longer has a role; no-one needs her so she no longer counts in the household. From that moment she is condemned to being 'une ombre familière qui passait inaperçue' (NA 61). The invisible daughters also feel a sexual imbalance: what they lack most is being desired by a male. This is especially serious for the 'dévorante' Barbe. It is time for her father to marry her off before her sexual appetite leads to a scandal. The story only ends when her father restores her visibility and finds a husband for her.

This feeling is even stronger in 'Le Couple'. Valérie does not dissociate from the body of her lover simply because it is unnatural for two people to share one body. Aymé is quite explicit about her reasons:

> Valérie, elle, ne trouvait pas dans cette unité la promesse d'une vie sociale, à la fois établie et enracinée, ni la perspective d'un foyer, d'une famille à défendre . . .[29]

In Valérie's case it is a sort of predestination that someone further to the left than Aymé might call repressive social conditioning. Elsewhere it is an order, a hierarchy, a system whose strength is being demonstrated. But the system is not always attractive or just. Aymé is seldom more ironically incisive than in 'Dermuche', where the harmony upset is not so much social as bureaucratic. Certainly Dermuche upsets physiological laws when he is transformed, but his jailers do not guillotine him for that. His metamorphosis represents anything that 'rocks the boat'. They might want to be merciful to the new-born baby that now occupies the cell but that would create complications, shake the system, stop the cycle of upward promotions, not only for the warden but also for his political superiors:

> l'époque n'étant pas à la tendresse, ils tremblaient pour leur avancement qu'on ne vînt à les suspecter d'être bons. (VP 127)

There is a remarkable tension in the stories of Marcel Aymé, the tension of a struggle between Aymé's heart and his head, between the curious inventor and the conservative moralist. This tension can explain not only variety but contradiction. Aymé's head tells him that reality must be restored but his heart often goes out to his victims in their efforts to escape it. Aymé restores the ignoble cycle only because it is insidiously strong. He does not often praise it.

It is almost as if to make up for the regrettable necessity of guillotining Dermuche that Aymé allows the select few of his characters to defy all notions of order and reality beyond the end of their story. Several of Nature's laws are ironically thwarted in *Les Contes du chat perché*, where it seems to matter less. Just as a pig can escape the butcher's knife on magic wings, so Delphine and Marinette are occasionally spared a punishment they deserve. And when they are eaten by the wicked wolf they are simply cut out of his stomach before the end of the story. It is this same lack of seriousness that leads Aymé to upset ordered reality by allowing Duperrier's halo to remain, Lafleur's 'art efficace' to become a permanent movement or young Antoine to go striding off in his seven-league boots.

This occasional contradiction of securely founded trends in Aymé's work, this denial of ordered reality, is less disturbing than it might seem. Firstly, Aymé is very conscious of contradicting himself.[30] He does it partly to confound those who might seek theories with which to tie him down. Furthermore, such unpredictability makes for good short story endings and a pleasant change from the rather depressing returns to reality. But most important, letting the escapist succeed, the disorder remain, the unreal survive, underlines another theme that gives unity to Aymé's work. Physical fantasy is so often brought into the lives of Aymé's protagonists to show that, despite our inability to manipulate it with anything but the most disastrous of results, fantasy is a necessary part of life. Aymé further protests that the unreal is a valid mode of expression, a valid subject, indeed a necessary counterweight to realism in literature.

Man's catastrophic brush with the unreal is generally the result of an excessive reaction after a complete lack of fantasy. Aymé's ideal seems to be that even physical fantasy should be accepted as a natural part of life, that we should free ourselves from too strict a dependence on realism and reason. In this way they never become too excessive or provoke an extreme reaction towards chaos and unreason. Aymé's greatest reproach to his era, an era of science that wanted to unveil and explain all things, was that it stressed reason too much to the detriment of instinct and fantasy. Some of Aymé's more comic scenes occur when his characters apply reason where it has no currency: the American scientists trying to analyse Lafleur's talent for nourishment, the vet who is summoned when Delphine and Marinette transform the animals, the gendarmes who are nonplussed by Aristide and Udine, and above all the philosophy teacher looking for the 'raisons raisonnables' when faced with a student who turns people into birds.

Aymé's work is clearly a study of the intrusion of the unreal into our lives. He is certainly a moralist here. Through Samson's father he tries to persuade his hero that man should accept the many things in this world that he does not understand or cannot control. *Les Contes du chat perché* are in a way seventeen little skirmishes in the continuous war between reason and instinct, between reason and the unreasonable. Many of Aymé's protagonists are forced during the course of their story to 'admettre l'inadmissible' (the words are those of Cérusier in *La belle image*) by being so closely concerned. Aymé's stories are seldom long enough to allow him to be didactic about this, but there are passages in some longer texts that provide illuminating glimpses of his goals. He wants to provoke a consciousness of the unreal in his reader too. Aymé sees our reason

> comme le chien de garde qui aboie et tire sur sa chaîne quand les rôdeurs longent la clôture, et qui ferme sa gueule ou se contente d'un grognement quand ils passent au large. (BI 188-9)

Through another character in the same novel he criticizes

> la vision d'un monde aux mailles serrées ne laissant point de place aux vérités d'un usage trop restreint. (BI 53)

Valentin, the young man who changes his friends into birds and snails, is probably Aymé's best evangelist on this theme. An agent of poetry, like young Isabelle in Giraudoux's very similar *Intermezzo*, Valentin breaks the chains of reason that bind the Cartesian teacher Chabert. Chabert is a clear representative of reason; he surrounds his verifiable world with high walls for security, so Valentin neatly puts a hole in the wall:

> Ce n'est pas d'illusion qu'il s'agit, mais d'un trou dans le mur, d'une brèche éternellement béante. (OL 263)

Chabert, like so many of Aymé's protagonists as well as his readers, is obliged to accept a 'nouvelle réalité', but Aymé would prefer it to be accepted as prevention rather than cure. 'Pastorale' and 'Oscar et Erick' are both explicit about this. The interlude of disorder that is brought to an end at the close of 'Pastorale' is one of excessive reason. In the skyscraper Dulcène, where all is reasoned control and nothing is left to chance, instinct or whim, excess poets are ostracized or brain-washed into scorning poetry as a threat to 'le bon ordre'. After a particularly savage campaign there are no poets left to maintain the spark of life and love. All that remains is an apathetic society of automata so uninterested that even sex is no longer a joy. There is something of a parallel here with the interlude brought about by the decree in 'La Carte': the activity of artists, sculptors, writers and musicians was restricted in the name of rational order. Finally the exiled poet Belin, a missionary like Aymé, returns to revive the spark of life with his unreasoned poetry and his primitive seduction of the first Dulcénienne he meets. He awakens the desire for love and life in her and she gives birth to a poet whose cries shake the skyscraper from its torpor. The interlude is over: 'Le Chef, extasié, regardait renaître la vie' (PI 126).

'Oscar et Erick' brings Aymé to the necessity, or more particularly the justification of such fantasy in art. This story has been seen as a heritage of the 'Art et scandale' chapter in Aymé's *Silhouette du scandale*. Oscar's paintings are the case in point:

> Sur toutes les toiles s'étalaient des objets d'une forme absurde, monstrueuse, auxquelles leur couleur verte semblait vouloir conférer la qualité de végétal. Certains de ces monstres étaient constitués par un assemblage d'énormes oreilles d'ours, vertes, hérissées de piquants. D'autres ressemblaient à des cierges et à des chandeliers à plusieurs branches. (EA 13)

When his friends reproach him with painting what they consider to be scandalous absurdities, Oscar defends himself and Aymé: 'Telle est maintenant ma vision de la nature et ni vous, ni moi n'y pouvons rien' (EA 14). The objections of Oscar's father are even more precise: 'On n'a pas le droit de peindre autre chose que ce qu'on voit' (EA 15), and so is Oscar's defence: 'Mais si Dieu n'avait créé que ce qu'il voyait, il n'aurait jamais rien créé' (EA 15). Aymé's more directly personal defence can be seen in one of his magazine articles: 'le romancier est dieu, ne connaissant dans sa création d'autres lois que celles de sa propre logique'.[31] Oscar and Aymé are of course vindicated by Erick's return with the objects (bananas, cacti, pineapples) that prove that the imaginary can be real.

For Aymé, fantasy in literature is a complement to realism and intellectualism, for which he has often shown scorn. Aymé makes this point in his preface to Perrault, who made his children read fairy stories instead of *La Mort de Brutus*, and reinforces it when young Valentin makes the schools inspector concede:

> Je puis vous assurer que, désormais, Jules Verne et la comtesse de Ségur remplaceront aux programmes des lycées Racine et Corneille. (OL 262)

Aymé's collections of short stories are invariably made up of a sprinkling of fantasies sandwiched between solidly real anecdotes. In his world the real and the unreal are not as separated as we might suppose, and this is part of its unity too. Not only does each collection need a ration of both to be balanced, but within his most outrageous short story the absurdity is constantly framed, accentuated or tempered by reality.

Given Aymé's preoccupation with the movement between real and unreal, there is a strange lack, in the stories seen so far, of those level-headed characters like Oscar and Valentin who are at ease in both worlds. This is probably because of the strength of the physical absurdities involved. The gap between our reality and Aymé's faerie or fantastic propositions is just too wide. Yet these stories of physical fantasy are only half of his world, a complement to a corpus of quite realistic tales where the crises and reactions are less extreme, where the demarcation between real and unreal is disturbingly fluid, where a more moderate and subtle use of the unreal is possible.

The last major thematic current underlying Aymé's physical absurdities also serves as an excellent link to this realistic side of his work. In many short stories based on absurd metamorphoses, powers and disappearances Aymé seems to be demonstrating the domination of the material world by the spirit; his physical absurdities most often originate in the mind. The most striking examples of the powers of the mind are those phenomena provoked by a concentration of the will. The little hen's metamorphosis in 'L'Eléphant' is a direct result of the need to find an elephant for the game of Noah's ark. The hen is delighted to be elected and is given a picture-book so that she can learn how to be her new self:

> La poule blanche regarda l'image avec beaucoup d'attention et de bonne volonté, car elle avait très envie de faire l'éléphant.

> — Je te laisse un moment dans la chambre, (. . .) regarde bien ton modèle.
>
> La petite poule blanche prit son rôle si à coeur qu'elle devint un véritable éléphant, ce qu'elle n'avait pas osé espérer. (CP 213)

This concentration of the will is seen again in 'L'Ane et le cheval' where it is Delphine and Marinette who are transformed. They fall asleep just as they are thinking how nice it would be to be a donkey and a horse respectively. Of course they can hardly believe their eyes next morning. Things do not turn out very well in the animal kingdom and their unhappiness changes them back again in the end. Just as Valentin's power to change people into birds starts unconsciously and comes under the power of his will, so, to a lesser extent, Valérie dominates her condition in 'La Fabrique'. We have seen that her first nocturnal movement back in time is not so much a direct concentration of will-power as an escape reflex, but her subsequent return from a harsh reality to her own era is a clear example of the power of the will:

> elle réussit, au prix d'un immense effort, à reprendre pied dans le temps qu'elle avait quitté. (EJ 144)

The mental activity in 'Les Bottes de sept lieues' is a combination of will and belief reflecting the Tinker Bell principle that fairies are only visible to those who believe in them. Antoine and his companions need to believe in the facetious descriptions attached to the bric-à-brac and they need to believe in the magic of the seven-league boots. The concentration involved in the literary creation in 'Le Romancier Martin' provides a much more graphic example of the mind's domination over matter: Aymé's novelist puts so much effort into his writing that his creations are too complete; they are endowed with a will-power independent of his.

The mental activity in 'Dermuche', 'La Liste' and 'Fiançailles' remains at the unconscious level and yet is still strong enough to trigger off a physical absurdity. Thus Dermuche's moral innocence is projected on to his body, and Noël Tournebise's daughters disappear because their father no longer remembers their names. They have lost mental existence in their father's mind and that leads to a feeling of uselessness, which in turn effects the physical disappearance. And just as Valentin's changes in *Les Oiseaux de lune* are inspired by his reading of Jules Verne and the comtesse de Ségur, so books about Greek mythology are the source of Aristide's existence in 'Fiançailles': Estelle reads so many of them while she is pregnant that she gives birth to a centaur. Mental existence precedes physical existence.

Aymé has described an astounding variety of relationships between the mind and the physical world. One of the more disturbing phenomena is encountered by the lovers in 'Le Couple', where the communion of minds leads directly to the fusion of bodies. Naturally, when the mental harmony ceases so does the physical union. *Les Contes du chat perché* provide some of Aymé's more lighthearted examples of the link, from the transfer of blindness by telepathy in 'Le Chien' to the whimsical changes resulting from the drawings in 'Les Boîtes de peinture': once the animals see the sketches of themselves the images impose themselves through their minds on to their bodies. Not only do the white cows disappear (they are offended because they seem invisible on the white paper) but the horse ends up smaller than the rooster and the donkey has to make do with only two legs.

These stories based on psychosomatic phenomena lead directly to the complementary, more realistic side of Aymé's literary creation. All their key elements — concentration leading to imbalance, physical disorder, chaos and a forced return to reality — are elsewhere applied to stories where there is absolutely nothing that is physically absurd. Aymé's fantasy stories often show mental existence of the fantasy leading to physical existence, but there is no need for that mental unreality to attain a physical dimension before Aymé considers it worthy of his attention.

3
Illusion

C'est folie de rapporter le vray et le faux à notre suffisance.   Montaigne

Once we leave physical fantasy and rejoin what we normally accept as reality, many of Aymé's stories still seem surprisingly familiar. They are parallel in many respects to his faerie and fantastic interludes except that they are concerned solely with unrealities of the mind. Aymé's subjects are no longer fairies and manipulations of the clock but misconceptions, illusions and obsessions. The resulting situations are just as disquieting even though the unreality is much harder to define. We are still dealing with an invented reality but it is no longer just Aymé who is inventing; the creations are in the minds of his protagonists. Nevertheless they are still ideally suited to being the premise for one of his short stories. These mental unrealities, more than the physical absurdities, can be treated as real because they are always real to the mind that creates them.

Very early in his literary career Aymé showed a penchant for exaggerating certain psychological complexities and displayed the interest in the powers of the mind that is evident in his fantastic images. In his first novel, *Brûlebois*, he proposes a character who was, in retrospect, an early spokesman. Rodolphe divides humanity into two categories: 'les dos ronds' and 'les dynamiques', contrasting those who dissipate themselves in 'Pluriels ondoyants, moelleux' (BR 48) and those who concentrate their mental and physical energies in one direction. Of course he regards himself as a 'dynamique'. Rodolphe concentrates on a Balzacian quest for an algebraico-alphabetical absolute that he calls God. His concentration becomes obsession and then madness and he is taken away in a strait-jacket. Rodolphe and his spiritual cousin Johannieu who, in *La Rue sans nom*, retreats further and further into a private dream world obsessed by an ideal woman, provide psychological parallels to the frantic acceleration of some of Aymé's physical metaphors.

A parallel plot in *Brûlebois* shows mental concentration producing more direct physical results. For reasons of social prestige, the Reboudin couple have adopted the idea that they are suffering from asthma. A contest develops between husband and wife to see who can be the sickest and therefore the most talked-about. Inevitably they end up really believing they are sick. The sickness born in their minds is transferred to their bodies by a psychosomatic process and they actually die. The same fatality rounds off a sub-plot in *Le Vaurien*. Grelin's dead wife Lisbeth lives on in his mind, until he starts to believe quite strongly that she is dragging him down into the grave with her. This finally unbalances his mind and he does die. This sub-plot, developed by Aymé as support for a realistic novel, might easily have made an independent short story. Much the same could be said of the disorder explored in the plays *Clérambard* and *Les Maxibules*.

A more subtle example of the mental unreality that Aymé was to refine into short stories can be seen in his second novel, *Aller retour*. It is not a particularly good novel but deserves close examination because it is a prototype that was strongly to influence both structure and theme of many short stories that followed it. The structure and theme are condensed into the return-trip image of the title. It is the story of the rise and fall of a very ordinary *pauvre type*. Every day the lifeless Justin Galuchey takes the same bus to the same office and every evening home to the symbolic rue des Vertus, where the homely Apolline and domesticity await him. A minor humiliation triggers off Galuchey's consciousness of his mediocrity and he revolts:

> Tiens, je crache sur Galuchey de un à trente, je le jure! Je crache sur ce Galuchey domestique, je le piétine. Et maintenant, ça va changer... (AR 30)

Galuchey is ambitious but his horizons are sadly limited. His revolution starts with pathetic gestures that are simply a break with habit: lying to his wife and staying out half an hour later than usual. After several minor failures Galuchey decides that his metamorphosis needs the support of a physical dimension, so he has his moustache shaved off, orders a flamboyant suit and replaces his bowler hat (surely Aymé's symbol of the *pauvre type*) with a sporty cap. Mask and disguise are complete. Deciding to put his new self to the test, he sets about seducing the worldly Raymonde, who lures him away from his shabby apartment to the unfamiliar décor of the casino and the race-course. He rejects his professional role in the same way: the office whipping boy suddenly revolts, gains the respect of his mocking colleagues and humiliates his doddering superior into retirement. Galuchey replaces him and the power structure is neatly reversed.

Galuchey soon acquires a taste for this new, unreal life and feels the strain of the conflicting demands of his old and new selves. His old existence is an embarrassment whose presence, usually in the solidly pregnant form of Apolline, is too real. He rejects her more and more, feeling increasingly threatened by the constraints that she represents, and reaches out for the ephemeral freedom that he sees in the fleeting, irresponsible Raymonde. He even starts talking of divorce. Galuchey's professional security is threatened as he absents himself more and more from his office. It is clear to all around him that he is heading for a fall. This fall is finally engineered by his uncle Suprême, who decides that Galuchey is making a fool of himself. He gives Galuchey a rather muddled sermon on the caprices of fate and on man's incapacity to grasp the happiness that is near at hand. Then, in a terribly public humiliation scene, Suprême 'accidentally' shows Raymonde a photo of the Galucheys on their wedding day. The photo cruelly distils the mediocre essence of a 'couple hébété, triste, bénéficiant de cette nuance attendrissante qui peut être au ridicule [sic]' (AR 217). Raymonde bursts into laughter and destroys Galuchey's dream. Tail between legs, he returns to the domestic fold in utter despair.

The main elements of *Aller retour* were all to recur in Aymé's short stories. The most universal legacy is the feeling that this kind of revolt is doomed from the start. Galuchey's metamorphosis is essentially the story of 'un gardeur d'oies qu'une fée eût couronné roi' (AR 136). Galuchey is simply a peasant's son who arrives in the big city with paternal counsel of chastity, frugality and fidelity ringing in his ears, dons the bowler hat and joins the daily round. Unfortunately the link between this Galuchey and the big spender in the 'Cercle vert' is elastic but very strong; when stretched such a long way it does not snap as Galuchey would wish but jerks him back to his proper station in life. Aymé exaggerates each aspect of his situation to show how social necessity and human nature chain Galuchey to a fixed rung on the social ladder. The pages that prepare us for his revolt are very explicit: he is a mediocre clerk whose 'dîner à quatre francs le situait exactement dans la hiérarchie sociale, le rangeait dans une catégorie besogneuse' (AR 9), and whose wife is a perfect match: 'Leur vie était parfaitement régulière, parce que leurs pensées et leurs désirs, ignorants de la fantaisie, étaient un jour comme l'autre' (AR 28). Aymé is perhaps too insistent on the strength of what Galuchey is reacting against; during the course of the novel he constantly reminds us that Galuchey is struggling in vain. Little images of failure keep cropping up to show us the unreality of his escape. When he tries out his new masculinity in a bar fight his failure is prefigured the moment he walks in the door:

> Sitôt qu'il fut entré, son exaltation tomba. Evalué par le regard du garçon et des consommateurs, Justin se sentait ramené à ses proportions d'antan. Vingt années d'habitudes et de résignation lui tombaient sur les épaules. (AR 31)

Every time he goes to the races or the casino with Raymonde he makes himself look ridiculous and each episode warns us that something is wrong. It is obvious that Galuchey is not only chained to reality on a physical plane, by the Church and by the law, but on a mental plane too. He can physically escape Apolline for a while but she keeps reappearing in his mind.

One of the more influential aspects of *Aller retour* is the means used by Galuchey in his escape attempt: the mental creation of a second self. Like Gide's Michel in *L'Immoraliste*, Galuchey is convinced there is a new self to be freed from the former being. This new Galuchey is the focus for an egoistic drive towards self-fulfilment. At first the two selves cohabit with only occasional conflicts:

> Galuchey sentit en lui comme un deuxième Galuchey — l'ancien — qui se contractait dans la gêne d'être en retard sur l'heure accoutumée. D'un coup de cognac, Justin le réduisit au silence et sortit (AR 53).

It seems there might be room for both of them in his life because no one really takes the new one seriously. He sees Raymonde from time to time but still does his job and goes home to Apolline at night. But inevitably Galuchey loses his balance and decides to live his new self, seeing it, alone, as 'véritable' and rejecting all that is associated with his previous love and life.

Very early in the novel Aymé describes Galuchey thus: 'Inhabile à pénétrer l'harmonie intime des êtres, il chercha simplement à les différencier d'après leur aspect' (AR 10). Galuchey's belief in external appearances shows up in his desire to make physical reality conform to his mind's image of it, to make his new self be what he thinks it already is. We see this in his desire to change his external appearances. The interplay between mental and physical reality in *Aller retour* is very important, especially in the mind's refusal to accept any reality other than its chosen version. We are made aware of this play with reality every time Galuchey 'sees things'. He has visions of Apolline, whom he has decided to reject. His mind betrays his resolve and conjures up Apolline to follow him around and make him angry and afraid. He is finally so confused that he accuses her of following him in person. His paranoid outburst is quite pathetic:

> Tu étais à Saint-Cloud, tu me flanquais ta blanquette et ton avorton par le nez, dans l'autocar; tu étais sur la pelouse; et dans le taxi, tu t'étirais en pâte de guimauve. Est-ce que tu n'auras pas bientôt fini de m'épouser, hein? (AR 134)

Galuchey's confusion about what is real is further aggravated by a very revealing dream in which Apolline ceases to exist, even in the past, and Galuchey is 'bien aise'. The same means of speeding up the realization of a particular fantasy by giving it immediate existence in the mind is visible when Galuchey starts consciously referring to his wife in the past tense and feels immediately reassured. The fantasy forms of speech recur when they meet on the way home: to Apolline home is 'chez nous' while to Galuchey it has become 'chez toi'.

There is a strong sexual element in the motivation of Galuchey's illusion. There is simply no passion in the reality that Galuchey reacts against. His love has long since been constrained by conjugal habit. One of his first acts of consciousness is to see that his wife is ugly, and his war-cry, 'Je crache sur Galuchey de un à trente', is preceded by the revelation that he has 'mis trente ans à [s]'apercevoir que le corsage des femmes était rond'. Galuchey's whole revolt can be seen as a sexual affirmation. Even in the early stages, before he decides to take a mistress, his tentative revolt is described ironically in sexual terms: 'Ce "Tonnerre de Dieu", il l'érigeait comme un phallus de scandale dans sa vie d'autrefois' (AR 29). Similarly, his bar fight is evoked as a test of masculinity: he is seen going in 'comme pour une prise de possession' (AR 31). Galuchey obviously sees Raymonde as a sexual proving ground. She is to be an 'accomplissement', but ironically enough she is using him in exactly the same artificial way, having decided it would be a challenge to tear him away from Apolline. Raymonde is used in a sexual image that neatly sums up Galuchey's adventure; she excites Galuchey and abandons him just as his fantasy does:

> Sur la dernière marche, il se retourna vers elle. Alors Raymonde se laissa tomber sur lui. Dans son manteau de fourrure ouvert, elle l'enveloppa, se l'appliqua sur le corps, le mordit aux lèvres. Puis, de sa main gantée, elle lui tira son chapeau sur les yeux et s'échappa dans la rue en jetant son rire où tremblaient des promesses. (AR 151)

The presentation of Galuchey's illusion with its solid background of reality, its detailed sub-plots, long drawn out contrasts between characters and décors, its warning figures and images of failure, is rather too explicit. This is aggravated by Galuchey's unlikely demonstration of subtle strength and self-analysis. His musings are not only rather gratuitous after Aymé's very explicit contrasts and imagery, but are quite out of character. His moments of introspective lucidity are no more convincing and serve no purpose except to make his blindness all the more tragic: he clearly knows he is prey to an illusion but cannot help himself. This is pathetically brought out in the sad encounter he has with the little prostitute who sees through him as clearly as Bombé does. She easily sees he is married and chides him for being a 'rond d'cuir' too. Galuchey feels the full weight of his destiny and reacts with pathetic violence: 'Je te défends de dire ça, tu m'entends? Tu n'as pas le droit de savoir que je suis marié' (AR 159).

The reader almost feels thankful when the rather hypocritical Suprême brings Galuchey's fragile house of cards crashing around his ears. In condemning Galuchey, Aymé makes his point rather too well, but this is a fault he was to rectify by developing separate components of his prototype situation in individual stories. Many of the short stories reflect *Aller retour* quite explicitly. Its influence on his novels is less direct, the Galuchey figure usually being scaled down and appearing only in a sub-plot. Only once, in *La belle image*, was Aymé to base a whole novel structure on the rise and fall pattern, but despite his progress in subtlety between these two novels the situation is still stretched too far. The short story was to serve Aymé much better in exploiting the basic *Aller retour* plot and in proposing variations on its key themes.

The second-self and metamorphosis motifs were to become the backbone of many subsequent stories. In 'La Canne', a few years after *Aller retour*, Aymé describes the rise and fall of Galuchey's closest spiritual brother, Sorbier. We witness the mental metamorphosis of another *pauvre type* dominated by his wife and mocked by his children. In many ways 'La Canne' provides a mental parallel to Dutilleul's reversal in 'Le Passe-muraille'. One day Sorbier suddenly decides to take the late uncle Emile's walking stick on his usual Sunday stroll. This gives the meek Sorbier a new lease of life and he decides the time has come to wear the pants in the family. For a while he wins his wife's grudging admiration for his new self, but quickly makes a fool of himself and is taken in hand once more. This story reflects most of the key themes of *Aller retour* but without the sometimes tedious lengths of Aymé's explicit comments, without Suprême's theorizing and without the distraction of weakly integrated sub-plots.

The second-self motif is present in several variants, not only in novels like *Le Moulin de la Sourdine* and *Le Boeuf clandestin* but above all in short story form. The dream frame in 'L'Huissier' and its faerie décor and accessories are just a storyteller's ruse to show the mental metamorphosis that is provoked by Malicorne's experiences at the gates of heaven, and its accompanying state of illusion. Like Galuchey and Sorbier, Malicorne firmly believes he can create a new self. He wakes up in the morning firmly resolved to become a new man, determined to reverse his evil reputation throughout the town. He wants to be called 'bon'. Malicorne fails to see that his good deeds are quite illusory, that they are phony, insincere acts carried out simply in order to have something to write in his tallybook. The entries themselves clearly show the way he plays with words to bolster his illusion: 'J'ai, spontanément, augmenté de cinquante francs . . .' He is eventually gratified when the townspeople start using the expressions 'Bon comme Malicorne' and then 'Bon comme un huissier', but of course these too are just a form of words. Malicorne mistakes words for concrete reality. His whole metamorphosis is illusory but he believes in it wholeheartedly, secretly hoping that one day he may even become a saint. Not all the townspeople share his vision of course; most of them have no illusions. Knowing him better than he knows himself, they interpret his acts quite cynically, assuming that he is preparing a future bid for public office. At one stage his wife looks as though she might be going to attack his illusion: 'Tu achètes ta part de paradis', she complains rather crudely, but instead of going on to criticize him on moral grounds as we might expect, she continues 'mais tu ne me donnes pas un sou pour la mienne' (PM 240). So Malicorne's illusion continues until he dies again.

In 'La Statue' the second self is introduced from the outside. Julie Pinton, an admirer of the inventor Martin, suggests to the incognito celebrity a new version of his past. Martin is far from satisfied with his present existence and promptly adopts the new past, finally believing his life was quite different. 'Rue Saint-Sulpice' takes the motif further to portray a miserable ex-convict, beset by poverty and solitude, whose face is so marked by suffering that he gets a job posing as Christ for a religious statue-maker. He sees so many images of his own face on statues that he ends up identifying with his role and his mind totally eclipses his real self.

Aymé is interested in the mental creation motif in general and certainly does not limit himself to the second-self aspect. Personality doubling becomes tripling in 'Le faux policier' when Rodolphe boosts his ego and his income by adding to his initial, colourless self the role of fake police-officer and then that of movie-actor playing the role of fake police-officer. In 'L'Individu' it is another person rather than a second self that is created. Here, Aymé exploits the subjectivity of our emotional judgements of others: Marcelin invents a new version of his neighbour by simply overinterpreting the neighbour's real words and gestures. The reader's position is more objective—we see the real neighbour side by side with Marcelin's imaginary one.

Mental creation is much more complete when young Antoine in 'Les Bottes de sept lieues' invents an uncle for himself, an uncle who embodies all of his emotional needs. His desire for a good-fairy figure becomes belief and produces some very tangible results. 'Les Clochards' describes mental activity being focused on a thing rather than a person. A group of tramps sheltering from the cold night in a *métro* entrance huddle together for warmth and take refuge in dreams of riches. Maillard's mental concentration is so strong that he soon 'hears' the jingle of coins and the rustle of bank-notes; his new-found riches have become very real to him.

Often it is not a person or a thing that is invented in these stories but simply a non-existent situation. Aymé's interest in the relationship between real and unreal produces a series of stories describing illusions or obsessions, or simply built on less tangible misunderstandings and misinterpretations of reality. Martin's illusion in 'L'Ame de Martin' is typical. He fails in a suicide attempt but is quite convinced he is dead, his soul departed and his body therefore invulnerable. Too late, on the scaffold for murder, he sees his mistake. His name-sake in 'Le Dernier' is the victim of an illusion that becomes obsession. Martin is now a racing cyclist who always comes last. The more he races, the more confident he is that he will win next time, and the further back behind the second-last he actually finishes. His obsession with winning finally kills him. The starting-point of 'Le Vin de Paris' is a dream that becomes an obsession: Duvilé's dream of food and wine during the rationing period marks him so much that he eventually mistakes his father-in-law for a bottle of burgundy and tries to uncork him!

Not all of Aymé's descriptions of mental activity are as extreme as these last few cases. 'Le Proverbe' simply sketches a man whose emotional well-being depends on a flattering but entirely false image of himself as wise father and respected spouse, and 'Deux victimes' exposes a fine upstanding *bourgeois* living a similar lie but for much more hypocritical reasons. Both explore the processes whereby the mind sustains such comforting illusions. In 'La Lanterne' Aymé sums up this mental activity in a succinct image of misinterpretation. Diogène wanders through Athens with his lantern telling people simply: 'Je cherche un homme.' Each person he meets interprets this declaration quite differently, projecting his own preoccupations and desires onto Diogène's search.

The maintenance of a comforting illusion is one of the themes Aymé is attempting to illustrate throughout Jules Flegmon's diary in 'La Carte'. This is a particularly dense story; not only is it a biting fantasy indictment of collective racism and egoism, but also an extremely concise psychological study of the vain, self-satisfied, role-playing diarist Flegmon. After all, what can a diary hope to reveal better than its author's soul? Flegmon's diary is a narrative device which lays bare his hypocrisy as he describes what he sees around him; above all as his comments often reveal far more than he intends. 'On ne flétrira jamais assez cruellement l'égoïsme des humains' (PM 74), mutters Flegmon indignantly, but a mere page later we learn that he has applied for his personal case to be given special consideration. And just over the page he is taking advantage of his friend Roquenton's absence to seduce his wife. She soon leaves him for a young blonde fellow; good riddance, muses Flegmon, quite blind to the implications of his thought, she never had any taste anyway!

Flegmon is one of those who need to believe in their probity and importance; without this illusion they crumble. By far the best example of Flegmon juggling his scruples to justify his actions is the superb dinner-party scene that is one of the highlights of the story. Over cocktails, Flegmon declares his indignation about the shameful black-market. There follows a stony silence; all the bourgeois socialites are participating in it but 'On parla d'autre chose'. Poor Flegmon had hoped that his moral stand might impress the bishop, a fellow guest who might support his candidature for the Académie Française. Marcel Aymé never misses a chance to *bouffer du curé*: as it turns out, His Grace is more a realist than a guardian of morality. After dinner, Flegmon's hostess tries to convert the discomfiting do-gooder by attacking his weak point, vanity: she declares that it is the duty of a talented writer to take every opportunity to extend 'une existence consacrée à l'enrichissement de la pensée et à la grandeur du pays' (PM 87). Such is Aymé's irony that she even manages to refer to Flegmon's participation in the black-market in human life as an 'obligation morale'. The bishop, called upon to back her up, side-steps the moral responsibility of direct comment. He expresses his opinion by twisting a parable to suit the occasion: an energetic farmer buys unused land from a lazy neighbour, works hard at cultivating it 'et récolte de grasses moissons qui profitent à tout le monde' (PM 88). Certainly the parable is only as relevant as the assembled guests wish to make it. This openness to interpretation has of course always been the virtue of parables. The hypocrite Flegmon clearly wants it to be relevant. The next few lines of strained self-justification have brought him through a full moral circle in the space of one page:

> Je me suis laissé persuader par cette brillante assemblée et ce matin il me restait assez de conviction pour faire l'achat de cinq tickets de vie. (PM 88)

In their hypocritical connivance, Flegmon and his hostess are playing with words just as much as Malicorne.

* * *

The development of these mental creations into a viable short story reflects the structures and some of the techniques that Aymé applies to his physical absurdities, but there are fundamental differences in the presentation of the material. Aymé's stories of illusion and obsession tend to be more serious than his ventures into Fairyland or even his fantastic intensifications of aspects of man's condition. Despite certain similarities, the concept of the short story has changed. The unreal is not so much a means to illuminate the real; it is now much more thematic. We are dealing with less tangible situations. Aymé is more interested in man's motivations and processes of creation than in his own invention of striking metaphors. He is a psychologist more than just a storyteller. His goal here is not so much to shock or amuse us as to present a situation of potential disorder and involve the reader as it grows. The unreality is no longer such a surprise and is visible not so much by its nature as by its growth.

Aymé's illusions originate within his protagonists. The unreality is not a fantastic gift imposed from outside with a magic wand. The birth and growth of these psychological situations must be much slower if they are to be realistic. This poses few problems with longer texts like the plays *Clérambard* and *Les Maxibules* or the novels *Le Rue sans nom* or *Brûlebois*, but is much harder with the length restrictions of a short story.

Several stories show remarkable concision in the preparation and presentation of the illusion, which allows Aymé to describe the complete evolution despite his length restrictions. 'La Canne' shows the whole evolution of a fantasy by closely following the classic presentation, development and dénouement of the physical absurdities. Sorbier is immediately described as timid and uninspiring. His brief opening exchanges with his wife make us quite aware of the unreality of the new man that he tries to become. We understand at once that language like 'dignité', 'fermeté', 'homme libre', 'chef de famille' and 'mâles responsabilités' is quite out of place, and we easily follow the swift development of his metamorphosis right up until his catastrophe. He takes the stick despite Mathilde's protests and sets off down the 'pente redoutable' that she fears:

> Mathilde garda un silence contraint, elle craignait un coup de tête. On achète d'abord une canne, on prend le goût de la dépense, on a des maîtresses . . . (NA 33)

He flirts with the women in the park and begins to assert himself over the bewildered Mathilde, insisting that they take refreshment in an expensive boulevard café instead of the usual smelly bar. We are made to feel more and more that Sorbier is out of his depth in this role, just like Dutilleul in his role as burglar, Galuchey in the 'Cercle vert' or the narrator astride his two time zones in 'Le Décret'.

'L'Ame de Martin' does not follow Aymé's standard fantasy structure as closely as 'La Canne' but still manages to describe quite succinctly the motivation, birth and evolution of Martin's illusion. Aymé teases us with a gratuitously shocking opening:

> Martin abattit sa femme et ses beaux-parents à coups de revolver et poussa un soupir. Tout s'était passé normalement, mieux même qu'il n'avait osé espérer (DM 137)

but he soon provides the motivation for the crime: Martin feels humiliated when he discovers that his wife has been cuckolding him with the complicity of her parents and the knowledge of the whole neighbourhood. For the moment, what interests Aymé is to sketch Martin's relief, indifference and his rather blank state of mind — a mental vacuum that is about to fill with illusion. Martin's immediate reaction is to attempt suicide, and when his revolver fails to fire he thinks he feels his soul departing regardless. The illusion grows stronger: 'je ne compte plus', he muses, and assumes he now has only temporary possession of his body. He believes he is dead. He empties his wallet into a priest's eager hand to assure the salvation of his soul for a hundred years and, his illusion fortified, calmly allows himself to be condemned to death. 'Mon affaire est réglée sur la terre comme au ciel' (DM 153), he assures the prison chaplain, but the illusion comes full circle in the end. Aymé ironically rounds off the tale by making Martin realize on the steps of the guillotine 'qu'il s'était forgé un conte' (DM 153).

Despite the length restrictions of the short story, Aymé's interest in the birth process of an illusion leads him to forego the expedient of starting his story with the statement of an existing illusion. His usual solution, combining this interest with his desire to show the illusion's dénouement as well, is to construct the story simply as a slow realization of the fantasy, a combined presentation and development of the illusion. This produces stories which at first seem rather anti-climactic to the reader attuned to Aymé's more startling announcements. He starts with a quite acceptable situation and then pursues it until it becomes unacceptable. The story tends to start in a very banal fashion and to become quite complex by the end. 'La Statue' is typical of this: Aymé has arranged the tale into a smooth rise towards full revelation of the extent of Martin's fantasy. He evolves from being a simple physical manipulator (inventor of gadgetry like the 'pandemonium mirabile') towards being one of Aymé's more subtle mental inventors. Martin loves Julie Pinton, but she loves another, a Martin of the past whose glory is made permanent by the statue in the park. Martin at first reacts physically, clambering up onto the pedestal and trying to be like the statue, and then mentally, adopting the version of his past that Julie suggests:

> Il oubliait peu à peu sa laideur et lui substituait sans le vouloir l'image d'une créature jeune, gracieuse, qu'il croyait retrouver au fond de sa mémoire et qui n'était en réalité que la dernière et la plus belle de ses inventions. (DM 209)

Haunted by these new possibilities, he rejects his present real self. He sells his junk, his furniture, his tools (his life) and ends up on the streets begging in animal solitude while in his mind the fantasy lives on, totally eclipsing reality:

> A l'âge de trente-quatre ans j'ai épousé une veuve très riche. Une femme millionnaire. J'avais hôtel particulier, domestiques, voitures, un château en Touraine, des villas au bord de la mer. Je portais un monocle. Je semais l'or à pleines mains... (DM 218)

It is not often that Aymé provides as complete an account of the birth of an illusion as in 'L'Individu'. Marcelin is initially described as a *pauvre type* quite satisfied with his own mediocre joys and successes. The story then recounts several very real events which we, and even he at first, observe quite objectively, but which Marcelin slowly distorts beyond all recognition. The reality: Marcelin is kept waiting by a tobacconist who is flirting with a well-dressed and gallant customer who follows Marcelin into the shop. Marcelin admires the other customer in spite of himself and dismisses the incident because the man lives on the first floor of Marcelin's building and he wants to remain on good terms:

> Celui-là, d'ailleurs, ne paraît pas désagréable. Il parle bien. Il a une bonne balle souriante. (PI 150)

Once within the building, the other resident jokes amiably with the concierge about the broken-down lift while Marcelin is put out at having to climb seven flights and is insulted by the concierge when he grumbles.

During his seven-storey climb, Marcelin has time to reflect on all this. The illusion: by the first floor his co-resident, who is already at his door, becomes 'cet animal-là'. By the third floor Marcelin has exaggerated the concierge's remarks and begins to suspect the probity of the 'gros feignant'. By the fifth floor he is reflecting again on the incident in the tobacconist's:

> il a fallu que ce cochon-là me passe sur le ventre, il a fallu qu'il se fasse servir avant moi qui attendait [sic] depuis vingt minutes. Et avec ça, il me ricanait dans le nez. Et quand je suis passé devant lui, cette manière qu'il avait de siffler en me regardant monter mes sept étages . . . (PI 152)

and soon he is convinced they are all in league against him. Reality has been totally deformed and reinterpreted:

> 'ma parole, il m'a presque bousculé . . . il m'a bousculé.' Donc, cet individu l'avait bousculé avec l'approbation de la buraliste; après quoi, dans la rue, il avait joué avec sa canne et fredonné une chanson, par bravade. Passant devant la concierge, il tenait des propos badins au sujet de l'ascenseur détraqué; et l'exemple de sa détestable complaisance compromettait d'avance toutes les justes réclamations; la concierge, par le jeu d'une comparaison forcée, n'avait d'ailleurs pas manqué d'en tirer argument. (PI 153)

Once Marcelin gets home, the 'individu' has become a totally imaginary scapegoat figure, the direct cause of all of Marcelin's failures in life.

This development pattern of a rise towards a climax of illusion is also the basis for Aymé's description of an alcoholic delirium in 'Le Vin de Paris'. Again he prepares his starting point well by setting his tale in the rationed post-war years and choosing a protagonist with a particularly strong thirst for wine. Not only is wine very scarce, but Duvilé's thirst is aggravated by a nagging wife, noisy children and a hypercritical, parasitic father-in-law. Aymé has carefully prepared Duvilé for a frustrating dream where he wanders in a labyrinth of fountains of wine and tables groaning under food but where he cannot derive any satisfaction from what he eats and drinks. Like Bradley in 'Le Mendiant', Duvilé wakes to be more and more obsessed by what he has seen. One of the last images of the dream was a vision of his father-in-law as a bottle of burgundy. Aymé has cleverly staged a metamorphosis: much to the surprise of his family, Duvilé actually begins to like his father-in-law. His solicitude for the man he alone sees as a large bottle of wine provides some very comic moments as Aymé directs his dramatic irony towards the knowing reader. When his children play too roughly with their grandfather he scolds them: 'Voyons, (. . .) ne le secouez pas comme ça. Il faut le laisser reposer' (VP 111) and decides to stay at home in case his beloved father-in-law falls and breaks! Aymé soon speeds up Duvilé's tragi-comic delirium: memories of how his former sergeant used to knock the tops off bottles of wine pushes him to try the trick on the old man. In the end Duvilé sees everyone else as bottles and rushes out into the street amazed at the variety:

> Des dizaines et des dizaines de bouteilles, des crus les plus divers, déambulaient sur le trottoir, les unes solitaires, les autres par rangées. Un moment, il suivit des yeux avec amitié le couple charmant que formaient un bourgogne râblé et une fine bouteille d'Alsace au col élancé. (VP 113-14)

When the police arrest him for trying to molest one of the bottles he tries to drink the inspector!

This acceleration movement, already familiar from Aymé's fantastic stories, seems even more natural in stories like *Aller retour*, 'La Canne', 'La Statue', 'L'Individu' and 'Le Vin de Paris', where Aymé develops his situation by simply allowing the illusion or obsession to run its full course. The length of a novel or play gave Aymé more scope to bring out the full extent of the illusion without it dominating the story too much. In *Aller retour* and *Brûlebois* he had room to give the mental fantasy a strong reflective background and a feasible physical dimension to bring it into relief: Rodolphe expresses his madness in strange clothes and decorations for his house and Galuchey changes his physical appearance and rents a bachelor flat. Aymé is also permitted the luxury of a secondary plot so that we are brought back to reality from time to time to see how the dreamer is changing.

Aymé's most successful short stories manage to underline the illusion without succumbing to the dangers of the novel's extra length.

Although by the very nature of the fantasy Aymé is now denied the ruse of the first-person narrative and has to content himself with the artificial author-observer point of view, he tries to restrict or disguise his own direct comment as much as possible and let the illusion reveal itself. The key mechanisms here are a simple increasing conflict and the separation of real and unreal. As with the fantastic stories, we often see the victim removed from his niche, transformed and replaced. Again we see Aymé letting his dreamers wander against a briefly sketched background of reality. A faded marriage and browbeaten home life coupled with the mediocre routine of 'métro-boulot-dodo' are the background that shows up the dreams of 'La Canne', 'L'Individu', 'Le Vin de Paris' and 'Le Proverbe'. The darker reality of 'Les Clochards' (cold, windswept streets and the miserable existence of the hungry tramps) and 'Rue de l'Evangile' (marshalling yards, gasometers, shanty towns and racism) provide a sharper contrast for other illusions.

One key development technique that is not simply an extension of those used for Aymé's physical metaphors is a subtle contrast of secondary characters and their differing visions and interpretations of reality. Aymé's use of Dominique in 'Les Clochards' is a very positive character contrast. Like the ox which does not get an education in 'Les Boeufs', he is an unchanged control figure who is quickly established as a realist to act as foil to Maillard's optimism. All the tramps rave except him. He reminds them of the ever-present reality that will reassert itself with the dawn:

> — Bien sûr, approuva Dominique d'une voix calme, nous voilà riches, comme tu dis. (. . .) Ne remue pas comme ça, le vieux, couche-toi et puis reste bien tranquille. Il fera jour demain. (PI 138)

He repeats this evocation of the dawn several times in the course of Maillard's dreams. Machelier's madness is also brought out by a contrast in vision: he doesn't see himself as we do. Machelier sees himself as Christ and we see a tramp. His evolution parallels the increasing friction between the neighbour Marcelin sees and the one Aymé shows us. The other characters in the short story can be effective witnesses too: Marcelin's wife obviously agrees with our simpler vision, but Marcelin heeds her indirect warning no more than Machelier realizes that the passers-by are laughing at him.

Irony is one of the characteristic elements of Aymé's work, but one whose function has seldom been analysed. Here it is the weapon of a storyteller who is denied the direct narration of a Jules Flegmon or the victim in 'Le Décret'. Irony is the solution for a writer who is too conservative to attempt a Robbe-Grillet or Butor type dissection of the consciousness, who is content to describe from the outside of the mind and yet seeks a more subtle means of expression than a direct narration of events and thoughts. Aymé, too, depends on reader participation for the success of his tale. His physical inventions provoked this quite easily but in his stories of illusion it is left to the irony. It is the superb description of Marcelin's drift away from reality that induces us to participate in his creation, the ironic language where Aymé pretends to espouse Marcelin's vision in the narrative between bursts of dialogue:

> Enfin, on ne pouvait accorder au gros homme le bénéfice d'avoir agi par imprudence, puisque ce salopard-là, tandis qu'il fourrageait dans son trousseau de clés, avait regardé son voisin peiner sur la rampe d'escalier avec une ironie à peine déguisée; il sifflotait. On ne sifflote pas en cherchant une clé dans un trousseau; il y avait là une affectation d'insolence. (PI 153)

Dramatic irony plays an important part in inducing the reader to judge Aymé's hapless dreamers. He is very fond of exploiting the contrast between his own description of a protagonist and that character's vision of himself. In 'Le Proverbe' the contrast is particularly marked: Aymé sees Jacotin as 'injuste' and 'tyrannique' while Jacotin regards himself as 'ridiculement bon'. When Machelier asks plaintively 'Pourquoi est-ce qu'ils ne me reconnaissent pas?' (NA115), he leaves passers-by and reader conspiring together against him in pitying humour. A dramatic irony worthy even of Molière is wielded against the obsessed racing cyclist for the same reasons. Martin starts by being simply optimistic and determined to try harder even though he always comes last. Soon his optimism grows to be an obsession but at the same time we clearly see that he is losing by more and more in each race. It is his blindness that provokes the dramatic irony. When his colleagues laugh at him he wants to share their joke and naïvely joins in the laughter. Aymé even creates a burlesque situation where 'une femme de mauvaise vie' tries to seduce him: Liliane asks for a demonstration of a massage and then wants to see him in his racing shorts, and suddenly appears herself 'vêtue d'un costume plus léger encore que le sien' (NA 276). But Martin continues to be blissfully unaware of her real designs.

The humorist in Aymé certainly shares the stage with the serious psychologist in most of these stories, but his humour now appears mostly as comic relief. Once the reader is engaged by comedy, Aymé steers Martin towards tragedy. When the spectators laugh and joke derisively about him he compensates with imaginary headlines:

> Martin enlève l'étape Poligny-Strasbourg; après une course mouvementée, il est vainqueur au sprint. (NA 274)

From then onwards, the story is Martin's downhill slide away from reality. When he meets his wife by the roadside after a few more years of losing he does not even recognize her. He is totally cut off from life by his obsessive 'Je m'entraîne' and 'Je vais me rattraper'.

* * *

In these descriptions of illusion Aymé continually explores the difference between what is commonly accepted as reality and the extremely subjective vision of it nurtured by certain individuals. His subject is still, and much more seriously than when he was using fairies and metamorphoses, man's relationship with the unreal. Aymé repeatedly stresses that none of us really sees reality in the same way as others. Just as his physical fantasies work towards blurring the demarcation line between the real and the unreal, so these images of exaggerated mental activity underline the difficulty, or even the impossibility, of our determining just what is real and what is not.

A dominant pattern in these psychological studies, a theme which links them strongly to the fantastic imagery, is of course the accelerating movement away from commonly accepted reality. Without naming it or becoming didactic in any way, Aymé has constructed a multi-faceted study of the psychosis of schizophrenia with its intense interior existence and its corresponding loss of contact with reality. The psychologists tend to make this sort of activity their private domain. Aymé intrudes into their domain and returns a human dimension to it.

The movement away from reality is clearly visible in the evolution through rejection, forgetting and suggestion to creation in 'La Statue', as well as in the accelerating, obsessional optimism of the cyclist in 'Le Dernier'. Marcelin ('L'Individu') and Johannieu *(La Rue sans nom)* are excellent examples of the interference of emotion in the objective apprehension of reality. Both are emotionally involved, Marcelin by inferiority-fed hatred and Johannieu by idealistic love, with the objects of their more and more subjective vision. The movement away from reality is essentially a refusal that reflects man's hidden desires but it is more subtle here than when expressed through physical metaphors. Aymé no longer explores general aspirations to know the future or traverse solids, but more personal and intimate desires.

A strong common element of these illusions is their frequent reflection of sexual desire, a theme also implicit in many of Aymé's physical images. The sexual revolt of the senators in 'Rechute' or of Dutilleul in 'Le Passe-muraille', like fantasy in general (and the two are strongly linked in 'Pastorale') can often be seen as the reintroduction of the spark of life into an existence which has become devoid of interest. This desire for sexual fulfilment, coupled with situations of sexual disorder or imbalance, colours many more of Aymé's stories of illusion and provides a complex exposition of sexual order and reality.[1] Already in the prototype *Aller retour* Galuchey's dreams are predominantly sexual. The challenge of the haughty princess, the knightly trial of strength in his office, the secret trysts, the 'garçonnière capitonnée' are all manifestations of a sexual revolt. Galuchey's fantastic extension, Cérusier, never expresses so openly his desire to become seductive, but we suspect it because one of the first things he notices after this change is the way women have started to stare at him. He decides to seduce his wife incognito as a test, and then sets out to conquer the girl of his dreams. Both are reduced again to sexual anonymity by acts of humiliation: just as Cérusier is ignored by la Sarrazine near the end of *La belle image*, so Galuchey is revealed to his mistress and her laughter destroys him.

Sorbier's sexual reversal in 'La Canne' is the closest realistic development of the prototype. Uncle Emile's stick symbolizes *panache* and virility when Sorbier turns to it to escape routine and his wife's domination. On his Sunday stroll with the stick in hand he gains the strength to express his hidden frustrations. He highlights his wife's insufficiencies by commenting on the naked statues in the park:

> A plusieurs reprises, Mathilde l'entendit prononcer d'une voix saccadée: 'La cuisse, l'épaule, le ventre, le jarret' (. . .) 'Et les seins, nom de nom! les seins.' (NA 38-9)

Sorbier has the bit between his teeth and subjugates Mathilde even further by flirting with two young women. Once he drags his family into the expensive café it is clear that he is heading for a fall. He contracts a loss of vision similar to Galuchey's and starts to flirt with a young woman whose very ancient profession Aymé leaves in no doubt. Sorbier sees only her façade of respectability and sets out to impress her with his stick. Mathilde sees his foolishness and warns him, but to no avail: he is 'impressionné lui-même' by his performance. His inevitable end is just as dramatic as Galuchey's: trying to impress the prostitute, he waves the fateful stick to call the waiter and shatters a large mirror. There is a 'tumulte de rires' and Mathilde capitalizes on his humiliation. With a cruel laugh, she reasserts her domination and order is restored. She leads him away in a 'reprise de possession définitive' (NA 53).

To a certain extent the same desire for sexual amelioration is a key to 'La Statue', where Martin's adoption of a different past is partly to gain the affections of Julie Pinton. The theme is more explicit in 'L'Individu' when the *pauvre type* Marcelin seeks relief from his nothingness in the creation of a new neighbour who shoulders the blame for his insufficiency. The description of Marcelin's dreamy revenge is the only time Aymé ever (albeit ironically) mentions Freud in this connection:

> Dans la nuit, il eut un rêve satisfaisant: à califourchon sur le dos de son insolent voisin, il gravissait un escalier vertigineux, interminable, tel qu'on imagine à un gratte-ciel de soixante-quinze étages. M. Marcelin, qui n'était pas freudien pour un sou, goûtait simplement le plaisir d'humilier le gros homme qui respirait comme un soufflet de forge et demandait grâce avec une voix usée. (PI 156-7)

The illusion is only terminated by the birth of Marcelin's child, an emotional shock but perhaps also an affirmation of his virilité.

Aymé often describes sexual illusions which do not really reflect the revolt pattern of *Aller retour* but which are simply part of the broader, unifying vein of consolation in escape from reality. Abd el Martin's escape from misery in 'Rue de l'Evangile' reinforces this theme. By day he wanders in the bleak décor of the Porte de la Chapelle and by night he gives himself the illusion of humanity by dreaming of the ugly Madame Alceste. She dreams of a handsome young legionnaire who will carry her off, and takes refuge with the handsome young men in the movie magazines. They both dream of simple human contact. Abd el is so desperate that he even extracts warmth from the graffiti on the dirty walls: a human hand, a brother, made the marks. Veiled by the night, the two bodies meet on Abd el's three steps of cold stone. The illusion is consummated. 'Mon légionnaire!', sighs Madame Alceste, and Abd el is not even sure it is her. The only real communication is the transfer of several fleas to Madame Alceste. This is the ironically bitter Aymé at his best.

The escapists' refusal of reality is clearly one of the stronger thematic links between Aymé's diverse creations. From the blatant escapism of 'Le Décret', 'Les Bottes de sept lieues', 'Conte du milieu' and even *Les Contes du chat perché*, Aymé moves towards a more honest, less gimmicky exploration of the same theme. Abd el's movement towards dream to escape physical misery is reflected again in 'Les Clochards'. They, too, escape solitude:

> — Ah! parle-moi . . . dis-moi seulement que tu m'écoutes, rien que ça. Voilà quinze jours que personne ne m'écoute. (. . .) je voudrais que tu me parles, je voudrais que tu me demandes comment je m'appelle, d'où je viens . . . Il y a quinze jours que personne ne m'a dit mon nom. Je m'appelle Maillard. C'est facile à retenir, hein, Maillard . . . Maillard . . . (PI 128-9)

But it is Maillard's dream of money that is the real escape. Having convinced himself, he spreads the dream around him. Aymé describes the illusory wealth as being almost messianic, using words like 'annonciation', 'délivrance' and 'extase'. The miracle gives hope to other tramps, who flock to the Bethlehem *métro* entrance where it all started. Maillard is transported:

> — C'est fini, disait-il, fini de traîner sa gaîne par les rues au milieu du monde qui ne vous regarde pas. On est riche pour toujours. C'est fini d'être tout seul, et puis d'avoir peur. Plus de fatigue, plus de vieillesse. (PI 137)

Dawn comes, of course, with its cold grey reality, but Maillard does not want to open his eyes, physically or mentally. 'Je veux rester riche'. 'Les Clochards' describes one of the more striking nights of fantasy, but we can suppose that every night is an interlude of escape, just as every Saturday night's alcoholic stupor is an interlude for the Italian workers of *La Rue sans nom*. The current is very strong throughout Aymé's work.

Hardship and misery are far from the only triggers to activate Aymé's mental escapists. For the murderer in 'L'Ame de Martin' it is the more personal shame and ridicule of being publicly cuckolded that provokes a departure from reality, and in 'Le Vin de Paris' it is the combination of wine rationing, black-market food prices, shortages of fuel for winter and a nagging father-in-law that trigger Duvilé's alcoholic alienation. Aymé's most explicit description of a physical escape — Antoine's departure in his magic boots — partly obscures a more subtle escape: his mental creation of an uncle to dull his feelings of inferiority. Antoine is a younger version of Sorbier, Galuchey and so many different Martins. Closed up in the hospital ward with his injured friends, the underprivileged, fatherless Antoine is made all the more aware of the gap between him and his friends Nodier, Huchemin and Baranquin. His mother sacrifices her meals to bring him sweets and oranges but this hardly makes up for the procession of relations surrounding his friends. Worse: one by one the others announce that Mum or Dad or a kindly aunt is going to buy them the coveted boots. To put himself on an equal footing with them, Antoine spontaneously invents an Uncle Victor:

> un être prestigieux, beau, brave, généreux, fort, ayant son certificat d'études, tuant une personne par semaine et jouant délicieusement de l'harmonica. Assurément, il était homme à se couper en quatre et, en cas de besoin, à passer sur le ventre d'une famille innombrable, pour procurer à son neveu les bottes dont il aurait envie. (PM 221)

Antoine's friends question him more and more about his uncle, necessitating more lies, and Antoine soon realizes that Victor is getting out of hand. He tries to decreate the uncle but Victor now has an existence of his own:

> L'oncle Victor était gênant, lourd, indiscret, effrayant aussi par l'importance qu'il avait déjà. Antoine essaya de l'oublier, mais l'oncle avait une personnalité forte et originale qui s'imposait. (. . .) l'oncle Victor lui apparaissait maintenant redoutable. (PM 221-2)

But Aymé smiles upon his young apprentice inventor: the boots will be his.

Consolation for insufficiency is a more serious theme in Aymé's description of the alienation and vengeance of the tax collector in 'Le Percepteur d'épouses'. Gauthier-Lenoir takes it to heart when he is ill-treated by his fellow citizens, especially as he has difficulty in paying his own taxes! He wanders sadly alone in the rain and begins to resent those who do pay their taxes, especially Rebuffaud, who always pays up smilingly and on the first day. Gauthier-Lenoir's mind slowly and illogically twists the actions of the threatening Rebuffaud until by paying his taxes promptly he is actually evading his social duty. Not content with letting Gauthier-Lenoir dream quietly in his corner, Aymé then has his wife elope with a handsome cavalry lieutenant. This finally unhinges him and he is beset by 'toutes sortes d'idées étranges'. His pride cannot accept that his wife has left because of any insufficiency of his own, so his mind invents another solution: 'sa femme lui avait été prise par le fisc' (PM 177). This illusion gives Aymé the chance to exploit some excellent tragi-comic scenes: Gauthier-Lenoir writes complaining letters to himself and finally stages a mock interview with himself, changing chairs in his own office according to the role he is playing. When he gets no satisfaction from this charade the two separate movements of his mind come together: he will inflict the same penalty on his fellow tax-payers, starting with Rebuffaud of course!

The escape from anonymity or mediocrity is a familiar trigger for mental creation. When the Martin of 'Le faux policier' indulges in illusory and hypocritical 'oeuvres de justice', it is compensation for his moral cowardice during the Occupation, an escape from the compromises and privations he endured as well as from his fears of Liberation reprisals. To a lesser extent the same motivation is visible in the escape from anonymity and mediocrity in 'La Statue':

> Humilié par sa misère, il enviait l'homme de bronze d'avoir su arrêter le temps et de s'être figé dans un moment glorieux, tandis que lui-même s'était laissé prendre à l'habitude de vivre. Il l'accusait de lui avoir dérobé sa chance et ses forces les plus précieuses. (DM 211)

This 'habitude' is also a strong motivation for Galuchey's revolt and is certainly instrumental in provoking Sorbier too:

> Il semblait bien que la promenade dût être ce qu'étaient toutes

> les promenades du dimanche: deux heures d'ennui coupées par une station silencieuse autour d'une canette de bière. Le père dit: 'En route, mauvaise troupe'. C'était l'habitude. (NA 32)

It is immediately after this moment that Sorbier decides to take the uncle's walking stick.

Aymé clearly realized how serious his canvas of alienation and madness had become. In 'Héloïse', he anti-seriously tries to redress the balance by beginning another Martin story with two false starts that are reminiscent of the *anti-conte* 'Le Vin de Paris':

> Il y avait à Paris, dans le quartier des Enfants Rouges, un nommé Martin qui croyait être un balai neuf et qui aurait voulu que sa concierge l'eût en mains à tout instant.
> On l'enferma dans un asile et on n'en parla plus. Dans le quartier de la Goutte d'Or, il y avait un autre Martin qui se prenait pour un calembour, s'irritait de ne pas voir les gens éclater de rire à son approche. On l'enferma aussi.[2]

It is only after all this that our *conteur* begins his fantastic tale about Martin's sex-changes: 'Le Martin que je veux dire, c'est celui qui ...'

The dénouements of Aymé's stories of illusion are often less abrupt and more explicable than the sudden reversals of the fantastic. They evolve from the accelerating obsession and, as with the physical mode, most involve a termination of the unreality. The tramps' dawn will come as it comes every morning to tear them away from their comfort, and the emotion of his daughter's birth will coax Marcelin back to reality. Hardly any of Aymé's dreamers are realistic enough to return to reality on their own; they need Aymé's intervention. Sorbier's dream is shattered with the café mirror, Duvilé is swiftly removed to an asylum and Martin the murderer is guillotined.

The ending of 'Le Dernier' shows one of the more inexorable fates reserved by Aymé for those dreamers who, despite warnings from those around them, move faster and faster towards catastrophe. Martin simply will not accept the truth. From being a day late in Marseilles, he is a week behind in Roubaix. Soon he is still completing last year's Tour de France and the children are shouting 'Au fou! à la ferraille! à l'hôpital!' Still blind to reality, he dies at the handle-bars:

Comme il enfourchait sa machine, au sortir de la porte Maillot, un camion le projeta sur la chaussée. Martin se releva, serrant dans ses mains le guidon de sa bécane fracassée, et dit avant de mourir:
— Je vais me rattraper. (NA 283)

As Aymé so ironically puts it at the beginning of the story: 'Les personnes qui ont un idéal ne peuvent pas vivre comme tout le monde, c'est compréhensible' (NA 272). Death might seem a fitting retribution to terminate 'L'Ame de Martin' but it seems a little harsh for Martin the cyclist and above all for Machelier. He could have heeded his employer's suggestion that he become John the Baptist for a while and model different poses, but it is too late. He is already identifying too closely with Christ. He wanders down to the Seine and tries to walk across the water to reach his friends on the other bank.

These endings consistently underline the theme of man's *bêtise*. The theme runs more seriously through these psychological studies than it does when Aymé gives man a special gift to tempt him. He is still concerned with man's obstinate misuse of unreality, and also with his stubborn refusal to see reality as it really is. Hypocritical refusal of reality is the target of the pitiless satire in 'Deux victimes'. Here Aymé reveals the subtle movements and motivations of Vachelin's mental juggling in order to highlight the dangers inherent in such activity. While his psychosomatic images often show the strength of man's mental concentration, he now underlines the basic weakness of our mental perception.

Vachelin sees himself as a fine upstanding bourgeois 'âme d'élite'. His fight with the Devil begins when a pregnant young girl writes to tell of his son's wild ways as a young medical student. She appeals to Vachelin's sense of duty. He is immediately tempted to judge that she is after his son's name and security. Thoughts of the boy's ruined career and a social scandal pass through his mind and he resolves to punish his son. Vachelin's mental gymnastics start with the nature of the punishment:

> il ne songea plus qu'aux moyens de punir le vice. C'est pourquoi il s'interdit de marier Lucien avec l'apprentie. En effet, le séducteur (et la lettre le disait expressément) adorait sa victime et ne demandait qu'à l'épouser. En consentant à cette union-là, M. Vachelin eût récompensé le coupable, ce qui était pire

119

que de l'absoudre, et contrarié les desseins de la Providence, lesquels ne pouvaient être que de châtier le criminel. (NA 81)

He goes off fishing, congratulating himself in another bout of hypocritical semantics about the unfortunate girl:

> 'Dieu merci' songeait-il 'je ne suis pas de ces bourgeois aux idées étroites, qui considèrent qu'une jeune fille est déshonorée parce qu'elle a un enfant'. (NA 81)

Another letter comes from another young victim of Lucien's debauchery. Vachelin is now comforted by the illusion that it is certainly the women who are debauching his innocent son, but eventually makes a show of accepting the truth, only immediately to apply illusion to his reaction. Still upset by thoughts of social scandal and the threat to his daughter's coming engagement, Vachelin comes back from fishing having decided once more that 'Lucien paiera'. Thinking in noble terms to bolster his own confidence as well as to impress his wife, he sets the scene for a letter to his son. We almost hear Aymé's ironic drum-roll and clash of cymbals as Vachelin's fine-sounding phrases announce his paternal indignation and pass sentence:

> 'Mais ton châtiment ne serait pas complet, s'il ne t'atteignait pas plus personnellement. J'ai donc décidé de réduire à la somme de dix francs les cent cinquante francs que je t'allouais mensuellement pour tes menues dépenses. Ainsi, tu n'auras plus le moyen de céder aux dangereuses tentations qu'une bourse bien garnie propose aux jeunes gens de ton âge, et ton travail en ira mieux.' (NA 95)

Vachelin's semi-conscious self-delusion is a sickness shared by the Martin who turns from being a mediocre junior accountant to the role of fake police-inspector. In reality, Martin is a robber, confidence-trickster, extortionist and sadistic murderer. The mind games of the story are his excuses and justifications for his conduct. Aymé ironically shows Martin turning to crime as a sad necessity:

> Loyalement, il s'était obstiné à nourrir ses trois enfants des valeurs morales les plus solides, les plus éprouvées, et devant les petits visages blêmes, les pauvres poitrines étroites et toussoteuses, il avait fini par pressentir qu'un régime de viandes

rouges les mettrait à même d'assimiler plus complètement ses robustes enseignements. (VP 155)

He fights down his honesty ('il faut bien vivre'), laments the fact that war destroys all possibility of virtue, and turns extortionist with a will. He appeases his conscience somewhat by telling himself he chooses his victims from among black-marketeers and corrupt officials (his best success is to have tricked a gang of 'faux policiers') and by convincing himself that his actions are deeply patriotic! With the Liberation, Martin rejoices that what he sees as his 'fausse existence' can end and he can return to his simple joys. This is further self-delusion of course: not only has Martin started to believe his own patriotic fervour (he starts to denounce his fellow Parisians for their conduct under the Germans) but his wife has developed a taste for luxury and his salary will only just pay for her cigarettes. So Martin goes sadly back to work.

Martin's mental juggling continues much further than this. He robs a wartime denouncer and then strangles his victim in order to atone privately for his crime by an act of patriotism and justice. Aymé applies his familiar acceleration pattern again: Martin kills more and more, believing more and more firmly in his 'oeuvres de justice'. He suffers more and more subjective vision, seeing collaborators all around him:

> Parfois en flânant dans la rue, il lui semblait reconnaître un trafiquant du noir à l'insolence de son ventre, ou un collaborationniste à la lueur perverse d'un regard et il sentait à son poing frémir le glaive d'un archange. (VP 160-1)

Martin's role-playing now multiplies as he pretends to be a movie-actor playing the role of 'faux policier'. His mistress Dalila soon sees through his act, telling him 'Ton film est terminé depuis longtemps'. She makes her Samson shave off his moustache and change his police disguise ('imperméable vert et chaussures à tige') for a more stylish outfit; Martin's next victim simply laughs at him and moves back one level of reality to call the real police. Martin's interlude of delusion ends in jail.

To some extent Aymé's exaggerated returns to reality show man still searching for happiness but still unable to profit from his own imagination. The three wishes motif of Fairyland literature, where the recipient usually shows his unworthiness, is more clearly visible in 'Les Bottes de sept lieues'. Aymé offers the boots to young Antoine and his friends. Certainly they all dream of trips to exotic lands but their individual imaginations are depressingly cautious and reality-bound. Frioulat would like to win all the world sprint records while Rogier would use the boots to do his mother's shopping more cheaply in the provinces and pocket the few francs difference. Here, too, Aymé's rather medieval moral streak shows through. It is Antoine who proves worthy of succeeding in the quest. Only he thinks of someone else in imagining a use for the boots: he would buy food and clothes for his poor mother and even steal the rent (from the rich of course) so that she would be spared the concierge's condescension.

It is tempting to feel that there must be a guiding theory behind Aymé's recurrent tail-between-legs returns to reality. No individual story harbours much theorizing but in the final scene of the prototype *Aller retour* uncle Suprême formulates ideas that obviously dominate the short stories that followed. Suprême is the most theoretical and outspoken of Aymé's agents. He even goes as far as to give the dreamer Galuchey a fairly explicit lecture before he brings him crashing back to reality. He reverses Galuchey's metamorphosis partly because his god-son is making a fool of himself, partly because he finds the Galuchey-Raymonde couple aesthetically displeasing and partly out of a sense of social justice. He might even be seen as a symbolic social figure acting to cover up the scandal of a wayward member of society. But the real reason for the little soirée that Suprême has engineered is almost philosophical. He believes in an ordered world where roles are determined by a kind of grace, and he judges the dreamer not to be 'élu de Dieu'. The conversation centres on whether happiness is within easy grasp or whether it is simply not of this world. Just before destroying Galuchey, Suprême speculates on the fragility of happiness that is at the mercy of 'quelque circonstance imprévue et fort mince' (AR 213). Finally he asks his guests:

> Mais ne pensez-vous pas qu'il existe, entre ces circonstances infimes et les individus qui en sont victimes, une relation spirituelle (. . .) qui s'exprime peut-être constamment par une loi d'aptitude et où le hasard joue normalement entre des limites bien assises. (AR 213)

His comments suggest that Aymé's dreamers fail because of a lack of grace, because of 'notre impuissance ou (. . .) notre inaptitude au bonheur convoité' (AR 214). Ironically enough, Suprême shows that it is only because he, the guardian uncle, judges Galuchey to be undeserving that the 'accident' of the photo was arranged. Suprême was right but for the wrong reasons; perhaps that is why he was to be the first and last of Aymé's theorizing spokesmen in this domain.

The elimination of these scandalous illusions is not only esthetically satisfying as a dénouement but also continues to demonstrate the strength and (perhaps again reluctantly) the necessity of the order that was so strong in Aymé's physical fantasies. The psychological images expressing this order are not as explicit as the concrete metaphors for the upset of natural order and its accompanying roles and hierarchies, yet Aymé's preoccupation with the theme is still evident. Perhaps there is not much threat to stability when a born loser like the cyclist Martin makes an all-out effort to win, but the threat is stronger in 'La Canne'. Sorbier's predetermined position is that of the dominated partner. The disorder upsets family and sexual stability. Reality and order return when Mathilde reasserts her domination. 'Le Proverbe' relates a similar threat to the family order that is based upon Jacotin's figurehead position.

With our move away from physical imagery to psychological complexities Aymé seems to become less dogmatic about terminating the unreality. He does not always feel obliged to inflict retribution in his quest for a satisfying ending. After all, we do dream, we do fool ourselves, we do become alienated from our surroundings, and our society's increasingly tentative attitude towards normality and madness allows the alienated dreamer that hides in many of us to be tolerated more and more. So Aymé grants some of his illusionists a dispensation from the irony-tipped shaft that is so often used to burst the bubbles of illusion. His justice grants a moment's pleasure and warmth to Abd el Martin, the 'moment de délire sans lequel il n'y a pas de vie' that Claude Damiens underlines in his brief study,[3] and the tramps can dream of riches again tomorrow night. 'La Statue' is perhaps a more tacit admission of our need to dream: the story moves steadily towards construction of the inventor's final illusion and his departure into the unreal and an unknown fate:

> Quelques jours plus tard, le hasard conduisait Martin sur la petite place où il s'était assis si souvent. Il la traversa sans la reconnaître ni prendre garde à la statue et ce fut à peine si une obscure inquiétude lui fit presser le pas. (DM 218)

This is still a satisfying and realistic dénouement.

To allow Vachelin's hypocritical, bourgeois façade to continue undisturbed in 'Deux victimes' may seem strange but Aymé is still just being realistic. He obviously realizes that the Vachelins of this world will always surround themselves with comfortable walls of illusion and that no matter how often they are told the truth they will be deaf to anything they do not want to hear. It is no use knocking down their protective walls; they will rebuild them straight away. This need to delude ourselves despite the hazards involved is clearly another theme uniting Aymé's diverse imagination. His expression of it here is much more honest and less marred by antiserious gimmicks. It is the need to dream, not so much to escape reality (as indeed so many of his accident-prone victims do) as to balance reality that Aymé still advocates. Admittedly Antoine escapes at the end of 'Les Bottes de sept lieues' but his invention of an uncle and the boys' games of imagination are more important than his dreamy voyage in the magic boots; it is they that really balance reality. Like so many of Aymé's characters, Antoine and his young friends create a supplementary 'poetic' dimension for their lives. They need to believe the labels on the objects in the old man's shop-window:

> le moulin à café de la du Barry, le porte-savon de Marat, les charentaises de Berthe au grand pied, le chapeau melon de Félix Faure, le tuyau de pipe de la reine Pomaré . . . (PM 192)

but are certainly not going to get carried away by them. 'Les Bottes de sept lieues' contains some surprisingly acute observations on the world of children and on the importance they attach to the imagination. The language that Aymé uses to describe the boys juggling the relationship between truth and imagination reveals, in a series of suggestive phrases, his profound understanding of the boys' attitude to the magic of the boots:

> une autorité presque incontestable. Peut-être (. . .) ne croyaient-ils pas positivement (. . .) Ils soupçonnaient même que (. . .) mais n'en ayant pas la certitude, ils composaient facilement avec leurs soupçons. Pour être en règle avec la vraisemblance, peut-être aussi pour ne pas s'exposer à voir la réalité leur infliger un démenti, ils admettaient que la vertu de ces bottes de sept lieues s'était affaiblie ou perdue avec le temps. En tout cas, leur authenticité ne faisait aucun doute. (PM 194)

'Les Bottes de sept lieues' describes the rather sad gap between children's and adults' ways of looking at the world. When Frioulat is out playing soldiers in the yard he drops a bottle of cognac that was serving as a machine-gun: 'La vache! il m'a flanqué une balle en plein dans ma mitrailleuse' (PM 218). His mother's point of view is of course totally lacking in this fantasy: she sees nothing but a broken bottle of cognac whose price had just gone up ten per cent. Mme Frioulat's soulless, rational outlook on life is also the reason why she offends the strange old shopkeeper playing chess and arguing with a stuffed bird:

> Je ne vais tout de même pas perdre mon après-midi à attendre votre bon plaisir. J'ai autre chose à faire. (PM 215)

Germaine Buge seems (albeit unwittingly) to bear with the madman's fantasy a little more, and it is she who is allowed to buy the boots. Playing the game is capital. We first appreciate this when we meet the band of *copains* during their adventurous after-school expedition through a coldly real Montmartre. Their games depend on a pretence that there is danger all around them, so when Antoine is sent out on reconnaissance he plays the game:

> Au retour, Antoine rendit compte de sa mission, d'une voix sobre.
> — Je n'ai pas été attaqué, mais rue Saint-Vincent, il y a du louche.
> — Je vois ce que c'est, dit Frioulat, mais j'ai pris mes précautions. (PM 188-9)

Poor Baranquin lacks the necessary imagination to dress up reality:

> Au cours de sa reconnaissance, il n'avait rien vu de suspect et le déclara tout innocemment. Choqué par ce manquement aux règles du jeu, qui révélait une absence du sentiment épique, Frioulat prit ses compagnons à témoin. (PM 190)

When Baranquin defends his realism, the leader of the little band reiterates Oscar's defence in 'Oscar et Erick' by forcefully stating their need to pretend:

> — Alors quoi, si on s'occupe de ce qui est vrai, y a plus moyen de rien faire, dit-il. (PM 190)

So the game continues.

Another child of about the same age, Jacotin's son in 'Le Proverbe', is accorded the same gift of lucidity. Lucien Jacotin and his father are a development of the Rigault pair in *Le Moulin de la Sourdine*. Lucien sees through and coldly dissects his father's need to dream and his dependence on the saving lie that props up so many of Aymé's hollow men. Lucien's father is a tyrannical and rather unjust *père de famille* caught up in play-acting and delusions about his own devotion to and unappreciated sacrifices for his family. Like Marcelin and Galuchey, he needs to blame his mediocrity on someone else and feels menaced by all around him. This produces the tension which is suggested in the very first drily realistic scene of the story:

> Dans la lumière de la suspension qui éclairait la cuisine, M. Jacotin voyait d'ensemble la famille courbée sur la pâture et témoignant, par des regards obliques, qu'elle redoutait l'humeur du maître. (PM 127)

Aymé's story, covering a week that elapses before we return to the same meal-time scene, is a concise psychological portrait of a crumbling *petit-bourgeois*, and a study of the complex, ignoble thoughts that masquerade as family love and harmony.

Rather paranoid feelings of inferiority in Jacotin cause a familiar misinterpretation of the reality that surrounds him. He feels that every word, every silence is a veiled attack on his efforts or his authority. The other members of the family are quite conscious of the play-acting that maintains family harmony and they are careful to do or say just what is expected. The wayward Lucien is Jacotin's most convenient scapegoat, providing many opportunities for tyrannical outbursts. Even the fact that his son has not done his homework seems a threat to Jacotin's well-being; of course Lucien has been off skulking with the dunces of his class while the dux, Béruchard, has been studying. And Jacotin has to put up with the condescension of Béruchard's father at his office. Jacotin consoles himself by blaming fate: 'Je n'ai pas la chance, moi, d'avoir un fils comme Béruchard' (PM 133) and by deluding himself that although Béruchard's son may be brighter than Lucien, he, Jacotin, runs rings around the father:

> Qu'est-ce que c'est que Béruchard? je parle du père. C'est l'homme travailleur, si on veut, mais qui manque de capacités.

> Et sur les idées politiques, c'est bien pareil que sur la besogne. Il n'a jamais eu de conceptions. Et Béruchard, il le sait bien. Quand on discute de choses et d'autres, devant moi, il n'en mène pas large. (PM 132-3)

In these psychological studies, Aymé reduces his overt, personal intrusion into the text as much as his penchant for ironic sniping will allow. He has an excellent ear for idiomatic language and uses dialogue to great effect in getting inside his protagonist and revealing his foibles. In one of his tirades Jacotin raves for more than two pages almost without taking a breath (PM 132-3). He seems to be talking about his son but is in reality revealing much more about himself.

The crucial moment for Jacotin's delicate ego comes when he decides he will bolster his self-esteem and win Lucien's respect by doing his son's homework. Lucien has left it until the last minute to write his composition on the theme 'Rien ne sert de courir, il faut partir à point'. Here, Jacotin is out of his depth, as Aymé's understated irony subtly suggests:

> La mine soucieuse, il relut plusieurs fois le proverbe et murmura:
> — C'est un proverbe. (PM 139-40)

Of course Jacotin does not see the relevance of the dictum to what he is doing; he does not even see the connection with the fable of the Hare and the Tortoise! He composes an absurdly lyrical text that is just one more example of the way he dresses up reality:

> — Par cette splendide après-midi d'un dimanche d'été, virgule, quels sont donc ces jolis objets verts à la forme allongée, virgule, qui frappent nos regards? On dirait de loin qu'ils sont munis de longs bras, mais ces bras ne sont autre chose que des rames et les objets verts sont en réalité deux canots de course qui se balancent mollement au gré des flots de la Marne. (PM 142)

His lucid son hesitates before handing in what he sees as 'faux' and 'discordant'. Of course Béruchard gets thirteen and Lucien only three, plus a lot of humiliating laughter from his classmates. The dénouement is final proof of Aymé's realism and compassion. When Jacotin asks what mark his efforts earned, the story has reached its climax. The whole story leads up to this moment. Will Jacotin's illusions, upon which he is so dependant, be shattered or reinforced? We expect a crashing return to order and reality but Aymé defuses the situation. In the potentially explosive pause between the question and the answer, Lucien describes a whole family of Ayméan anti-heroes:

> Il comprenait que, depuis de longues années, le pauvre homme vivait sur le sentiment de son infaillibilité de chef de famille et, qu'en expliquant le proverbe, il avait engagé le principe de son infaillibilité dans une aventure dangereuse. Non seulement le tyran domestique allait perdre la face devant les siens, mais il perdrait du même coup la considération qu'il avait pour sa propre personne. Ce serait un effondrement. (PM 147)

Lucien tells his father he got thirteen, just like Béruchard. Aymé has worked an ironic reversal on Jacotin: the father thinks he has taught his son a lesson, where in reality Lucien has understood much more than his mentor. There is an ironic twist reserved for Lucien too: because of his apparent success, a glowing Jacotin replies that henceforth they will always do Lucien's homework together!

This subtle ending is only equalled by the irony that Aymé has in store for his ambitious bailiff in 'L'Huissier'. We are expecting Malicorne to be recalled for judgement to have his phony metamorphosis ridiculed, but the storyteller has other plans. Aymé's idea of justice is to engineer an unconscious, gradual and real metamorphosis to terminate Malicorne's conscious, artificial one. This second metamorphosis occurs as Malicorne continues his rounds dispensing money. During his normal visits, he doles out his money with a few perfunctory words of encouragement and then swiftly records his deed in the credit column. On the fateful day, Malicorne wanders into a tenement as if in a dream, notices the squalor and poverty for the first time (Aymé treats us to a particularly sombre two-page description of misery) and feels guilty and intimidated without knowing what is happening to him. Malicorne is moved by physical contact with a child who comes to sit on his knee. He does not even think of reaching for his wallet this time but wishes he had lollies to give the child instead. The bailiff feels shame and is saved by his first truly spontaneous act—his physical defence of the mother and child when the brutal Gorgerin comes to collect his rent, and his cry of 'A bas les propriétaires'. Only now is Malicorne's metamorphosis truly complete. His one authentic good deed is a guarantee of heaven: he, a bailiff, dies defending penniless tenants against their landlord. 'Que c'est beau', murmurs God, and opens wide the pearly gates.

Although the psychologist Aymé is dominant in these stories of illusion, the entertainer has not entirely faded from sight. With this gentle upwards stroke instead of the usual downhill slide and thump at the end of his story, Aymé provides that final twist that he is so fond of, a twist that leaves the tale 'up in the air'. He softens Duvilé's madness in similar fashion in the last paragraph of 'Le Vin de Paris', leaves us wondering just what Lucien Vachelin is really like in 'Deux victimes' and teases us by suggesting that Gauthier-Lenoir's little illusion might just have caused a major tax upheaval had the war not broken out. These endings, too, reflect Aymé's penchant for the 'brume de mélancolie'.

4

Reality

Ma matière, ce n'est ni le merveilleux, ni la réalité, mais ce qui change de la vie.   Marcel Aymé

Given the strong current of physical or mental fantasy in Aymé's work, it is tempting to suppose that stories based on the ordinary reality which satisfied so many of his friends like Céline, Blondin and Nimier might not interest him. Plain realism is obviously less intriguing than his flights of fancy, and indeed Aymé's realistic stories have provoked much less critical comment. Yet reality is just as important to Aymé as fantasy, both as a mode of expression and as a subject. Aymé revels in tales of Montmartre concierges, Clichy prostitutes, Montparnasse black-marketeers, Jurassian peasants and harassed schoolmasters, tales that have the most solid air of reality about them. He often uses his realism to pursue the same themes with similar structures. Aymé's realistic stories are a complement to the more spectacular side of his work, often reflecting the same special world but without the fantastic and psychological exaggerations. They also reflect the same harsh reality against which so many of his chosen victims react.

Aymé matches his psychological studies with a series of realistic vignettes, tales of country and city life that amount to a modest human comedy. Aymé is much less ambitious than Balzac; his characters and settings provide far less than a cross-section of his age. Certain milieux and character types are completely absent while others get far more than their share of attention. Aymé restricts himself to writing about what he knows best, and above all those settings where he finds life's little people, the lower orders in society that he prefers. The upper classes and their preoccupations are almost absent from Aymé's work. His world is not sexually balanced either. The few women who are accorded an active role in his stories often tend to be rather stereotyped — old maids, *dévorantes* or prostitutes. Otherwise, women are often reduced to the role of observer-wife in their husband's crisis. This is rather surprising, given the important part played in Aymé's upbringing by his grandmother, his aunt Léa and his sister Suzanne.

Aymé's Montmartre, the solid background for so many of his faerie and fantastic adventures and several tales of illusion, is not so much in evidence here, but he still exploits the familiar village in 'Le Mariage de César' to provide a frame for the blossoming love between his 'bougnat vertueux' and the innocent daughter of the hypocritical *bourgeoise* Madame Dupin. Between Madame Dupin's acquaintances and the customers of César's little bar and brothel, the only Montmartrois absent from the tale are the painters and the tourists. Just as Aymé's backdrop for fantasy is often the occupied Paris of 'La Carte' and 'Le Décret', so daily life in occupied Montmartre is the subject of Aymé's Chaucerian collection of anecdotes in 'En attendant'. From the desperate fantasy of the story's beginning:

> Pendant la guerre de 1939-1972, il y avait à Montmartre, à la porte d'une épicerie de la rue Caulaincourt, une queue de quatorze personnes, lesquelles s'étant prises d'amitié, décidèrent de ne plus se quitter (PM 247)

Aymé quickly descends to the driest realism. 'En attendant' is a group of varied images within one story, much like Aymé's collections of stories. In age and occupation, the fourteen people are almost a microcosm of Montmartre, and their tales of woe are arranged in varying length, style and seriousness for the maximum contrast effect. A retired shop assistant spends five pages relating the ambitions, the sacrifices and the petty consolations of his marriage as a prelude to a description of how his wife's cherished fox-fur, a luxurious symbol of all that they had strived for, was lost in the war. The fox was lost in a sadly ironic way. When her husband fell sick the wife sold the fur to buy food on the black-market, saving his life but breaking her own heart. Only later, when she was on her death-bed, did her husband discover that the fur was innocently sold for 800 francs when it could have fetched 10 000. Aymé follows this tragedy with a superbly stated one-liner: 'Moi, dit un enfant, j'ai faim. J'ai toujours faim' (PM 252), and then a young prostitute tells at some length of her problems with uncooperative café-owners, the Germans and her deformed pimp Fernando. It is particularly difficult for her to earn a living now that it is winter: the cold forces her to ply her trade in cafés where not only are the overheads very high but she has difficulty advertising. Her best assets are her legs, she explains, and she cannot show them off to advantage sitting at a table. Aymé contrasts the prostitute's daily fight for survival with a young girl's melancholy at seeing all the young men, whose flowers and wolf-whistles made life so worth living, disappearing to the front and an old lady's exaggerated distress when her only problem is her difficulty in finding tasty titbits for her cat. 'En attendant' is a war story with a difference. The adversary is not enemy soldiers but other Frenchmen: the resourceful, the rich, black-marketeers and even civil servants. There are no bombs and bullets; the destruction is psychological and moral rather than physical. The fourteen people in the queue are refugees simply because there is nothing but solitude, hunger, cold and despair awaiting them at home.

Aymé often chooses as a frame for his stories this tense moral and psychological atmosphere of the Occupation that he describes so well in *Le Chemin des écoliers*. He is extremely frank and objective in his descriptions of the ordinary Frenchman, but this quality won him more enemies than friends. It was not only because Aymé defended Brasillach, Bardèche and Céline that his work was subject to a certain stigma and not only because he chose to continue writing and publishing during the Occupation. It was also because of the painful truth of his portrait of those tormented years. It was because of his understanding of the plight of those who were forced to compromise their scruples in order to survive; and it was his understanding of that twilight zone where peaceful coexistence becomes collaboration. Unfortunately for Aymé, he was writing at a time when such understanding was often misconstrued and when unthinking approval of even the most irresponsible acts of terrorist resistance had become the fashion.

Black-market profiteering is one of Aymé's prime targets. Having sniped at Flegmon's hypocrisy in 'La Carte', he now shows the dilemma of a young mother struggling to find 'nourriture nourrissante' for her four remaining children. He describes the depths which desperate thoughts will plumb by showing her railing against hypocritical 'grossiums' and 'profiteurs'. She is already looking forward to settling accounts:

> Marchez, la guerre, ça durera pas toujours. Quand les Allemands ils partiront, on aura des comptes à régler. Tous ceux

qui auront la gueule fraîche et le ventre sur la ceinture, on aura deux mots à leur dire. Pour chacun de mes gosses qu'ils m'auront assassiné, il m'en faudra dix. A coups de galoche dans la gueule, que je les tuerai, et je mettrai du temps, je veux qu'ils souffrent. Les cochons, ils ont le ventre plein quand ils viennent nous causer honneur, loyauté et tout le tremblement. (PM 257)

Then, by describing the young mother's temptation to steal prisoners' Red Cross parcels, Aymé probes the nerve of jealous resentment that must have hidden behind much of the self-righteous indignation thrown at the *débrouillards*. Aymé uses a similar theme, setting and cast for one of his longer and more famous stories, 'Traversée de Paris', which Claude Autant-Lara, Jean Gabin and Bourvil turned into a very successful film. This *nouvelle*, featuring a well-known Montmartre 'character' called Henri Marchénoir, relates a trek across occupied Paris with suitcases full of contraband meat. On the surface there is a certain humour in the rather picaresque tale, but at its heart there is a despair reminiscent of the more sombre stories of Carco or Mac Orlan: it is an atmosphere piece describing the dog-eat-dog world of the black-marketeers and their double-dealing, suspicion and murder.

This oppressive atmosphere accentuates Rodolphe's hypocritical mental juggling in 'Le faux policier', and it is an integral part of 'L'Indifférent'. This story, written against the background of the Petiot scandal in Paris, is based on a wartime criminal confession set on the boulevard Rochechouart and dominated by a sinister *éminence grise* controlling murderous extortionists and unscrupulous profiteers with *milieu* names like 'Médé Clin-d'oeil' and 'Christophe-le-Belge'. The story is made up of petty bravadoes, pretence, outright treachery and callous violence. 'L'Indifférent' with its theme of the lack of human solidarity, reinforces the atmosphere of *Le Vaurien* and looks ahead to *Les Tiroirs de l'inconnu.*

Some light relief is found when Aymé turns his attention to the countryside and the lives of the Jurassian peasants that he knows so well. Here we find the villages, fields and farmhouses of his youth, filled with poor but stoical farmers so often called Félicien, Maximilien, Honoré, Léontine or Félicie. Colourful material from Aymé's Jurassian past finds its way into novels like *Gustalin*, *La Table aux crevés*, the supernatural *La Vouivre* or the ribald *La*

Jument verte; Aymé allows himself several *scènes de la vie de campagne* in his short story collections too. Chekhov often maintained that a good short story should have neither beginning nor end. Aymé would most certainly not have agreed wholeheartedly — beginnings and above all endings are very important to him — but in his more realistic vein he does occasionally approach Chekhov's ideal by composing short vignettes without much plot or shape, simple evocations of a moment, a feeling, a fragment of life. 'Les Chiens de notre vie' is a rural vignette with no hidden sting or ulterior motive. It is pure storytelling for its own sake, using the pretext of a rural grandfather telling his grandchildren a story before they set about their chores. His tale of the various dogs that have been in the family is nothing more than a series of pegs on which to hang his reminiscences and his homespun philosophy as he moves towards an ironic comparison between the dogs and their human masters. 'Les mauvaises fièvres', like the very similar 'Le Puits aux images', brings us to a more personal level in its brief description of the twisted relationship between a Jurassian husband and wife. Poor, browbeaten Maximilien blames all the calamities of his 'saleté de vie' on his wife Esther, and when she falls sick he prays that perhaps she may be allowed to die during the night. Esther has only a passing malaise but Maximilien tries to convince her, himself and everyone else that she has the dreaded 'mauvaises fièvres'. He even has recourse to a sort of psychosomatic voodoo, trying to speed things up by making the official declaration of her death!

Country scenes like this provide the simplest and often the shortest of Aymé's stories, displaying tighter unity of time, place and action than many of his fantasy stories. Yet even in these short rural pieces Aymé cannot often resist sniping at man's personal or institutional foibles. 'Sporting' belies its ironic title, as Aymé is really using the tale of two rural sports clubs as a simple political allegory in much the same way as he uses his physical imagery to illuminate reality. Before the local elections, the radical socialist candidate founds a gymnastic club and his right-wing opponent, not to be outdone, turns to rugby. Aymé gives vent to his satirical vein as sports tempers cloud the election issues and political points are scored on the sports field. One suspects that never has the region seen such impassioned electioneering!

The last of Aymé's recurrent settings is the classroom, the battleground for dunces and pedantic teachers. Aymé clearly had a very rich store of memories from his days at the Collège de l'Arc in Dôle.

'A et B' and 'L'Elève Martin' both develop conflicts within this setting but the simplest, most poignant tableau of school life is found in 'La Retraite de Russie', where Aymé uses his country school to frame an outsider's revenge on life. He sketches a basic contrast between the large but not very bright Léon Jars and the smart but self-conscious little red-head, Petit-Doré. The resentful Léon betrays the unwritten rules of his peer-group in arranging for Petit-Doré to become the victim of the teacher's injustice and scorn, as well as ridiculing his red hair: 'Les rouquins, ça ne pourra jamais pisser haut, c'est bien connu' (PI 37). The discouraged victim muses on the absurdities of life and on the uselessness of education in a world where one is judged on how high one can urinate or the colour of one's hair:

> Pourquoi faire, mon Dieu, apprendre la division, l'orthographe et tant de choses compliquées? Et pourquoi triompher en calcul mental ou en géographie, puisque tant de savoir ne prévaudra pas contre l'insolente mauvaise foi d'un Léon Jars. (PI 37)

Then, in one of his better reversal endings, capturing the essence of the schooldays he is describing, Aymé allows Petit-Doré his revenge on the cruel world. Asked by the mocking teacher to dissert on Napoleon's retreat from Russia, the red-head concludes with Marshal Ney:

> Napoléon l'a appelé le brave des braves. Le maréchal Ney s'était battu sous la Révolution. Il était né à Sarrelouis et il avait les cheveux roux ...
> (...)
> — Il avait les cheveux roux, et dans toute l'armée, il pissait plus haut que n'importe lequel. (PI 39)

There are no more metamorphoses here, no misconceptions or violent obsessions, yet some of Aymé's more drily realistic stories, even novels like *La Rue sans nom*, *Le Chemin des écoliers*, *Le Vaurien* and *Travelingue*, have still provoked critics to use terms like 'merveilleux', 'fantaisie' and 'irréel'. There is something unreal underlying his realism too, and the key once more lies in disorder. Aymé's *comédie humaine* is not very objective. His canvases still betray his own preoccupations, above all a continuing preference for situations which in some way reflect the disorder-discipline and scandal-façade motifs. Within this group of more realistic stories there is more variety of plot, setting and character than within the physical and psychological groups, but Aymé's realism is still to some extent an extension of their ordered, hierarchic world. Both sides of his basic paradox concerning the strength of order and the need to dream are still present even though his mode of expression has changed since 'Le Passe-muraille' and 'La Canne'.

The same familiar *pauvres types* called Martin (with a sprinkling of Rodolphes, Luciens and Valentins) inhabit Aymé's real world: hen-pecked husbands, ridiculed adjutants, despised neighbours, junior clerks, dunces and tramps, who wander the same impersonal cities, rejected, alienated or lost. Their antics produce a clash with an ordered reality. They provoke unsettling situations which have little in common with Johannieu's madness, the cyclist's optimism or Galuchey's naive ambition and yet their tales are often singled out by Aymé for the same interlude stamp. There are no face changes and lecherous ogres, yet there is something just as 'wrong' that often leads Aymé to treat them in the same way as his confrontations with absurdity or obsession: exploitation of the tragi-comic consequences and a 'righting' of the situation once it gets out of hand. Their structure parallels the intrusion of magic or madness into everyday life, and their key theme of disorder stretches all the way back through Sorbier to Dutilleul and the water-sprite Udine.

*   *   *

Aymé's realistic stories may seem far removed from our starting-point — the effect of an absurd metamorphosis — but he is often exploiting an analogy between the effect of a physical absurdity on people used to reality and another of his favourite themes: the effect of a social scandal that threatens an ordered façade. The unreality or disorder is now above all social. One of Aymé's strongest images of social scandal is too complex to be contained in any but the longest *nouvelle*. It found expression in the play *Louisiane*. Here Aymé starts with a rich Southerner with a bitter sense of humour who leaves his plantation to his relatives on condition that they live there all together for a while. The catch: one of them is coloured. Their cohabitation is an emotionally and physically violent interlude. As soon as it begins there are the inevitable murmurings from local society and the situation explodes when the white cousin becomes romantically involved with the black one. The police chief is quickly sent in to restore order and murders the unfortunate negro. Aymé uses a truth drug to provoke more social disorder in *Les quatre vérités*: for the duration of the drug's effect we witness a chaotic interlude of confession where everyone reveals his true feelings, thus threatening the social fabric and obliging Aymé to call a halt. The façade of hypocrisy and flattery stripped away by the truth drug is quickly restored. In Aymé's world, 'La police est bien faite à l'égard des songes. La société prend toujours sa revanche'.[1]

These two plays provide striking lessons in order and are a guide to the interpretation of several of Aymé's more subtle short stories like 'En arrière' and 'Traversée de Paris'. 'En arrière' is the ironic title given to a reactionary review founded by five millionaires' sons. These scions of a capitalist system that thrives behind a façade of hypocritical lip-service to socialism start writing articles with seditious titles like 'Assez de gâtisme révolutionnaire!', 'Que les pauvres se débrouillent!' 'Aimons les riches!' and 'Nous ne voulons plus feindre pour le prolétariat un amour que nous n'éprouvons pas' (EA 252-4). They want to tear away the façade erected by their fathers and openly admit the truth. Their fathers move swiftly to stop the scandal, cutting their sons' pocket money to only 50 000 francs a month and pleading with the idealistic youths: 'D'être pour le peuple comme tout le monde, d'être révolutionnaire comme nous tous.' (EA 255) The sons are finally recuperated; the prodigals return to the fold, dutifully voicing their love for the masses.

Aymé explores a more complex disorder in Martin's situation. It is he, the son of a 'petit employé mal payé', who most believes in the review's ideology. Once abandoned by his rich backers, he is befriended by their secretary Ginette and they conveniently win the lottery. Aymé's irony flowers here as Ginette persuades Martin that security comes first; they invest in a safety-pin business (the pun on security works in French too) and make a fortune. Then Martin, too, hypocritically abandons the review: he is for the people like everyone else . . . Yet the cynical Aymé has not finished. The crack in the façade is still there at the end of the story to tease us. Martin, the agent of Aymé's disorder, the 'garçon méphistophélique', the 'nature perverse' with his 'petit rire sec qui faisait froid dans le dos' (EA 252) is still a threat. He is occasionally heard to criticize the masses under his breath, and Aymé ironically speculates that one day Martin may rock the boat again:

Moi qui le connais bien, je me demande avec une certaine

anxiété s'il ne donnera pas un jour au monde le spectacle, difficilement imaginable, d'un homme richissime confessant publiquement ses vrais sentiments à l'égard des masses. (EA 264)

The murder at the end of 'Traversée de Paris' is not so clearly an image of society taking its revenge or preserving its façade (society does that by quickly arresting the murderer), but is nevertheless a demonstration of the same vein of Aymé's justice. Martin finds out that the trendy young painter has been feigning companionship for him, slumming and dabbling in the black-market dangers for thrills. The resentful Martin angrily restores order to the class separation by stabbing Grandgil.

Several short stories about more personal disorder are strongly illuminated by Aymé's almost ideological play *Vogue la galère*. This contains one of his most explicit statements of man's need for a disciplinary force of order, in this case blatantly political. The basic situation described is a revolt aboard a slave-galley. Once the slaves are all free and equal there is no-one left to row or steer so Aymé's ship of state drifts aimlessly until Simon rises from the ranks to take power. He releases the key officers, presses them into service and step by step oppresses his colleagues once again. First they are set rowing, then chained up, and finally we see them obeying the disciplinary whistle drill that opened the play. Order is restored.

Aymé's choice of physical image for the cycle of revolution was perhaps a little facile but quite striking. His superficial moral seems to be that as long as the slaves are kept chained up all will be well. This is certainly the lesson that young Frioulat tries to impress upon his followers in 'Les Bottes de sept lieues' after the band splits in two and is involved in an accident outside the curiosity shop:

> Tirant la leçon des événements, Frioulat exaltait les principes d'ordre et d'autorité et soutenait que rien ne fût arrivé si la bande avait gardé son chef. (PM 207-8)

But there is a deeper order upset in *Vogue la galère*, an order that goes beyond the physical chains to the mental relationship between oppressor and oppressed. In the final, humiliating whistle drill it seems as though the slaves accept their lot; they are born slaves just as Simon is a born master. There is an incident which suggests that the condition of slave is much more in the mind than around the ankles: the imprisoned captain gives an order and a freed slave rather slowly obeys, for the ordered habit of chains is much stronger than the confusion of freedom.

It is the freed slave Main-Gauche who first expresses the desire for discipline and order among his fellows. Here he talks of their former pirate captain:

> Du moment qu'il me laissait gueuler, je gueulais. Je ne suis pas un enfant de choeur, moi. Je prends toute la place qu'on me laisse prendre. Mais dire que ça me plaît, non. Justement, j'aime me sentir bien calé entre des bornes solides. C'est là que je me retrouve et que je me reconnais. (VG 164-5)

There is something unreal about the slaves' freedom. When Simon takes power and ends the chaos, promising to be just as cruel as his predecessor, they seem numbly thankful. The noble Lazare's ideas of fraternity and liberty for all are ridiculed and forgotten; it is not with them that Simon can maintain order.[2] For Aymé, slaves cannot handle freedom any better than Johannieu can handle the powers of his mind. Main-Gauche is once again Aymé's spokesman when he talks about the paradoxical liberty they felt under the harsh disciplinarian; his comments could well apply to many of Aymé's adventurers:

> sous son commandement on se sentait nettoyé de toute une saloperie de petites peurs, de brouillard, de doutes merdeux qui barbouillent le coeur et la cervelle. On était net, propre comme des sous, comme des anges du ciel, nom de Dieu! Tenez, on était des hommes libres. (VG 166)

The mental conditioning shown in *Vogue la galère* explains the conduct, bewilderment or resentment of several of Aymé's *pauvres types*, but in particular the play helps interpret the long story called 'Josse'. Growing disorder is felt throughout the story but only towards the end is the reader aware of just what is wrong. Adjutant Josse retires from the army and goes to live with his spinster sister Valérie. There is immediate tension between them which grows into open hostility until Josse shoots her and is taken away to prison. The police-inspector has a superficial interpretation of events:

> La vérité c'est qu'il a vu rouge parce que le vieux chameau a dû lui en faire endurer au-delà de ce qu'il est possible d'endurer.

Son cas est celui de tous les braves types qui finissent par tuer leur femme (EA 209-10)

and superficially he is right. Josse and Valérie bicker and fight about everything from the military souvenirs in his room to the weekly brothel visit that she finds so disgusting:

> elle se mit à brailler des injures, le traitant de débauché, de coureur de chiennes, de bête lubrique, et crachant les mots avec une délectation malpropre. (EA 185)

She spies on him and searches his room, and he annoys her with rather childish practical jokes. Valérie is intent on dominating Josse to the extent of making him eat and dress sloppily and even trying to confine him within the house.

There is a deep disorder in Josse's new life. He has been an exemplary adjutant all his life, methodical, rather anti-social, supremely unsentimental, living on 'ordre', 'discipline' and 'dureté'. Valérie's rather harsh verdict is that he is 'dépourvu de toute humanité' (EA 179). Aymé has retired Josse out of his masculine barracks context and thrown him on the tender mercies of his capricious, frustrated sister. Aymé has also taken him from a life of continuous action and chained him to enforced boredom. Josse tries to survive by strolling past the local barracks and watching nostalgically from the café opposite, but this is artificial and he ends up feeling ridiculous.

Josse is alienated, lost in the real world where he does not really belong. He cannot go back to the army and he cannot cope in Valérie's world; she is destroying him by breaking down his self-discipline. When he does try to adapt and, for the first time in his life, becomes attached to another human being, he becomes emotionally dependent and makes himself even more vulnerable. Valérie exploits this. This is when Josse reacts, shoots her and tries to incriminate himself. It is the final description of his motivation that is most revealing. He has found a new life of discipline:

> Dans sa cellule, Josse pensait avec satisfaction aux années de bagne qui l'attendaient. Il lui semblait renaître à un monde cohérent où les hiérarchies et les consignes calaient sa conscience et le protégeaient contre les aventures sentimentales. (EA 210)

Given the thematic clarity of *Vogue la galère* and 'Josse' it is hard not to suspect a moral behind the whimsical façade of 'Conte de

Noël'. With the intervention of 'l'enfant Noël' distributing 'bonnes pensées' (he cannot afford more solid gifts) in a barracks and a brothel, this story might seem to rank among Aymé's physical fantasies, but its true place is here as one of Aymé's more explicit images of an ordered world. 'Conte de Noël' uses a barracks setting to show order and hierarchy being threatened once again. The protagonist is an adjutant like Josse and the story describes his attempts to suppress the barracks trouble-maker Morillard. In a way the barracks is Aymé's whole world and the adjutant is a control figure whose job it is to maintain discipline. Morillard is the cross he has to bear, a personification of disorder: 'un défi à la bonne ordonnance'. The adjutant even tries to persuade Morillard not to re-enlist at the end of his term. Morillard does, of course: the threat of disorder is ever-present, like Martin's true feelings lurking at the end of 'En arrière'.

The mental conditioning of 'Josse' and *Vogue la galère* and the social conditioning of 'En arrière' reinforce the feelings of belonging that pervade Aymé's world. His short stories make up a panorama of rather Jungian wanderers in search of their souls. Aymé's preoccupation with this theme may well be traceable to his early political, geographical and professional wanderings. This feeling of belonging has already been seen as natural law in Aymé's fantastic stories and even as destiny in 'Samson' and 'Le Romancier Martin'. It recurs in less supernatural form in Galuchey's insidious attachment to the rue des Vertus and to his role as office butt, and in Sorbier's role as cringing spouse. Josse and Main-Gauche belong in their secure routines and discipline.

Several different kinds of attachment are felt in Aymé's realistic stories. Samson's destiny is felt on an almost geographical plane by Coindet in *La Table aux crevés*. He elopes with Jeanne Brégard despite the violent disapproval of her hot-blooded family, and they leave their villages to take refuge in the town of Dôle. Coindet knows that his return for an encounter with the Brégards is inevitable, but the novel takes us much further than this feeling of a personal 'show-down'. Coindet's return to the reality of his village is the result of geographical ties just as strong as Galuchey's social attachment. Not only do Aymé's characters seem immobile in the vertical plane but horizontally too. Coindet and Jeanne are country people and quite out of place in the city. They are used to striding around the open fields. Aymé's image of what happens to Coindet in their urban lodgings is quite explicit. He does not belong:

> Il lui fallait marcher avec prudence pour ne pas bousculer un meuble ou casser quelqu'objet [sic]. Les murs se touchaient, autant dire, et il avait chaud rien qu'à respirer. (TC 189)

Once Coindet and Jeanne are removed from their normal context their life and love change utterly: 'les heures leur paraissaient vides, ils n'avaient presque rien à se dire' (TC 183). Their return to the land is a restoration of order.

Gustalin provides a mirror image of Coindet's disorder. Sarah and Victor Jouquier provoke chaos when they bring their city mentality to the country. Jacques Teynier has underlined the ridiculousness of Victor trying to apply his artificial urban vision of reality to the country village:

> la plus pertinente image du déplacé, esthète à la campagne, qui ne voit dans tel pré fleuri qu'un Monet très réussi, et s'extasie, avec des gloussements dans la voix, sur les *adorables petits anges au cul rose* de l'église ou le *pittoresque* de l'épicier ventru. Sur tous ces personnages, Aymé venge une passion du vrai que leur goût du faux bafoue.[3]

Victor's wife Sarah is just as clumsy, failing to understand the subtle harmonies of the country. She invites the local peasants to a tea party, tries to emancipate the stoical Marthe and wants to talk philosophy with the simple curé. The harmony of the little community is quite upset. Marthe is seduced by Sarah's words and leaves Gustalin for the town; she dies for her transgressions, failing to see Aymé's necessary separation of town and country.

This sense of belonging can apply even within the frames of country and city. In *La Table aux crevés* we see a sharp distinction between Coindet's and Brégard's villages; in *Le Moulin de la Sourdine* we feel a definite attachment in the inhabitants of the Malleboine; and in *La Rue sans nom* Méhoul is suspicious of someone 'qui n'était pas de la rue' (RN 7). Even within this street we sense a strong separation between the immigrant Italians and the native French. Cruséo dies trying to bridge this gap, the postman Capucet (the only real link between Cessigney and Cantagrel) dies when Coindet faces Brégard, and David dies when black and white come together in *Louisiane*. Aymé's point is taken.

Aymé seldom tried to bring out this ingrained geographic attachment within the confines of a short story, but it is a closely related notion of belonging that makes Josse shoot at Valérie to return to a secure cocoon, and a parallel attachment to ideas that leads to the recuperation of the wayward millionaires' sons in 'En arrière'. In fact this last story depends for its main interest on an attachment between class and idea that has been ironically reversed to stress it. Aymé's eye for appropriateness would normally decree that the right ideas for millionaires' sons should be the fervent praise of capitalism that their fathers outwardly deplore, and that their youthful indiscretions should entail flirting with socialist revolution. The initial reversal of this expected situation is a typical Aymé ploy.

This reversal of belonging is the key to the whimsical 'A et B'. This time Aymé sketches the disorder that ensues when the A class is temporarily mixed with the B class. Worse: this brings Latinists and mathematicians together. Petty squabbles and disturbances, clumsily handled by the partisan teacher, explode into physical violence between the students and angry recriminations between the teachers and the *surveillant-général* (the agent of order) who tries to restore the balance and defend the rights of the oppressed mathematicians. Here, as in 'Josse' and to a lesser extent 'En arrière', Aymé's construction of the story hinges on his favourite technique of placing in close proximity people or groups who are in some way opposites. Instead of real and unreal forming the conflict, both sides are now solidly real, so Aymé strengthens the contrast by moving it onto another plane (in 'Josse' the mental and the physical complement each other) or increasing the conflict (in 'A et B' the original confrontation between the trouble-maker Salignon and the Latin teacher soon involves the two classes and then two sets of teachers). In each story, the growing disorder is underlined throughout. The thematic and structural parallel between Aymé's physical unrealities and these stories based on social or personal suitabilities is obviously very strong. Even where the belonging is an attachment to habit more than to a function or a place, the link is still visible. Galuchey was condemned partly for breaking with all his secure routines. Jean Cathelin has pointed out a similar return to routine after the interlude of *La Mouche bleue* and habit is, of course, the security that Josse and Main-Gauche seek in discipline.

Aymé's man belongs to a personal routine or role. More than this, he actively needs one to belong to. 'Engagement' and 'enracinement' are security. Valérie makes this quite clear in 'Le Couple'. The disappearance of Barbe in 'La Liste' is a strong metaphor for this need and the necessity is underlined more subtly by

Valentin's confusion at having his dwarf status revoked. 'La Clé sous le paillasson' is essentially the story of a man trying to belong somewhere (he is searching for his real family) and in a more realistic mode *Maison basse* almost provides a political version of the same feeling. The vacuum is well described in the novel *Le Vaurien* where the protagonists are rather spiritless characters with little function, involvement or belonging. The 'vaurien' himself is described as an 'être sans habitudes'; he hardly exists.

Aymé explores this emptiness in two of his more pessimistic short stories, 'Je suis renvoyé' and 'L'Indifférent'. The first portrays a *pauvre type* in the mould of Sorbier and Galuchey who is abruptly fired from his office job. He wanders aimlessly, feeling that he cannot go home because it is a bread-winner that belongs there, and knowing that he no longer has any role in his office either. Aberdame is tempted by the uncommitted life of a tramp. Finally he rejects his former self, squashes his bowler hat, leaves his money and identity papers to be stolen by a prostitute and wanders off into the vacuum:

> Il avait changé de mémoire, et ne savait plus rien, sinon qu'il errait dans la ville depuis toujours, cherchant la vie au ras du sol, sans peur et sans espoir. (DM 67)

Aberdame's situation, a realistic parallel to Valentin's predicament in 'Le Nain', is also rather similar to the role vacuum experienced by two of the people in the grocer's queue in 'En attendant'. One of them was a seamstress before the war but now there is no demand and no cloth. From making ball-dresses, she has been reduced to patching worn-out garments and altering hand-me-downs. She lives in a past where she felt she was someone ('Mlle Duchat, robes, manteaux, tailleurs', PM 260) because now she has lost this identity and feels she has ceased to count:

> J'ai soixante-cinq ans, je n'ai jamais été jolie, et si je comptais pour quelque chose, c'est parce que j'avais un métier, un vrai. (DM 260)

The young girl dreaming of the eternal springtime when she was sixteen before the war experiences the same malaise: her whole life revolved around being smiled and whistled at by adoring young men. Even if she was only a sex-object belonging to the boys, at least she felt she existed then:

> Les jeunes gens qui restent, on en rencontre quelquefois, ils ne pensent pas à nous. Ils ne nous voient pas. Les rues sont vides, les agents sont vieux. (PM 267)

An extreme picture of a voluntary rejection of belonging occurs in 'L'Indifférent', where the murderer expresses total lack of commitment to anything except chance and pleasure:

> Je lui expliquais brièvement que les scrupules m'étaient aussi étrangers que les remords (. . .) que je réglais mes actions sur mon bon plaisir plutôt que sur les raisons et jamais sur des principes. (. . .) j'avais pensé à m'engager dans les rangs des terroristes, mais je suis imperméable à l'idée de patrie comme à celle de justice sociale. (VP 14-15)

This turns into one of the most darkly pessimistic scenes from Aymé's human comedy.

In addition to underlining an ordered reality braced by suitabilities or attachments and defended by agents of order, Aymé's realism also continues to some extent his exploration of man's relationship to reality. Man's difficulty in apprehending reality and his occasional refusal to accept it are both themes which still recur although in much less striking form. Part of Josse's struggle was to come to grips with the real world, the uncertainties and the responsibilities from which he was sheltered by the army's categorizing uniforms and protective rank:

> Josse rougit et se sentit nu comme un ver. (. . .) Il éprouvait pour la première fois que le retour à la vie civile, en le privant des prérogatives de son grade et de la protection tutélaire de l'armée, l'avait rendu vulnérable au monde extérieur, et combien il se trouvait diminué. L'univers hiérarchisé dans lequel pendant plus de trente ans, il avait trouvé un recours en toutes circonstances, cet univers-là était fermé, et il lui semblait n'avoir aucune prise sur le monde étrange et chaotique où l'avait jeté sa mise à la retraite. (EA 188-9)

Josse is totally lost in the real world just as Aberdame has difficulty in confronting the reality of insecurity once he is dismissed. Josse can withdraw into his previous existence, or at least a substitute, but Aberdame has nowhere to go. He opts for the rather inconclusive 'chute qui le dispensait de lutter' (DM 55) and takes refuge in self-abandonment:

> Engourdi sur le siège, il lui semblait être très loin du monde, et abrité de la société pour toujours. Son rêve de solitude se confondait avec la réalité présente, et il lui plaisait de croire qu'il était dégagé, vis-à-vis d'autrui, de toute espèce d'obligation. (. . .) il appelait l'instant où, le cerveau vide de toute préoccupation, il serait délivré de l'habitude de penser et deviendrait un être libre. (DM 56)

Aymé is almost as inconclusive in another of the sketches in 'En attendant'. Superficially this is the story of a wife coming to grips with her husband's absence, but more importantly she has had to come to grips with the reality of herself and her new freedom. The little manifestations of this freedom are

> Lire au lit, sortir en cheveux, me lever tard, me coiffer dans le dos, aller au théâtre, être en retard aux rendez-vous, et tant d'autres choses défendues (PM 253)

but the more serious change is her abandonment of play-acting. She no longer has to play the social game by smiling at her detested in-laws or lying to her husband about how much she likes rugby and his crude friends. She can now be her real self, no longer having to 'se façonner à un homme'. As she puts it: 'Dans mon existence de femme seule, j'ai (. . .) appris à ne rien me cacher' (PM 255). The hypocritical compromises are over, but what will she do when her husband returns from prison camp? Her liberation coupled with despair, rather analogous to Aymé's earlier sorcerer's apprentice motif, is paralleled by Aberdame's: neither quite knows what to do with the new freedom.

Aberdame's almost suicidal gestures are reflected by Martin's despair at the full realization of reality in 'Traversée de Paris'. Aymé's Martin appears here in a rather unaccustomed role: instead of wondering what to do with a fantastic gift, he has undertaken to transport black-market meat across occupied Paris with a chance acquaintance called Grandgil. The resulting *nouvelle* provides Aymé with a chance to indulge in more detailed character analysis than is usually possible in short stories. Flashbacks, reflection, dialogue and action combine to reveal all. Martin is preoccupied with getting to know his mysterious companion, and through Grandgil he attains a self-knowledge that is not very palatable. Bit by bit we discover Martin's confusion in war, his mediocrity and lack of understanding of women, his lack of initiative masquerading as probity, his 'loser' mentality and finally his slow, reluctant awakening to the possibilities of life.

Grandgil's actions and comments throughout the night are the instrument of Martin's awakening. When Grandgil bluffs Martin's shrewd black-market boss out of ten times the price Martin had meekly agreed upon, Martin initially sees it as 'duplicité', 'perfidie' and 'déloyauté insondable', but under Grandgil's prodding he slowly reverses his previous vision of reality to agree that 'voler un voleur peut passer pour un acte de justice' (VP 45), partly as an attempt to impute moral coherence to Grandgil's actions. This initial step is complicated when Grandgil tempts Martin just as the Devil tempts so many of his namesakes: why not steal the meat and sell it on their own behalf? Martin is so out of his depth now that he is scared even to think about what he is doing:

> La conversation prenait un tour dangereux. Martin sentit la nécessité de repartir à l'instant même. Prendre du repos, pensait-il, c'est prendre du recul pour mesurer sa peine et sa fatigue et la tête se met à travailler, mais quand on est dans les brancards, on ne fait plus qu'un avec la besogne. (VP 47)

Martin's initial hatred of Grandgil slowly turns to reluctant admiration which redirects the hatred against Martin himself. This curious reversal is revealed as he involuntarily laughs at Grandgil's colourful scorn for the café owners who are just like Martin deep down. Grandgil further reveals Martin's real self to him by demonstrating how Martin's mistress is really only interested in his money.

Martin is understandably confused by Grandgil's bombardment, and this hinders his second struggle in the story: an attempt to come to grips with the reality of his companion. Since Grandgil is mysteriously silent at first, Martin's interpretations are extremely subjective. It is only when Grandgil begins to talk that his conduct takes on any coherence. But the *pauvre type* still cannot comprehend his companion's hilarity in the cellar and his scant regard for the dangers they run. And why, with 3000 francs in his pocket, does Grandgil not simply abandon the dangerous suitcases? Grandgil's amusement at the harsh denunciation potential of the café scene and his mocking insults of the proprietor, added to a mouthful of gold teeth, a silk shirt glimpsed under his rough jacket and his claim to be a painter, confuse Martin even more. He is troubled by

Grandgil's 'double personnalité' which he finds 'à la fois hermétique et transparente', and by a relationship that seems to be nothing more than a 'suite d'équivoques et d'incertitudes' (VP 70).

Martin's quest to penetrate and interpret appearances suddenly finishes when Grandgil reveals the truth during an overheard telephone call. He has been playing a role all night long:

> — Louise? disait Grandgil. Bonsoir . . . Je n'étais pas là . . . une soirée de vacances. Je me suis déguisé en gangster . . . ma parole, ne ris pas, j'ai même ramené un joli butin . . . j'ai joué au méchant, à l'anarchiste, au dur intégral . . . (. . .) Je dois te dire que j'ai joué aussi au démon tentateur . . . justement non . . . j'ai d'ailleurs fini par sombrer dans l'attendrissement . . . (VP 71)

Martin kills him in a blind rage but his naive world of appearances has collapsed. Companionship, solidarity, honesty, all is illusory. Martin is physically and emotionally exhausted. Aymé's final irony is that Martin is now so overtaken by life that he finds it hard to understand just why he killed Grandgil.

Man's relationship with reality is very important here. The world that surrounds Martin is the one described throughout Aymé's serious stories; like Maupassant, he is preoccupied by the reality that is camouflaged, the motivations that are masked by hypocrisy or unconsciousness, the real power that is wielded by sinister *éminences grises*, the truth that is methodically hidden by a hypocritical façade strongly defended whenever scandal threatens. The many stories that explore this theme, whether on a personal or a social level, complement Aymé's polemic articles, plays like *La Tête des autres* and *Les quatre vérités* and so many novels full of opulent façades, repressed desires, honours dishonourably won and scandals threatening to bring down the temple. The essay *Le Confort intellectuel* reinforces the theme by scourging an excessively literary interpretation of life and the Romantic camouflage of reality with fancy forms and hollow linguistic frills, while another essay, *Silhouette du scandale*, sets about analysing the lies that Aymé sees as 'une nécessité élémentaire de la vie en société'.[4]

Life in Aymé's human comedy is decidedly pessimistic. His world is often one of humiliations and defeats rather than successes:

> Les pères chaussent leurs souliers pointus pour distribuer des coups de pieds efficaces, les mères, esclaves serviles, mijotent

en douce de secrètes vengeances, les jeunes filles feignent de croire à l'amour mais n'écoutent que leur intérêt, les riches écrasent les pauvres, les puissants les faibles, et les lâches (soit l'humanité toute entière) applaudissent.[5]

Mauriac called Aymé 'un pessimiste qui se penche sur une humanité inguérissable'. Aymé denied that he had lost all hope for mankind. He accepts man but is just not prepared to disguise the vision he has. When writing of a similar pessimistic streak in his friend Céline, Aymé simply calls it honesty.

Aymé's realism describes above all the urban world of 'Les Clochards' or of Abd el Martin and his

> paysage littéraire où les promeneurs d'une âme sensible (. . .) se surprennent à prier Dieu pour que la vie ne soit pas démesurément longue. (DM 157)

This is the reality that provokes so many of Aymé's escapists. We find it again in the hazards, uncertainty and duplicity of 'L'Indifférent', in the absurdity that brings Aberdame's world crashing about his ears in 'Je suis renvoyé', in the oppressive solitude and silence that drive the alienated Martin to surrender himself at the end of 'Traversée de Paris'. 'Un Crime' is a darkly absurd two-page sketch of the same desperation. A man murders his wife and her lover only to be flabbergasted that he could take the time to eat a plate of cold meat before leaving the scene of the crime. It is his remorse about the meat that leads him to give himself up and accept his sentence without defence, and the meat finally leads him to escape from Guyana and brave the jungles of Venezuela to eat some more.

'L'Affaire Touffard' is an equally strange tale that pursues this oppressive atmosphere through an abstract Big Brother personification. In a pastiche of Conan Doyle's characters and style, Aymé's ace detective O'Dubois and his faithful companion proceed to the most fantastic solution of the most fantastic crime. O'Dubois decides that the only person to profit from the crime was the state. He evokes a personification of the state actually committing the crime and then stealthily watching for those who might be on its trail. The scandal cover-up is exercised once again as the cynical Aymé has O'Dubois conclude: 'Je n'ai pas envie de me faire de l'Etat un ennemi personnel. Tant pis pour la justice' (NA 164). So the criminal goes free. There is a certain black humour in this story that is rather uncharacteristic of Aymé.

It is the whole human condition that is abstracted in the sombre atmosphere study of 'Trois faits divers'. Aymé sketches two armed killers who meet at a crossroads one night in a climate of mutual distrust. Desperately they exchange stilted gestures and words, each trying to explain a crime he hardly understands himself. A weak sort of communication is established and the outcasts, 'heureux de ne plus souffrir de solitude' try to support each other's protestations of innocence of the 'crimes passionnels', agreeing with each other that the murders were in fact nothing more than 'faits divers'. They gladly welcome what they assume to be another outcast:

> L'homme était nu-tête et parlait en gesticulant. Sans comprendre le sens de ses paroles, ils entendaient sa voix rauque, tantôt plaintive, tantôt menaçante. Tout à coup, Finard serra les bras de Gonflier et murmura avec exaltation:
> — Il est des nôtres. C'est un malheureux comme nous. Regarde-le, écoute-le . . . (NA 199)

but when they discover that he has really committed no crime they re-inflate their own deeds and accuse him of still being acceptable to society at large ('les autres') and turn on him. This is a rather inconclusive, allegorical sketch somewhat reminiscent of 'L'Indifférent' and which could easily have become Theatre of the Absurd in the vein of Beckett or Ionesco. The only really typical element is Aymé's deflating, anti-serious ending: he has the killers turn on each other when their victim escapes.

It falls to the microcosmic 'En attendant' to represent Aymé's pessimistic world most fully. Here, again, there is an Absurd vein. The fourteen protagonists are waiting in a grocery queue, but the story goes beyond this level; they are not only waiting for food or even the end of the war, they are just waiting — for Godot, for an end to their suffering, perhaps for an end to life itself. The thirteen tales of misfortune, of which several have already been discussed, contrast petty but often exaggerated personal disasters with the understated tragedies of life. One man spends several pages lamenting the reduction of his wine consumption from six litres a day to one. Certainly he suffers personally from this, and even has to drink water ('Si c'est pas révoltant'), and the rationing provokes bitter fights with his wife when she has the effrontery to want to drink her ration without sharing it with him, but what distresses him more is the idea that a lack of wine may stunt the growth of his twelve-year-old son. The young mother beside him feels even more acutely that she is being prevented from fulfilling her role as mother and provider. She is being destroyed not so much by hunger as by the reproachful looks from her children when she comes home with an empty basket:

> Hier, mon sac il était vide, mais ce qui s'appelle vide, ravitaillement pas arrivé. De les voir venir tous les quatre, le coeur m'a comme éclaté, j'ai pleuré. Par-dessus tout ça, mettez pas de chauffage, par le froid, et la semaine passée, le gaz coupé huit jours, rien de chaud à leur mettre dans le ventre. De froid, ils en ont la peau grise, les yeux morts et l'air de nous dire: 'Mais qu'est-ce qu'on a fait?' (PM 256)

A young boy then only needs three lines to tell his tragedy: he has lost the whole family's bread coupons. And a Jew only needs one: 'Moi, dit un Juif, je suis juif' (PM 265). This is Aymé's most concisely ironic understatement. Yet he has still not finished harassing his victims. The fourteenth person in the queue, whose growing worries are summarized in two lines ('C'était une jeune femme, mari prisonnier, trois enfants, la misère, l'angoisse, la fatigue', PM 267), quietly dies while waiting; and still she has to wait because of a shortage of coffins! As the thirteen friends set out in search of a coffin we are made to experience the all-pervading, inhuman, unfeeling absurdity of the era, an absurdity in which man often seems determined to participate wholeheartedly:

> Borniol n'avait plus rien en rayon. Un confiseur offrit de procurer un cercueil en sapin pour une somme de quinze mille francs, (. . .) Un menuisier honnête homme proposa de fabriquer une bonne imitation en contreplaqué. (PM 267-8)

Jacques Teynier[6] has pointed out the brilliant concision of Aymé's suggestion and understatement in this final passage of 'En attendant'. Firstly the dignity of bereavement is shattered by the reduction of a respected funeral parlour to the level of a shop which has a temporary shortage of stock on the shelves (and there may just be a suggestion of coffins under the counter for a price). The first gleam of hope comes from a confectioner (a particularly absurd source for coffins) who offers to procure (as middle man of course) a pine coffin at a rather exorbitant price. The second proposal (and surely in normal times it would have been the first) is from an honest (no adjective was needed for the confectioner since he obviously has black-market connections) cabinet-maker who offers to make (as opposed to procuring) a realistic imitation (normally the domain of a *confiseur* while the carpenter should have had access to pine). The price is not mentioned; it will presumably be as honest as the tradesman himself. In these two simple sentences, where term is contrasted with term or term contrasted with meaningful silence, Aymé has very skilfully summed up the whole upside-down world of 'En attendant'.

Urban oppression preoccupies Aymé far more than rural misery. The lot of his peasants is certainly not luxurious but they are less frustrated, more stoical beings. Maximilien muttering about the harshness of his life with Esther in 'Les mauvaises fièvres' is an exception, and La Jouque's life in 'Le Puits aux images' is far from happy. Her husband lowers her down a well whenever the fancy takes him, and the consolations of her neighbour are not much help: 'Pleure pas, allons, faut te dire que ça ne durera pas toujours, cette vie-là' (PI 13). Even the fantasy of the local cinema is not really consolation, and it certainly does not match the images of smiling young love that her mind projects on the surface of the water in the well:

> sur la surface de l'eau froide, ses yeux suivaient un couple heureux pour qui le monde semblait fait tout exprès: une belle fille et un beau garçon, qui la regardaient avec sympathie, lui souriaient d'amitié. (PI 14)

So when punishment time comes around again she happily allows herself to be lowered away, and plunges into the water to join the smiling lovers.

Given what we have seen of Aymé's earlier escapists, it would be naive to look for a realistic reprieve from this harsh reality. Only La Jouque's suicide might be viewed as a truly realistic way out. But the storyteller — as if to prove that he has not succumbed to despair — is occasionally prepared to soften his realism with sympathy and humour. His whimsical overthrowing of his own realism — like Antoine's departure in his magic boots or Jacotin's saving lie — satisfies the storyteller if not the moralist. All the rules of Aymé's world say that Martin should not really be allowed to win the lottery and become rich in 'En arrière'. But Aymé is not always concerned with the rules. Defending his refusal of a moral ending for the play *Les Oiseaux de lune*, Aymé wrote in his *prière d'insérer*:

> La morale aurait voulu que cette grande foule d'oiseaux vînt crever les yeux de l'enchanteur, mais dans un simple divertissement, on n'est pas trop soucieux de morale.

Morillard's adjutant, the representative of harsh reality and order, is probably the closest Aymé comes to creating a mouthpiece for his own feelings about consolation for life's repressive systems and hierarchies. Constantin is a character whose heart and head are engaged in the same conflict as Aymé's:

> Il aurait aimé que chaque fantassin eût un cheval pour le porter et prît son petit déjeuner au lit, mais il comprenait bien que c'était impossible. Le militaire n'est pas fait pour s'énerver dans une existence de plaisir, au contraire. (. . .) C'est une question de principe. Il faut que chacun soit à sa place. C'est pourquoi l'adjudant Constantin punissait beaucoup. (. . .) Mais tandis qu'il faisait pleuvoir les punitions, son coeur saignait de pitié. (DM 183)

And so even though the moralist's head makes him throw Morillard in the guard-house, Aymé's tender heart still arranges for his Christmas gift to be delivered to his sweetheart.

The struggle described earlier between Aymé's head and his heart, between the moralist and the curious inventor, has here become more a struggle between the moralist and the pure storyteller. The moralist now loses more than he did before. Aymé seems more interested in providing intriguing, amusing endings to make up for drily realistic material. So it is that even Aymé's realistic Martins sometimes do inherit the earth. Morillard sends his Christmas present and César finally wins the approval of Madame Dupin and leads his beloved to the altar in 'Le Mariage de César'. Félicien, in 'Bonne vie et moeurs', is an unscrupulous good-for-nothing, so of course the local mayor refuses him a *certificat de bonne vie et moeurs* and laughs at the idea that Félicien aspires to marry his daughter. And yet Aymé allows Félicien to outwit the mayor, get his certificate and even marry Léontine into the bargain!

The schoolroom drama in 'L'Elève Martin' provides one of Aymé's more poignant reprieves. Martin this time is a young trouble-maker who has scrawled graffiti on the school urinal, insulting the pompous *surveillant-général* Escuelle. Escuelle is sniped at by Martin's teacher, Lamble, and browbeaten by the headmaster, so he takes it out on Martin. For personal revenge on Escuelle, Lamble gets Martin off the hook and the guilty pupil can hardly believe his luck. Aymé has a more personal interest in the fate of the troublesome Salignon in the very similar drama of 'A et B'. The young Aymé was very gifted at mathematics but had no penchant for literature. Thus when the rebel mathematician Salignon pits his talents against the arrogant classics teacher, Aymé takes sides with the mathematics class. Salignon carries out experiments on insects in his desk while Cicero is being translated and burns rubber on the heating furnace when the humanist denigrates the mathematicians temporarily under his command. Salignon finally persuades the headmaster of his innocence and humiliates his teacher in front of the whole class.

There is a kind of rough justice in these two classroom dramas, but other reprieves can be much less likely. It is the marriage of 'La Vamp et le Normalien' that provides one of Aymé's most improbable situations and one of his most idealistic consolations. Aymé's first fantasy here is a Normalien who cannot find a job in the civil service so he puts on a rough accent and takes a job as assistant to Aymé's own butcher in the rue d'Orchampt. The vamp is an even less likely proposition: she has made a fortune under the Occupation and men are still driven to despair and suicide by her fatal charm, and yet she, who failed the *baccalauréat* six times, falls madly in love with the penniless butcher's boy because of his erudition. This is almost a variation on the princess-disguised-as-a-cowgirl theme and the ironic Aymé pastiches the time-honoured 'Darling, there's something I should tell you . . .' situation particularly well:

> Adrien composa un bouquet d'Homère, de Sophocle, de Virgile, de Sénèque, et fit un exposé rapide et nerveux de la *Critique de la raison pure.* A toutes ces beautés, elle sentait s'ouvrir et fleurir son dur coeur de vamp comme s'ouvre et fleurit la corolle ennuitée à la caresse des rayons auroraux. (. . .)
> — Adrien, mon amour, murmura Eva, je vous dois une confidence. Je suis . . . mon Dieu . . . je suis une vamp. (. . .)
> — Je vous aime néanmoins, répondit-il, mais ne me cachez rien. (EA 217)

Aymé's third fantasy: the vamp is persuaded to mend her ways and give back all the money so that they can live idealistically on the butcher's meagre salary. The final twist: when she is spotted by the tax-inspector because she is giving away so much money, he is touched by her confession and, instead of enforcing the law, lets them live happily ever after:

> Emerveillé, il s'éloigna sur la pointe des pieds et, avant de sortir de l'église, glissa un billet de dix francs dans le tronc du denier de Saint-Pierre. (EA 228)

* * *

Aymé's more realistic stories suggest a slightly different orientation in his conception of the short story. The last few stories discussed, like 'Traversée de Paris', 'Trois faits divers', 'L'Affaire Touffard', 'En attendant' or 'La Vamp et le Normalien', individually reflect some thematic continuation of Aymé's two other groups but their great variety shows that this more realistic group of Aymé's stories is not nearly as structurally or thematically unified as his physical or psychological stories. The difference is above all a domination of the moralist by the storyteller. Aymé has much more freedom here; he is less restricted by the nature of his material and less dependent on the interlude structure with the surprise and consequences of the fantastic or the inexorable downhill slide of schizophrenia. Aymé's realism as a whole is not as single-minded or controlled and there is a less insistent drive towards a predictable, moral ending.

It is here that we find Aymé's most simple, traditional plots. 'Les mauvaises fièvres', portraying Maximilien's simple wish, the reasons for this wish and the way Maximilien goes about realizing it, is a concise movement from wish towards belief mirrored by his trip from his house into the village. 'Le Puits aux images' is just as simple in action and décor, and yet in its swift, uncluttered progression from La Jouque's imagination in the well, through her disappointment at the cinema to her final suicide it reflects the essence of Aymé's more complex escapes. 'Trois faits divers', too, could hardly be more concise an image, with its nocturnal meeting leading to a heated discussion, misunderstanding and murder. Even the apparently structureless storytelling frame of 'En attendant' with its fragmented tales alternating between long and short, contrasting the tragic and the pathetic, is strongly unified by its central theme of suffering and misery. Aymé exploits the same technique to unify the stream of consciousness monologue in 'Knate'. Here he has relinquished his usual third-person, past-tense narrative for a much more immediate mode. As Aymé's tailor measures a client, his banter roams from subject to subject: Jews, Franco-German relations, nobility, communism, his own nephew and religion, but Aymé's frame and a recurring theme of deceptive appearances maintains control over the rambling stream of language that constantly threatens to lead us off at a tangent.

Aymé's realism tends to be more analytical and less dramatically narrative than his fantastic stories. There is certainly less opportunity for the entertainer in him to alleviate the seriousness with the joyous piling up of words that characterizes the descriptions and narratives of stories like 'Les Sabines', 'La Fosse aux péchés' and 'Pastorale'. But where Aymé eschews his use of the fast-moving, almost picaresque, third-person narrative of his fantastic stories or the subtle complexity of the psychological studies, he gains in stylistic flexibility by his increased use of dialogue. In his realistic stories the world is not so consistently presented through the eyes of Aymé the storyteller. He uses monologue and dialogue to penetrate the psyche of his characters in a much less obvious way than in the first-person narratives of 'La Carte' and 'Le Décret'. The variety of style available to Aymé is astounding. The closest Aymé comes to verbal amusement now is the theatrical tirade where Grandgil gives his version of Martin's reality in 'Traversée de Paris', ridiculing the fearful drinkers in the café half-way across Paris:

> Regardez-moi ces gueules d'abrutis, ces anatomies de catastrophe. Admirez le mignon, sa face d'alcoolique, sa viande grise et du mou partout, les bajoues qui croulent de bêtise. Dis donc, ça va durer longtemps? Tu vas pas changer de gueule, un jour? Et l'autre rombière, la guenon, l'enflure, la dignité en gélatine avec ses trois mentons de renfort et ses gros nichons en saindoux qui lui dévalent sur la brioche. Cinquante ans chacun. Cinquante ans de connerie.

Encouraged by the stunned silence of the admiring Martin and the terrified café proprietors, Grandgil gives them more of the same:

> Qu'est-ce que vous foutez sur la terre, tous les deux? Vous avez pas honte d'exister? Mais non, pensez-vous, ils sont là, ils

s'installent. Leur gras double, ils vous le mettent dans l'oeil, dans la tête, dans l'air qu'on respire. Ils salissent tout, même les couleurs. Voyez le rouge sur les joues de madame: de l'écrasure de punaises pilées dans un fond d'abcès. Le blanc, le violet, le jaune, le gris, quand je les vois sur sa gueule à lui, je peux plus les pifer, je les vomis. Assassins, rendez les couleurs! (VP 56)

The drier, less personal side of Aymé's realism is exemplified by 'L'Indifférent'. It is a concise, confessional narrative, almost deadpan in tone, based on simple dialogue and action and completely devoid of direct author-comment. Happily for his readers, the ironic verbal humorist in Aymé was not often prepared to remain so aloof from his story.

Aymé's use of absurd faerie and fantastic material and his ambitious tableau of schizophrenia require different but particularly challenging linguistic skills. Aymé's realistic stories are perhaps not as demanding, although it can sometimes be a challenge to maintain the reader's interest after he has become used to magic wands and mental metamorphoses. But this certainly does not mean that Aymé's realism offered him no opportunities to display his linguistic cunning. Certainly the showpiece of Aymé's mastery of language, and dialogue in particular, is 'En attendant'. The Voltairian skill, already seen in Aymé's comments on the black-market coffin supply, is visible throughout the story.

Except for its framework, comprising the first sentence and the last three-quarters of a page, 'En attendant' is entirely composed of spoken French. It is a collection of thirteen monologues. Aymé has done his best to adapt style to character, even though the thirteen storytellers come from the same social class. The rambling, highly idiomatic monologue of the shop assistant and the blatant slang of the prostitute are contrasted with the much more structured speech and thought patterns of the young wife whose marriage is threatened; and the disjointed, often elliptical, emotional idiom of the drunkard sets off the slower, coldly lucid monologue of the despairing seamstress. The difference in length of the monologues further demonstrates Aymé's linguistic flexibility. The longer, rambling monologues create their effect by accumulation and repetition while the shorter ones display such economy that they often depend on just one word. 'Moi', says a child, 'j'ai faim. J'ai toujours faim.' The word 'toujours', like the word 'juif' in the twelfth monologue, has exceptional strength. The word 'nourrissante' attached strangely to the word 'nourriture' in the mother of four's monologue works the same way.

Aymé's shorter, three- or four-line monologues sandwiched in between the longer ones are quite meticulously composed. An old lady has two eggs, real eggs; in the word 'vrais' the whole ersatz existence of Occupied France is evoked by implication. When she drops them, her brief 'Je ne crois plus en Dieu' says it all. It must have been very difficult to evoke with such economy the extraordinary importance that Occupation life attached to such a simple act as dropping two eggs. Aymé manages the same sleight of hand in three crisp sentences when a young boy loses the family's bread coupons:

> Moi, dit un gamin, je voudrais bien que la fin du monde arrive avant midi. Je viens de perdre toutes nos cartes de pain. Ma mère le sait pas encore. (PM 260)

The strength here is in the reversal of normal priorities. The statement 'Je viens de perdre toutes nos cartes de pain' is the one that he should be most upset about, but for him the darkest aspect of the tragedy is the beating he is in for when he arrives home at lunchtime: 'Ma mère le sait pas encore.' The lad does not just want the world to end; he wants it to end 'avant midi'. The slightly longer but equally skilful monologue of the twelve-year-old girl is a similarly ironic manipulation of our expectations. She tells of a dark stairway, a sinister man in the shadows, her mother's warnings, her own fears, and finally an attack:

> Quand je suis passée, il m'a sauté dessus. Il m'a allongée de tout mon long sur la pierre. (PM 258)

We fully expect to read 'Et il m'a violée'. Instead, Aymé cleverly replaces 'violée' with a similar word: 'Et il m'a volé mes lacets de souliers'. This is a brilliantly concise evocation of the absurdity of the era.

Aymé the realist certainly does not abandon his favourite techniques for the construction of a successful short story.[7] This is evident in 'Josse' and 'A et B' where the fantastic story structures are reflected so clearly. The last few stories to be examined in any detail—the whimsy of 'Bonne vie et moeurs', 'L'Elève Martin' and 'La Vamp et le Normalien'—display definite similarities in Aymé's approach to his material. Aymé's standard plot here still reflects a desire to propose an intriguing, unexpected situation and let it develop to exploit humour or irony. A particularly characteristic element of his improbable situations is that they are reversals of expected situations. These reversals are often just as self-conscious as 'Le Passe-muraille' or 'Au clair de la lune':

> Il y avait au deux-sept-six d'infanterie un adjudant très bon et très doux qui s'appelait l'adjudant Constantin. (DM 183)

> Il y avait, dans un village du pays d'Arbois, un vigneron nommé Félicien Guérillot qui n'aimait pas le vin. (VP 101)

Aymé almost mockingly treats Félicien's problem as he did the fantastic afflictions. Like Duperrier with his halo in 'La Grâce' or Martin with his days of non-existence in 'Temps mort', Félicien is careful not to let the façade of normality break down and reveal his scandalous peccadillo. But the important aspect of this opening is that Aymé begins a discussion of the self-amusement goal that he claims lies behind his writing. After two pages of 'Le Vin de Paris', Aymé stops:

> Voilà une histoire de vin qui partait, en somme, assez bien. Mais tout d'un coup, elle m'ennuie. Elle n'est pas du temps et je m'y sens comme dépaysé. Vraiment, elle m'ennuie, et une histoire qui m'ennuie me coûte autant à écrire qu'un verre de vin à boire à Félicien Guérillot (VP 102)

and after discoursing on the potential outcomes of this situation, speculating just where it could lead him with its consequences, Aymé declares that he is not really in the mood for humour, and self-consciously switches stories:

> Je n'ai pas le coeur à parler de coteaux jolis, ni de vins gais. Conséquemment de quoi, je vais raconter une histoire de vin triste. Elle se passe à Paris. Le héros s'appelle Duvilé.
> Il y avait donc à Paris, en janvier 1945, un certain Etienne Duvilé, trente-sept trente-huit ans, qui aimait énormément le vin. Par malheur, il n'en avait pas. (VP 105)

Aymé usually follows up his inventions more faithfully than this. In 'Le Percepteur d'épouses' he proposes a tax-collector who has difficulty paying his taxes, and we have seen the outrageous fiscal innovations that this leads to. Behind Rodolphe's mixing of levels of reality in 'La Clé sous le paillasson' lurks another reversal situation. Aymé proposes in effect: 'Let's pretend a burglar turns honest, and see what happens.' It is no surprise to the hardened reader of Aymé to find that Rodolphe, like the deliciously beguiling wolf in 'Le Loup', has great difficulty in remaining honest. His new-found father quickly sets about exploiting him and disillusions him about the 'vertu' he thinks he has found. The cynical, grasping, hypocritical *bourgeois* disgusts Rodolphe so much that he burgles his money back from his father and disappears.

These situations are admirably suited to the short story but often seem out of place when Aymé inserts his reversals and unexpected combinations into his novels as comic relief for his socio-political criticism. The anti-serious inventor intrudes in *Travelingue* with a comic-strip barber who rules France from the backroom of his shop ('Moustaches—1F, Coupe—5F, Légion d'honneur—6F') and in *Uranus* with a bartender who composes alexandrines:

> Passez-moi Astyanax, on va filer en douce.
> N'attendons pas d'avoir les poulets à nos trousses.
>
> Mon Dieu, c'est-il possible. Enfin voilà un homme!
> Voulez-vous du vin blanc ou voulez-vous du rhum? (UR 264)

There is a clash of tone in these novels. The symbiosis of real and fantasy is imperfect. The contradiction is too obvious. Aymé's inventiveness is essentially a comic procedure depending heavily on style. The short story style is much smoother and softens the most violent contradictions. In 'Conte de Noël' there is a particularly good example of this stylistic deception which enables Aymé to perpetrate verbal contradiction even within one paragraph. The opening paragraph of the story begins by proposing an adjutant who is 'très bon, très doux' but by half-way through the paragraph, Aymé has managed to say 'C'est pourquoi l'adjudant Constantin punissait beaucoup' without its sounding at all unreasonable.

With the initial reversal of 'En arrière' Aymé relinquishes comedy for the rather cynical irony of his avant-garde review, but the comic streak reasserts itself in 'La Vamp et le Normalien'. The comedy is not so much in the movement of the Normalien downwards into the butcher's shop instead of upwards into the administration, or even in the irony of Eva Groubureau finally falling in love with someone who is penniless. It is more in the *volte-face* that Aymé inflicts on the vamp as she agrees to stop all her desperate lovers from committing suicide and redistribute all her ill-gotten gains to the widows and orphans of those who are already dead. There is a clear parallel here with the about-face in 'L'Huissier'. The vamp's reversal takes a week of frantic activity:

> Infatigable, elle allait par les rues et les ruelles, s'informant auprès des concierges et des garçons de café, coupant ici la corde d'un pendu qui respirait encore, ailleurs sermonnant un alcoolique passionnel ou arrêtant au bord du crime un père de famille consumé des feux d'un coupable désir. Son beau regard clair, qu'illuminaient maintenant le repentir et la compassion, apaisait le trouble des mâles, éteignait dans leurs yeux les sinistres lueurs de la concupiscence. (EA 225)

Aymé exploits her situation for comic contrasts as extreme as the waverings between sin and repentance in 'Les Sabines', but his irony supersedes his comedy once again at the end: Eva escapes the tax man's vigilance all the time she is making her fortune only to be caught when she tries to give it away!

Aymé's realism has not only replaced the initial surprise of the fantastic with comic potential and development of irony. There is also a more serious experimental vein in the realistic stories where he simply locks his victims into a crisis situation rather than inflicting on them a surprise or a reversal. As before, he will then sit back and wait for reactions and consequences. This crisis, tragic in the Greek sense, will have no easy solution. This is very much what Aymé has in mind with stories like 'Je suis renvoyé', where he proposes the initial shock of Aberdame's dismissal from the bank and then watches with a rather morbid interest as his victim struggles. Aymé might have followed the Galuchey-Sorbier-Duperrier pattern of removal followed by transformation and replacement, but here he is content with removal alone.

The same purpose seems to lie behind 'Trois faits divers', where Aymé throws the two murderers together just to watch their nervous suspicions grow into murderous combat. This reflects the plot structure of 'Josse' and 'A et B' where opposing people or groups that do not belong together are brought into conflict. Josse and his spinster sister or the mathematicians and the Latinists are enclosed in an artificial *huis clos* environment for added tension. The criminals are condemned to stay together as outcasts of society in 'Trois faits divers', the adjutant cannot escape Morillard in 'Conte de Noël' and

Petit-Doré cannot really get away from his tormentor in the closed school atmosphere of 'La Retraite de Russie'.

The developing contrast or conflict is still very much Aymé's mainstay. Above all he has a penchant for the more enclosed, personal conflicts seen in 'Josse', 'Trois faits divers' or 'La Retraite de Russie'. 'Traversée de Paris' is essentially made up of the personal contrast and conflict that Aymé has arranged between Martin and his mysterious companion. Their relationship fluctuates as Martin in turn fears Grandgil, admires him, resents him, despises him, vainly tries to understand him, argues violently with him, at last thinks he has found a friend and finally murders him.[8]

Aymé still sets up a conflict so that he can draw out all its consequences, and he is obviously enchanted if his irony can produce some that are out of all proportion to the initial clash. This is the success of 'L'Elève Martin', where Martin's confrontation with the supervisor first fills the classroom, gets out of hand to become a school-wide scandal, and culminates in a ridiculous public trial scene in front of the *vespasiennes* in the playground. 'Bonne vie et moeurs' is an even better example of the same technique. As in 'A et B', Aymé starts quite inoffensively. We detect personal animosity between the good-for-nothing Félicien and his prospective father-in-law, the mayor, when the latter tells Félicien that he can go and beg the curé for his character reference. This is all Félicien needs to play the curé off against the mayor using existing antipathy. The press supporting respectively the Church and the state takes up the cause, and what started as a personal squabble soon echoes throughout the *département* in a familiar acceleration and loss of control movement.

'Sporting' uses the same setting and conflict to expand the electioneering squabbles of left and right into the passionate arena of local sporting fixtures. Aymé gives free rein to his irony here as he allows the effect of campaign speeches to be linked to progress up or down a rugby field or skill on the vaulting horse. His final irony is to let the political fate of the region depend on the rise of sports entrepreneurs as much as on the skill of sportsmen, and then finally to expose the whole fabric to the fluctuations of the weather. It rains on the big day and the right-wing rugby rally is nearly deserted for the shelter of the opposition's gymnasium. Then, in a final reversal, everyone troops outside as the local rugby team defeats the pride of Paris.

With these whimsical endings, just as with 'il y avait . . .' beginnings, Aymé is openly hanging out a 'Beware, storyteller at work' sign. As with the dream of 'La Fosse aux péchés', the story-within-a-story façade of 'Conte du milieu' and 'Les Chiens de notre vie' and the false-start story of 'Le Vin de Paris', Aymé is very much the self-conscious storyteller who does not want to be taken too seriously. It is above all the irony of such endings that Aymé must have sought and enjoyed. As in his psychological stories, irony is the consolation of a *conteur* who has reluctantly forsaken the rather artificial satisfaction of creating an intriguing absurdity as a premise. He chooses to colour his realism with an ironic twist at the end instead; like O. Henry, Aymé is a master of the artfully concealed ending. The *élève* Martin is reprieved at the end of his escapades, but only because he becomes an unwitting pawn in the factional infighting of his teachers, and Petit-Doré turns defeat into victory after seeing his victory unjustly turned into defeat. The ironic twist that closes 'En attendant' touches on a black humour that Aymé usually avoids. After burying the unfortunate fourteenth member of the grocery queue, the remaining friends gather in a café. But their trials are not so soon over:

> Ils n'avaient pas fini de manger que l'un des convives fit observer qu'ils étaient treize à table et qu'il fallait s'attendre encore à des malheurs. (PM 268)

A grim smile must have played over Aymé's face as Finard and Gonflier set upon the defenceless Langelot at the end of 'Trois faits divers', only to let their victim escape at the last moment and watch from his hiding place as his assailants murder each other in a final misunderstanding:

> Il vit tournoyer un gourdin, briller la lame d'un couteau, et lorsque les deux hommes furent étendus sur la route, il rentra chez lui d'un pas vif et d'un coeur allègre, en jurant qu'on ne le prendrait plus à sortir le soir. (NA 209-10)

A more cynical irony colours the reversal ending of 'L'Affaire Touffard' when Aymé's Sherlock Holmes decides surprisingly against unmasking the author of the crime he has so laboriously solved. The whole story moves towards an expected unveiling but Aymé frustratingly refuses it. His dénouement is to be an anti-climactic reversal of standard detective-novel practice: 'Tant pis pour la justice'.

The final 'Mais la guerre est arrivée' that stops Gauthier-Lenoir's tax innovation filling his minister's bed with shapely contributions, or the reprieve accorded the vamp through being arrested by a tax-inspector who turns out to be as 'tendre' as Gauthier-Lenoir, are manifestations of the lighter-hearted irony that brings 'Le Mariage de César' to a close with the installation of a forty-two-year-old virgin as manager of a brothel. There is humour here in Aymé's reversal of his own standard story structure: he has taken the whole story to arrive at a situation that could well have been his opening gambit:

> Il y avait, à Montmartre, au 31 *bis* de la rue Caulaincourt, un vertueux bougnat nommé César qui tenait un bordel.

But there is a more cynical irony in the description of César's mother-in-law. She opposed César because of the ladies of doubtful morals who frequented his little bar, but once he is rich and established in the community he is immediately acceptable even though he makes his money as a brothel keeper.

Aymé allows himself the luxury of working a double irony on the King as the basis of his irreverent look at courtly love in 'L'Armure'. The King is privy to the death-bed confession of his seneschal: Gantus seduced the Queen one evening by keeping his armour on and imitating the King's voice. Since the seneschal is dying, the King does nothing except get a little jealous. But the next time he turns his attentions to Her Majesty in his slightly ridiculous fashion:

> — Adèle, murmurait le roi, je suis le gai rossignolet, rêvons à la fraîcheur des sous-bois printaniers. Mon amour est une eau vive qui se perd dans le lac de vos grands yeux de mystère. Je voudrais être une hirondelle . . . (NA 218)

she rejects his love-making. First irony for the King: she wants to be loved roughly, the way he (!) took her that night in his armour. Second irony for the King: Gantus recovers. So the King declares war to have Gantus (now a scandalous threat to his respect at court) killed off gloriously, and then he orders himself a new suit of armour.

The supreme combination of Aymé's penchant for the reversal ending, his sympathy for the down and out, and his taste for irony, is left to the ending of 'Bonne vie et moeurs'. It is not so much the fact that Félicien gets his certificate and his bride into the bargain despite the mayor's mocking refusals, it is the way he manages it that reveals the essence of Aymé's humour. Félicien simply gets Léontine pregnant and the tables are turned: the mayor not only has to beg Félicien to do the right thing by her but also has to consider a dowry! And of course Félicien would not dream of marriage unless his reputation was spotless and he had a good job to support her, and he cannot get a job without the certificate . . . . A smile flickers over Aymé's face at the end of so many of these tales, a wistful smile that seems to say: 'Life isn't really like this, but let's pretend it is.'

Conclusion

Marcel Aymé is a storyteller of unusual skill, variety and inventiveness. It is in his short stories rather than his novels that Aymé takes advantage of the greatest possible range of narrative form: fragmented diary entries, prose confession, recounted anecdotes, semi-epistolary story, ironic self-deflation, picaresque tale, realistic third-person narrative, stories composed largely of dialogue or rambling monologue, conscious parody of detective stories, Christmas tales, parables, legends, fairy stories and fables. In stories ranging from the driest realism, through the subtle machinations of the mind to the most dazzling absurdities, he has blended an astonishing range of material, tone and situation into a coherent whole. He has linked his stories with recurrent motifs and structures which supplement their individual themes.

Aymé's stories are unified in a general way by providing a multi-faceted perspective of man as an individual and as a social being. His fantastic images use special points of view and concretizations to allow us an oblique look at man's physical capacities and limitations; the psychological sketches stress man's relationship with himself and his perception of the world; the more everyday realism explores facets of his place in society. A further thematic unity is provided by Aymé's study of man's relationship with reality. The moralist accumulates his individual stories slowly working on a complex mosaic; each story's contribution to this mosaic is as important as its individual theme. His interest in man's desires and aspirations provokes a detailed exploration of our dealings with reality and fantasy. Aymé's mosaic includes many kinds of unreality, from mental and physical to social and even political. Man is frequently shown in a blind, accelerating movement towards a disordered and often catastrophic loss of contact with reality. Blending the disorder-discipline and scandal-façade motifs, a surprisingly disparate group of stories work together to build a highly

CONCLUSION

ordered world where an intricate pattern of harmonies, attachments, functions, hierarchies and cycles gives a secure discipline and sense to man's existence. The moralist sees this order as very strong, but he does sometimes draw attention to the repression of individualism and spontaneity that it involves, and pleads the cause of poetry, instinct and fantasy in a world becoming coldly rational.

Aymé's preferences as storyteller as well as moralist and his definite predilection for certain types of situation and specific ways of developing them transcend his different modes of expression and add significantly to the unity of his short stories. He frequently tests or tempts a character, locks him into a crisis situation or a context where he does not belong, or else places him in a situation of divided loyalties or desires where either solution is a compromise. The reversal motif is widespread too; Aymé upsets expected roles or attitudes to provoke conflict, or transforms his victim and replaces him in his social niche to watch the ensuing clash. These initial conflicts are heightened by contrasts. Consequences, both comic and sinister, are provoked by a growing separation of real and unreal, order and disorder. Acceleration or multiplication leads to a loss of control often described by ironic adoption of the victim's blindness in the narrative itself. The standard moral ending is balanced by Aymé's penchant for the reversal that provides an unexpected reprieve, the little ironic twist at the end which allows Aymé to express a forlorn hope for the 'loser' in an oppressively ordered world.

Aymé's short stories reveal the essential humanist who is bounded by the whimsy of 'Au clair de la lune', the pessimism of 'L'Affaire Touffard', the sympathy of 'Bonne vie et moeurs' and the objectivity of 'En attendant'. Aymé's variety and skill certainly resist formulae and generalization; yet, although slightly limited in their social range and dominated by recurring patterns, his short stories do form a reasonably complete and coherent world. Furthermore, they are thematically and technically an integral part of his work as a whole, completing the vision projected in more detail in his novels and plays.

The short story is an ideal medium for the writer who prefers to show many disjointed facets of his subject, the moralist who prefers to provoke quick reactions in his reader rather than convey a trite lesson. Aymé is very modern in his preference for a series of images rather than a reasoned analysis. This mode of expression enables him to exploit his very fertile imagination and bring together

CONCLUSION

extremely varied material—fantastic propositions, psychological complexities and subtle realism—which would otherwise be very difficult to unite in support of a common theme. Aymé's anti-intellectual image exploitation is very refreshing but sometimes frustrating: the individual themes raised are often quite serious and one feels that his deflating humour is a little out of place and his refusal to develop them rather irresponsible. Furthermore, in working by fragmented accumulation, Aymé occasionally contradicts himself. Individual stories stress different aspects of an overall position that sometimes seem incompatible: Aymé longs to see truth and idealism reassert themselves, but realizes the strength of social façades and hypocrisy, and sees them as necessary for man's social survival; the forces of order are seen as regrettably necessary but nevertheless repressive; man needs fantasy in his life but is incapable of controlling it and benefiting from it.

Aymé has a positive attitude to these contradictions. He wrote, with typical irony, about his collection *En arrière*:

> Chacune des pièces qui le composent correspond à l'idée et à l'humeur d'un moment, et il n'est pas possible de trousser à l'usage des critiques un très bref et très substantiel résumé qui les dispense de lire le volume.[1]

For Aymé, the collection of short stories was the ideal genre to express the diversity and the contradictions of life instead of imposing an artificial and coherent form on it: 'La vie est comme ça, elle a mille pattes.'[2] Aymé sees his contradictions as a necessary balance. In one story his head wins and the victim is brought crashing back to reality, while elsewhere a similar situation induces Aymé's heart to reprieve the escapist in the most unlikely way. It is this equilibrium that is one of the essential elements of Aymé's short stories. It is very hard to blend the moralist and the storyteller completely in any one story. But even if they remain separate, they complement one another overall. In his short stories, more than in his novels or plays, Aymé has achieved the balance he so often advocated. Behind the smiling grandfather hides the shrewd observer. Entertainer and moralist, joke and lesson, are complementary in his stories just as right and left are balanced in his politics. Aymé was not afraid of outrageous fantasy but also found joy in everyday reality. He liked to intrigue with frivolities but seldom shied away from the socio-political problems of his day. In individual stories the equilibrium may be lost, but overall the balance remains constant.

This is Marcel Aymé's enduring strength. It firmly situates him in a long and respected French moralist tradition. This tradition starts with the carefully balanced medieval *fabliaux*, and we then see it most clearly running through the work of one of Aymé's idols, François Rabelais, who was at times a solemn humanist expressing universal truths in simple images and allegories, and at other times a joker captivated by his own words. La Fontaine continued the tradition in his *Fables*, formulating a harmony between *plaire* and *instruire* that was to exert a very strong influence on the theatre of the seventeenth-century. Voltaire took up the ideal and consecrated the use of irony in its service. It is he who is Aymé's closest forbear. Like Voltaire, Aymé found a particular form—the short prose tale—in which he was able to develop his own unique language and in which he could achieve a balance between seriousness and irony, involvement and detachment, direct address to the reader and distance.

There are signs that Aymé's work has begun to come out from under the cloud that has for so long hung over it. Current expansion of the Folio paperback editions to include many of Aymé's works that were long out of print will surely allow a breath of fresh air into a literary atmosphere long preoccupied with ideas and theories rather than style. Recently there have been two new editions of his work, a prestige edition published by Michel de l'Ormeraie and a Flammarion edition of all his novels and short stories, illustrated by Roland Topor, which is to be followed by a similar edition of his theatre. In the same year, 1977, *Magazine littéraire* decided to 'faire le point' on this unjustly neglected writer and devote a whole issue to him. One sign that Aymé may truly be coming back into vogue: the issue contains a 'semiological' analysis of one of his plays! It is to be hoped that Marcel Aymé's reputation, not just as honest chronicler of his times and perceptive analyst of human nature, but above all as *conteur* in the tradition of Rabelais, La Fontaine and Voltaire will soon be restored.

Sources of Stories

A et B (PI)
L'Affaire Touffard (NA)
L'Ame de Martin (DM)
L'Ane et le cheval (CP)
L'Armure (NA)
Avenue Junot (EA)
Les Boeufs (CP)
Les Boîtes de peinture (CP)
La bonne peinture (VP)
Bonne vie et moeurs (NA)
Les Bottes de sept lieues (PM)
La Buse et le cochon (CP)
Le Canard et la panthère (CP)
La Canne (NA)
La Carte (PM)
Le Cerf et le chien (CP)
Le Chien (CP)
Les Chiens de notre vie (EA)
Au clair de la lune (PI)
La Clé sous le paillasson (NA)
Les Clochards (PI)
Le Cocu nombreux (DM)
Conte de Noël (DM)
Conte du milieu (EA)
Les Cygnes (CP)
Le Décret (PM)
Dermuche (VP)
Le Dernier (NA)
Deux victimes (NA)
L'Eléphant (CP)
L'Elève Martin (DM)
En arrière (EA)
En attendant (PM)
Enfants perdus (PI)
La Fabrique (EJ)
Le faux policier (VP)
Fiançailles (EA)

La Fosse aux péchés (VP)
La Grâce (VP)
L'Huissier (PM)
L'Indifférent (VP)
L'Individu (PI)
Je suis renvoyé (DM)
Josse (EA)
La Lanterne (PI)
Légende poldève (PM)
La Liste (NA)
Le Loup (CP)
Le Mariage de César (NA)
Le mauvais jars (CP)
Les mauvaises fièvres (PI)
Le Mendiant (EA)
Le Mouton (CP)
Le Nain (NA)
Oscar et Erick (EA)
Le Paon (CP)
Le Passe-muraille (PM)
Pastorale (PI)
La Patte du chat (CP)
Le Percepteur d'épouses (PM)
Le petit coq noir (CP)
Le Problème (CP)
Le Proverbe (PM)
Le Puits aux images (PI)
Rechute (NA)
La Retraite de Russie (PI)
Le Romancier Martin (DM)
Rue de l'Evangile (DM)
Rue Saint-Sulpice (NA)
Les Sabines (PM)
Sporting (NA)
La Statue (DM)
Le Temps mort (DM)
Traversée de Paris (VP)

Trois faits divers (NA)   La Vamp et le Normalien (EA)
Les Vaches (CP)   Le Vin de Paris (VP)

Samson: *4e Cahier de la Table ronde,* 1945.
Le Couple: *Festival du roman* No 72, September 1963.
Un Crime: *Aspects de France* 21 December 1951.
Héloïse: *La Nouvelle Table ronde* No 2, 1970. Also appeared in *Carrefour* October 1952.
Knate: *La Nouvelle Table ronde* No 3, 1971.

Notes

INTRODUCTION

1. G. Robert & A. Lioret, *Marcel Aymé insolite* (Paris: Ed. de la Revue indépendante, 1958), p. 21. Aymé quoted.
2. J. Cathelin, *Marcel Aymé* (Paris: Debresse, 1958), p. 11.
3. P. Hahn, 'Marcel Aymé: j'écris pour me faire plaisir', *Paris-théâtre* No 185 (1962), p. 20. Aymé interviewed. See also Aymé's preface to P. Véry, *Tout doit disparaître le 5 mai* (Paris: Denoël, 1961), p. viii.
4. Hahn, p. 22. Aymé interviewed.
5. M. Aymé, 'Les surprises du fantastique', *Arts* 28 December 1955, p. 1.
6. Hahn, p. 19. Aymé interviewed.
7. G. d'Aubarède, 'Rencontre avec Marcel Aymé', *Nouvelles littéraires* No 1377 (1954), p. 5. Aymé interviewed.
8. Aymé's *prière d'insérer* to *Travelingue*.
9. C. Perrault, *Contes* (Paris: Librairies associées, 1964), p. 11. Aymé's preface.
10. P. Vandromme, *Aymé* (Paris: Gallimard [Bibl. idéale], 1960), p. 50.
11. Hahn, p. 22. Aymé interviewed.
12. d'Aubarède, p. 5. Aymé interviewed.
13. Hahn, p. 20. Aymé interviewed.
14. F. Rabelais, *Les cinq livres* (Paris: Magnard, 1964). Aymé's preface.
15. P. Sérant, *Où va la droite?* (Paris: Plon, 1958), p. 6. Aymé's preface.
16. G. Rolin, 'Un Jurassien de Montmartre', *Magazine littéraire* No 124 (May 1977), p. 15.
17. J-L. Bory & J. Hurtin, 'Le pays derrière l'arbre', in ibid., p. 30.
18. Hahn, pp. 20-1. Aymé interviewed.
19. Vandromme, p. 271. Aymé interviewed by Gilbert Ganne. See also Aymé, 'La liberté de l'écrivain est menacée', *Carrefour* 26 March 1952; 'Liberté d'expression', *La Parisienne* January 1953; 'L'épuration et le délit d'opinion', *Le Crapouillot* No 11 (April 1950).
20. Robert & Lioret, p. 108. Aymé interviewed.
21. N. Debrie-Panel, *Louis-Ferdinand Céline* (Lyon: E. Vitte, 1961), p. 7. Aymé's preface.
22. Hahn, p. 21. Aymé interviewed.
23. *Magazine littéraire* No 124 (May 1977).
24. J. Teynier, *Le Passe-muraille* (Paris: Livre de Poche-Université, 1968), p. 264. (An edition with 70 pages of notes and commentary.)

25. A balance Aymé stresses in his prefaces to Rabelais, and to P. Dubout, *Dubout* (Monaco: Ed. Art et Technique, 1942).
26. Vandromme, p. 54.
27. Robert & Lioret, p. 110. Aymé interviewed.

1. PHENOMENA AND MOTIFS

1. R. Nimier, 'Une forte tête', *La Parisienne* December 1953; G-A. Masson, 'Le don', *A la façon de* . . . (Paris: Ducray, 1950); M. Perrin, 'Série noire et Bibliothèque rose', *Monnaie de singe* (Paris: Calmann-Lévy, 1952).
2. M. Schneider, *La littérature fantastique en France* (Paris: Fayard, 1964), p. 87.
3. I. Jan, *Essai sur la littérature enfantine* (Paris: Ed. ouvrières, 1969), Chap. VI.
4. Schneider, p. 87.
5. Aymé uses a setting called Poldavia to attack the French magistrature in his notorious play *La Tête des autres*.
6. M. Tillier, 'Je n'en croyais pas mes oreilles: Marcel Aymé parlait', *Le Figaro littéraire* No 910 (December 1963), p. 21.
7. Jan, p. 65.
8. J-L. Dumont, *Marcel Aymé et le merveilleux* (Paris: Debresse, 1970), pp. 87-8, on 'Le Chien' and 'Les Boeufs'; and Rolin, p. 16, quoting Robert Brasillach's interpretation of 'Le Loup'.
9. Rolin, p. 12.
10. Véry, p. ix. Aymé's preface.
11. P-M. Schuhl, *L'imagination et le merveilleux* (Paris: Flammarion, 1952), p. 8.
12. See Aymé's account of an execution, 'Une tête qui tombe', *Arts* 10 April 1952.
13. 'Samson', p. 141.
14. ibid., pp. 139-40.
15. Dumont, p. 208. Aymé quoted.
16. See Aymé, 'Le libérateur', *Défense de l'Occident* 21 February 1955.
17. Masson, p. 28.

2. TECHNIQUES AND THEMES

1. V. Propp, *Morphologie du conte* (Paris: Seuil, 1970), Chaps. 1-2.
2. J. Bellemin-Noël, 'Des formes fantastiques aux thèmes fantasmatiques', *Littérature* May 1971, p. 103.
3. J. R. R. Tolkien, *Tree and Leaf* (London: Allen & Unwin, 1964), p. 15.

NOTES

4. R. Brasillach, *Les quatre jeudis,* Oeuvres complètes, Vol. 8 (Paris: Club de l'honnête homme, 1964), p. 398.
5. H. C. Anderson, *Contes* (Paris: Livre de Poche, 1963), p. 11. Aymé's preface.
6. G. Simenon, *Le Chien jaune* (Paris: Livre de Poche, 1962), p. 11. Aymé's preface.
7. Teynier, p. 257.
8. Cathelin, p. 144.
9. 'Héloïse', p. 223.
10. Bellemin-Noël, p. 105.
11. Brasillach, p. 398.
12. Aymé, 'Les surprises du fantastique', *Arts* 28 December 1955.
13. Teynier, p. 258.
14. Brasillach, p. 399.
15. H. Scriabine, *Les Faux-Dieux* (Paris: Mercure de France, 1963), p. 53.
16. Aymé's *prière d'insérer* to *Derrière chez Martin.*
17. M. Ozeray, *A toujours Monsieur Jouvet* (Paris: Buchet-Chastel, 1966), p. 8. Aymé's preface.
18. Tolkien, p. 51.
19. Véry, p. ix. Aymé's preface.
20. 'Héloïse', p. 222.
21. P. Mabille, *Le merveilleux* (Paris: Ed. des Quatre Vents, 1946), pp. 68-9.
22. R. Caillois, *Images, Images . . .* (Paris: Corti, 1966), p. 34.
23. P. Mabille, *Le miroir du merveilleux* (Paris: Minuit, 1962), p. 280.
24. Teynier, p. 263.
25. Perrin, p. 29.
26. Hahn, p. 20. Aymé interviewed.
27. Vandromme, p. 133.
28. R. Caillois, *Anthologie du fantastique* (Paris: Gallimard, 1966), p. 8.
29. 'Le Couple', p. 1130.
30. Dumont, p. 215. Aymé quoted.
31. Aymé, 'Comment un romancier devient auteur dramatique', *Carrefour* 10 October 1951, p. 3.

3. ILLUSION

1. G. Lord, 'Sexual revolt in Marcel Aymé', *Essays in French Literature* No 12 (November 1975).
2. 'Héloïse', p. 222.
3. C. Damiens, 'Marcel Aymé approfondit Miller', *Paris-théâtre* No 142 (1956), p. 7.

4. REALITY

1. Vandromme, p. 88.
2. Aymé's pessimism here has been compared to the socio-political ideas of Hobbes. See E. Van den Haag, 'The soul recovers radical innocence', *Modern Age* No 3 (1959), p. 307.
3. Teynier, p. 261.
4. d'Aubarède, p. 5. Aymé commenting on *Les quatre vérités*.
5. Rolin, p. 11.
6. Teynier, p. 285.
7. See G. Lord, 'Aymé's interludes: structure and significance', *AUMLA* No 49 (May 1978).
8. The cinema adaptation by Jean Aurenche and Pierre Bost changes Aymé's ending: Martin and Grandgil are caught by the Germans, Grandgil is set free because of his connections but the eternal *pauvre type* Martin goes to prison.

CONCLUSION

1. Aymé's *prière d'insérer* to *En arrière*.
2. Teynier, p. 259.

Bibliography

BOOKS

Brodin, D. *The comic world of Marcel Aymé*. Paris, Debresse, 1964.
Marcel Aymé. Columbia essays on modern writers. New York, Columbia U.P., 1968.
Cathelin, J. *Marcel Aymé*. Paris, Debresse, 1958.
Dumont, J-L. *Marcel Aymé et le merveilleux*. Paris, Debresse, 1970.
Robert, G. *Marcel Aymé, cet inconnu*. Paris, Défense de l'esprit, 1955.
Robert, G. & Lioret, A. *Marcel Aymé insolite*. Paris, Ed. de la Revue indépendante, 1958.
Scriabine, H. *Les Faux-Dieux*. Paris, Mercure de France, 1963.
Teynier, J. *Le Passe-muraille*. (An edition with 70 pages of notes and commentary). Paris, Livre de Poche-Université, 1968.
Vandromme, P. *Aymé. Bibl. idéale*. Paris, Gallimard, 1960.

ARTICLES

d'Aubarède, G. 'Rencontre avec Marcel Aymé'. *Nouvelles littéraires* No 1377, 1954.
Curval, P. 'Marcel Aymé, le faussaire du quotidien'. *Magazine littéraire* No 124, May 1977.
Ganne, G. *Interviews impubliables* (a section on Aymé). Paris, P. A. Bonne, 1952.
'Marcel Aymé l'anticonformiste'. *Oeuvres libres* No 71, 1952.
Haag, van den, E. 'The soul recovers radical innocence'. *Modern Age* No 3, 1959.
Hahn, P. 'Marcel Aymé: j'écris pour me faire plaisir'. *Paris-théâtre* No 185, 1962.
Lord, G. 'Sexual revolt in Marcel Aymé'. *Essays in French Literature* No 12, November 1975.
'Aymé's interludes: structure and significance'. *AUMLA* No 49, May 1978.
Loy, J. 'The reality of Marcel Aymé's world'. *French Review* December 1954.
Nimier, R. *Journées de lecture* (a section on Aymé). Paris, Gallimard, 1965.

'Une étude sur Marcel Aymé'. *Nouvelle Revue Française* September 1969.

Rolin, G. 'Un Jurassien de Montmartre'. *Magazine littéraire* No 124, May 1977.

Temmer, M. 'Marcel Aymé, fabulist and moralist'. *French Review* April 1962.

Tillier, M. 'Je n'en croyais pas mes oreilles: Marcel Aymé parlait'. *Le Figaro littéraire* No 910, December 1963.

Index

'A et B', 135, 143, 154, 158, 161, 162
'L'Affaire Touffard', 149-50, 155, 163, 167
Aller retour, 5, 7, 96-100, 101, 109, 113, 114, 122-3, 141, 143
'L'Ame de Martin', 103, 106, 116, 119
'L'Ane et le cheval', 23, 34, 41, 62, 73, 75, 93
'L'Armure', 164
'Au clair de la lune', 22, 67, 90, 159, 167
'Avenue Junot', 11, 39, 59, 65, 76

La belle image, 5, 8, 40, 41, 44, 45, 55, 64, 69, 80, 81, 82, 84, 85, 86, 90, 100, 113
Le Boeuf clandestin, 5, 101
'Les Boeufs', 67, 75, 87, 110
'Les Boîtes de peinture', 33, 34, 61, 90, 94
'La bonne peinture', 39, 43, 65, 66, 73, 74, 76, 83, 89, 90
'Bonne vie et moeurs', 11, 153, 158, 162, 164-5, 167
'Les Bottes de sept lieues', 23, 67, 76, 77, 81-2, 89, 93, 102, 115, 116, 121-2, 124-5, 138
Brûlebois, 2, 95-6, 105, 109
'La Buse et le cochon', 34, 89

'Le Canard et la panthère', 60, 61, 87
'La Canne', 101, 105, 106, 109, 110, 113-14, 117, 118, 123, 136, 141
'La Carte', 36, 40, 44, 47-9, 50, 61, 62, 65-6, 73, 74, 79, 82, 83, 91, 103-4, 111, 131, 132, 156
'Le Cerf et le chien', 87
Le Chemin des écoliers, 5, 16, 132, 135
'Le Chien', 94
'Les Chiens de notre vie', 134, 163
'La Clé sous le paillasson', 54-5, 59, 80-1, 144, 160
Clérambard, 8, 9, 10, 96, 105

'Les Clochards', 102, 110, 115-16, 118, 123, 149
'Le Cocu nombreux', 53, 54, 56, 65, 72, 74, 76, 77
Le Confort intellectuel, 148
Consommation, 8
'Conte de Noël', 29, 141, 153, 159, 160, 161
'Conte du milieu', 11, 22, 58, 115, 163
Les Contes du chat perché, 9, 10, 16, 23, 30-6, 42, 43, 60, 69-72, 77, 81, 83, 89, 90, 115
La Convention Belzébir, 7, 36
'Le Couple', 11, 43, 88, 94, 143
'Un Crime', 11, 149
'Les Cygnes', 34

'Le Décret', 23, 38, 42, 43, 49, 50, 51, 54, 55, 61, 67, 73, 79, 80, 82, 83, 85, 106, 111, 115, 131, 156
'Dermuche', 29, 38-9, 63, 66, 67, 88, 89, 93
'Le Dernier', 103, 111-12, 113, 118, 123
Derrière chez Martin, 10, 74
'Deux victimes', 11, 103, 119-20, 124, 129

'L'Eléphant', 92-3
'L'Elève Martin', 11, 135, 153, 158, 162, 163
'En arrière', 137-8, 141, 143, 153, 160
En arrière, 10, 11, 168
'En attendant', 15, 60, 131-3, 144-5, 146, 150-2, 155, 157-8, 163, 167
'Enfants perdus', 84
Enjambées, 10

'La Fabrique', 10, 23, 41-2, 49, 58, 66, 75, 79, 83, 93
'Le faux policier', 30, 102, 117, 120-1, 133

179

'Fiançailles', 23-4, 43, 50, 63, 64, 76, 80, 90, 93, 94
'La Fille du shérif', 37, 39
'La Fosse aux péchés', 24-5, 29, 38, 58, 84, 156, 163

'La Grâce', 29, 38, 43, 59, 65, 67, 88, 89, 159
Gustalin, 4, 23, 133, 142

'Héloïse', 11, 53, 63, 65, 69, 78, 80, 118
'L'Huissier', 27-9, 38, 50, 66, 75, 77, 84, 101-2, 128-9, 161

Images de l'amour, 7
'L'Indifférent', 133, 144, 145, 149, 150, 157
'L'Individu', 102, 107-8, 109, 110, 111, 113, 114, 118

'Je suis renvoyé', 144, 145, 146, 149, 161
'Josse', 139-40, 141, 143, 145, 158, 161, 162
Les Jumeaux du diable, 30, 38, 45-6
La Jument verte, 2, 4, 9, 10, 31, 40, 134

'Knate', 11, 156

'La Lanterne', 103
'Légende poldève', 11, 25-6, 29, 38, 58, 75, 77, 82
'La Liste', 38, 58, 75, 88, 93, 143
'Le Loup', 34, 70-2, 75, 87, 89, 160
Louisiane, 7, 30, 136-7, 142
Lucienne et le boucher, 6, 7, 8

Maison basse, 4, 16, 144
'Le Mariage de César', 131, 153, 164
'Le mauvais jars', 32, 35
'Les mauvaises fièvres', 23, 134, 152, 155
Les Maxibules, 7, 96, 105
'Le Mendiant', 30, 58, 67, 109
Le Minotaure, 8
La Mouche bleue, 7, 8, 30, 143
Le Moulin de la Sourdine, 5, 101, 126, 142
'Le Mouton', 34

'Le Nain', 11, 41, 43-4, 51, 67, 80, 86, 87, 144
Le Nain, 10

Les Oiseaux de lune, 8, 41, 43, 68, 90, 93, 153
'Oscar et Erick', 56, 58, 91

'Le Paon', 35
'Le Passe-muraille', 52-3, 59, 64, 65, 66, 68-9, 75, 76, 77, 79-80, 81, 82, 83, 86, 101, 113, 136, 159
Le Passe-muraille, 9, 10, 82, 83
'Pastorale', 36-7, 38, 39, 47, 75, 91, 113, 156
'La Patte du chat', 34, 60, 75
'Le Percepteur d'épouses', 117, 129, 159, 163
'Le petit coq noir', 34, 35, 72, 87
'Le Problème', 33
'Le Proverbe', 103, 110, 111, 123, 126-8
'Le Puits aux images', 134, 152, 155
Le Puits aux images, 10

Les quatre vérités, 7, 8, 67, 137, 148

'Rechute', 10, 50-1, 61, 66, 73, 80, 86, 113
'La Retraite de Russie', 135, 162, 163
'Le Romancier Martin', 43, 46, 55, 58, 59, 65, 74, 76, 83, 93, 141
'La Rue de l'Evangile', 110, 114-15, 123, 149
'Rue Saint-Sulpice', 11, 102, 110, 111, 119
La Rue sans nom, 4, 95, 105, 113, 116, 135, 142

'Les Sabines', 53-4, 60, 63, 64, 65, 66, 68, 75, 80, 82, 83, 156, 161
'Samson', 11, 30, 42, 44-5, 50, 80, 90, 141
Silhouette du scandale, 16, 148
'Sporting', 134, 162
'La Statue', 102, 107, 109, 113, 114, 117, 123

La Table aux crevés, 4, 23, 133, 141-2
'Le Temps mort', 44, 46-7, 58, 67, 74, 75, 88, 159

La Tête des autres, 7, 8, 9, 16, 39, 148
Les Tiroirs de l'inconnu, 5, 7, 133
Travelingue, 5, 16, 135, 160
'Traversée de Paris', 11, 133, 137, 138, 146-8, 149, 155, 156, 157, 162
'Trois faits divers', 150, 155, 161, 162, 163

Uranus, 5, 16, 160

'Les Vaches', 32
'La Vamp et le Normalien', 154-5, 158, 164
Le Vaurien, 4, 16, 96, 133, 135, 144
'Le Vin de Paris', 60, 103, 108-9, 110, 116, 118, 129, 159, 160-1, 163
Le Vin de Paris, 10, 11
Vogue la Galère, 6, 7, 138-9, 140, 141
La Vouivre, 4, 23, 58, 82, 85, 86, 133

PQ 2601 .Y5 Z75x

Lord, Graham, 1947-

The short stories of Marcel
 Aymbe /